CCNP Cisco Networking Academy Program: Semester Six Lab Companion
Remote Access

Cisco Systems, Inc.

Cisco Networking Academy Program

Mark McGregor

Cisco Press

Cisco Press
201 West 103rd Street
Indianapolis, IN 46290 USA

CCNP Cisco Networking Academy Program:
Semester Six Lab Companion
Remote Access

Cisco Systems, Inc.

Cisco Networking Academy Program

Mark McGregor

Published by:
Cisco Press
210 West 103rd Street
Indianapolis, IN 46290 USA

Printed in the United States of America   1 2 3 4 5 6 7 8 9 0

First Printing   September 2001

ISBN: 1-58713-032-7

Warning and Disclaimer

This book is designed to provide information on networking fundamentals. Every effort has been made to make this book as complete and as accurate as possible, but no warranty or fitness is implied.

The information is provided on an "as is" basis. The author, Cisco Press, and Cisco Systems, Inc. shall have neither liability nor responsibility to any person or entity with respect to any loss or damages arising from the information contained in this book or from the use of the programs that may accompany it.

The opinions expressed in this book belong to the author and are not necessarily those of Cisco Systems, Inc.

Trademark Acknowledgments

All terms mentioned in this book that are known to be trademarks or service marks have been appropriately capitalized. Cisco Press or Cisco Systems, Inc., cannot attest to the accuracy of this information. Use of a term in this book should not be regarded as affecting the validity of any trademark or service mark.

Feedback Information

At Cisco Press, our goal is to create in-depth technical books of the highest quality and value. Each book is crafted with care and precision, undergoing rigorous development that involves the unique expertise of members of the professional technical community.

Readers' feedback is a natural continuation of this process. If you have any comments regarding how we could improve the quality of this book, or otherwise alter it to better suit your needs, you can contact us at feedback@ciscopress.com. Please be sure to include the book title and ISBN in your message.

We greatly appreciate your assistance.

Publisher	John Wait
Editor-in-Chief	John Kane
Executive Editor	Carl Lindholm
Cisco Systems Management	Michael Hakkert
	Tom Geitner
	William Warren
Managing Editor	Patrick Kanouse
Senior Project Editor	Sheri Replin
Product Manager	Shannon Gross
Copy Editor	Douglas Lloyd

About the Author

Mark McGregor, CCNP, CCDP, CCAI, is the regional coordinator for the Cisco Networking Academy Program at Los Medanos College in Pittsburg, California. He has taught in the Networking Academy program since 1997, and currently works for Cisco Systems Worldwide Education. Mark holds a bachelor's degree in English from the University of California, Davis, and has been an author and contributor for Cisco Press since 1998. As a public school instructor for more than seven years, he has enjoyed the opportunity to teach and learn from students of all ages and backgrounds. He lives in Antioch, California.

Acknowledgments

The labs and activities in this lab companion were developed and tested by a talented team of experts, teachers, and students. Much of the material included in this manual was contributed by my teammates at Cisco Worldwide Education: Todd White, Andrew Large, Scott T. Wolfe, Bob Larson, Jim Yoshida, and Torrey Suzuki. This book is a direct product of their diligence, inventiveness, and expertise.

Wayne Lewis, my partner at Cisco WWE, deserves special thanks for keeping this project on track and for keeping me sane (thanks to his concept of Hawaiian time). Also at WWE, Vito Amato, Dennis Frezzo, and Rick Graziani have each lent me invaluable support and guidance.

For the record, I am forever indebted to the fantastic team at Cisco Press, whose unenviable task has been to work with me in a deadline-oriented environment. This book owes its existence to the outstanding work of Carl Lindholm, Patrick Kanouse, and Doug Lloyd. I must also single out Shannon Gross for taking such great care of me. Above all, my editor, Sheri Replin, deserves recognition for her professionalism, creativity, and attention to detail.

Finally, I thank my colleagues at Cisco, Jody Mills and Eric Yu, for the significant technical contributions they have made to this book—above and beyond the call of duty or friendship.

Table of Contents

Introduction   1

Lab Equipment Requirements   3

Case Study: International Travel Agency   5

Introductory Lab 1: Getting Started and Building Start.TXT   7

Introductory Lab 2: Capturing HyperTerminal and Telnet Sessions   13

Introductory Lab 3: Access Control List Basics and Extended Ping   15

Lab 2-1: Configuring an Asynchronous Connection   21

Lab 2-2: Configuring an Asynchronous Connection on the AUX port   30

Lab 2-3: Configuring Asynchronous PPP   35

Lab 3-1: Configuring PPP Interactive Mode   41

Lab 3-2: Configuring PPP Options: Authentication and Compression   45

Lab 3-3: Configuring PPP Callback   49

Asynchronous PPP Challenge Lab   55

Lab 4-1: Configuring ISDN BRI   57

Lab 4-2: Configuring Snapshot Routing   64

Lab 4-3: Using PPP Multilink for ISDN B Channel Aggregation   69

Lab 4-4: Configuring ISDN PRI   74

Lab 5-1: Configuring ISDN Using Dialer Profiles   79

Lab 5-2: Using a Dialer Map-Class with Dialer Profiles   83

Lab 6-1: Configuring X.25 SVCs   89

Lab 6-2: Configuring X.25 PVCs   94

Lab 7-1: Basic Frame Relay Router and Switch Configuration   99

Lab 7-2: Configuring Full-Mesh Frame Relay   105

Lab 7-3: Configuring Full-Mesh Frame Relay With Subinterfaces   111

Lab 7-4: Configuring Hub-and-Spoke Frame Relay   115

Lab 8-1: Frame Relay Subinterfaces and Traffic Shaping   **121**

Lab 8-2: On-Demand Routing   **125**

Frame Relay Challenge Lab   **133**

Lab 9-1: Configuring ISDN Dial Backup   **135**

Lab 9-2: Using Secondary Links for On-Demand Bandwidth   **141**

ISDN DDR and WAN Backup Challenge Lab   **145**

Lab 10-1: Configuring Weighted Fair Queuing   **147**

Lab 10-2: Configuring Priority Queuing   **151**

Lab 10-3: Configuring Custom Queuing   **155**

Lab 11-1: Configuring Static NAT   **159**

Lab 11-2: Configuring Dynamic NAT   **164**

Lab 11-3: Configuring NAT Overload   **168**

Lab 11-4: Configuring TCP Load Distribution   **174**

NAT Challenge Lab   **179**

Lab 12-1: Router Security and AAA Authentication   **181**

Lab 12-2: Configuring AAA Authorization and Accounting   **187**

Lab 12-3: Using a TACACS+ Server   **192**

Appendix A: Command Reference   **195**

Appendix B: Adtran Atlas 550 Reference   **205**

Appendix C: Configuring the Cisco 700 Series Routers   **211**

Introduction

This lab companion provides a collection of lab exercises designed to supplement your study of remote-access concepts and the Cisco IOS. The concepts covered in these exercises include asynchronous dialup, dial-on-demand routing (DDR), PPP, CHAP authentication, PAP authentication, Multilink PPP (MLP), compression, ISDN, dialer profiles, X.25, Frame Relay, Frame Relay traffic shaping, ODR, WAN backup configurations, queuing, NAT, and AAA.

The labs are specifically written to supplement the Remote Access (Semester 6) course of the Cisco Networking Academy Program, but they can be used by anyone seeking hands-on experience and CCNP certification. Although the lab exercises contain brief explanations of key concepts, this is not a textbook. You will get the most out of these activities if you do them while concurrently engaged in formal study, such as an Remote Access Networking Academy class, a Building Cisco Remote Access Networks class (offered by Cisco's Worldwide Training partners), or self-study using one of the following Cisco Press books:

- *CCNP Cisco Networking Academy Program: Semester Six Companion Guide, Remote Access* (ISBN: 1-58713-028-9)

- *Building Cisco Remote Access Networks* (ISBN: 1-57870-091-4)

This lab companion includes a description of the lab configuration required to perform the exercises, a business scenario and WAN topology, an introductory lab, 11 groups of lab exercises, and 4 challenge labs. The appendixes contain a command reference, an Adtran Atlas 550 configuration reference, and a group of bonus labs for the Cisco 700 series routers.

Each lab references the fictitious International Travel Agency (ITA), which maintains a global data network. The ITA business scenario provides a tangible, real-world application for each of the concepts introduced in the labs. A diagram of ITA's WAN topology is included in this lab companion so that students can familiarize themselves with the company and its network.

An introductory lab precedes the lab exercises and is intended to refresh your basic router-configuration skills. Students who have just completed their CCNA studies can use this activity to better acquaint themselves with the lab environment. The introductory lab should be completed before you begin the lab exercises.

The lab exercises introduce you to advanced IOS configuration commands in a structured activity. They are grouped according to topic, corresponding to the chapters in *CCNP Cisco Networking Academy Program: Semester Six Companion Guide, Remote Access*. Each exercise group contains two to four labs:

- Labs 2: Modems and Asynchronous Connections
- Labs 3: PPP
- Labs 4: ISDN and DDR
- Labs 5: Dialer Profiles
- Labs 6: X.25
- Labs 7: Frame Relay
- Labs 8: Shaping Frame Relay Traffic
- Labs 9: WAN Backup Connections
- Labs 10: Queuing and Compression
- Labs 11: NAT
- Labs 12: AAA

If the concepts presented here are new to you, you should work through the exercises sequentially. After you are familiar with the concepts and essential IOS commands, you can focus your studies on particular exercises or challenge labs.

The challenge labs are an opportunity for you to apply the configuration concepts and commands introduced in the lab exercises. There are four challenge labs:

- Asynchronous PPP
- Frame Relay
- ISDN DDR
- NAT

You can use these as a culminating activity, a timed test, or a group project.

Finally, this manual concludes with the appendixes. You can use Appendix A, "Command Reference," as a quick reference or study guide. Appendix B, "Adtran Atlas 550 Reference," provides key lab configuration information. Finally, Appendix C, "Configuring the Cisco 700 Series Routers," offers bonus lab exercises for the Cisco 700 series routers.

Lab Equipment Requirements

CCNP Networking Academies

Each lab in this manual is written to accommodate the CCNP Academy lab pack, which CCNP Cisco Networking Academies are required to maintain. If your site has this lab pack, you can create up to three separate lab pods, provided you have the adequate access to a WAN simulation device.

WAN "Cloud" Simulation Using the Adtran Atlas 550

CCNP Academies are required to purchase at least one Adtran Atlas 550, which can serve as a POTS switch, ISDN switch, and Frame Relay switch. Essentially, this device simulates the carrier network, or WAN "cloud." No other WAN simulation device is required, although it's recommended that each pod be equipped with an Atlas 550.

The labs contained in this manual assume that the Atlas 550, and its bundled Hayes Accura 56 K modems, will be used. Where appropriate, explicit reference is made to the interfaces and physical configuration of the Atlas 550.

In the case of dialup lab activities, a single Atlas 550 can be shared among pods for asynchronous dialup and ISDN labs. When sharing an Atlas 550 among lab groups, at least one group must use alternate ports, phone numbers, and ISDN SPIDs, which are not labeled in the lab diagrams. An Atlas 550 configuration reference is included in Appendix B, so that alternate configuration information is readily available. The appropriate Atlas 550 configuration file can be downloaded by authorized Networking Academy instructors at cisco.netacad.net.

Alternatively, a Cisco router with at least three serial interfaces can be configured as a Frame Relay switch, and a single Atlas can be shared for dialup exercises.

Three workstations with terminal programs, Ethernet NICs, TCP/IP software, and a Web browser are also required in each pod. This manual assumes that you are using Microsoft Windows as your workstation's operating system.

Independent Lab Environments

If you do not have access to the CCNP Academy lab pack, you can build your own pod with the appropriate Cisco routers, modems, and a WAN simulation device. Two 2620 series routers (a single Fast Ethernet interface) and one 2621 router (dual Fast Ethernet interfaces) are recommended. In addition, you need the following:

- Three pairs of DTE/DCE cables appropriate to the serial interfaces on the routers you are using
- A device that can simulate a carrier network for POTS, ISDN, and Frame Relay (Adtran Atlas series is recommended)
- A pair of external modems for each pod
- An RS-232-to-serial cable (appropriate to your router's serial interface) for each modem
- A Cisco 700 series router (optional)

Other Considerations

These lab exercises were written and tested using Cisco IOS release 12.0(5)T. Although this release is not required to run these labs, note that features and command syntax change with each IOS release.

A physical diagram containing the essential configuration information precedes each exercise. Because the labs can be performed on a variety of equipment, the interface numbering labeled in the lab diagrams might not match your specific devices. Command output, when included in the labs, reflects what students see if they use the standard CCNP Academy lab pack.

Case Study: International Travel Agency

International Travel Agency

International Travel Agency, Inc. creates unique excursions throughout the world. Its innovative adventures include Saharan safaris, European museum tours, and Great Barrier Reef charters. Regional offices allow travel agents to personally coordinate every detail and guarantee customer satisfaction.

Based in San Jose, California, International Travel Agency maintains a comprehensive database of travel adventure packages. Graphic artists provide an interactive, media-rich Web site with "virtual excursions," which tempts potential clients. Also, in partnership with every major airline, cruise line, and resort, ITA is a leader in the use of extranets to cross-reference databases, allowing real-time updates for accurate reservations.

As a network professional with International Travel Agency, your responsibilities include creating and maintaining the San Jose campus network, connectivity to all regional headquarters, and Internet access via one or more service providers.

Company Structure and Locations

Corporate headquarters: San Jose, California, USA

- North American headquarters: San Jose, California, USA
  - East Tasman site
  - West Tasman site
  - Baypointe site
  - Vista, Montana site
- Asian headquarters: Singapore, Singapore
- Pacific headquarters: Auckland, New Zealand
- European headquarters: London, England
- African headquarters: Capetown, South Africa

Router Names

ITA North America	ITA International	Service Providers
SanJose1	Singapore	ISP1A*
SanJose2	Auckland*	ISP1B*
SanJose3*	London	ISP2*
Eastasman*	Capetown	
Westasman*		
Baypointe*		
Vista*		

* Not used in this course

The International Travel Agency (ITA) Remote Access WAN Topology

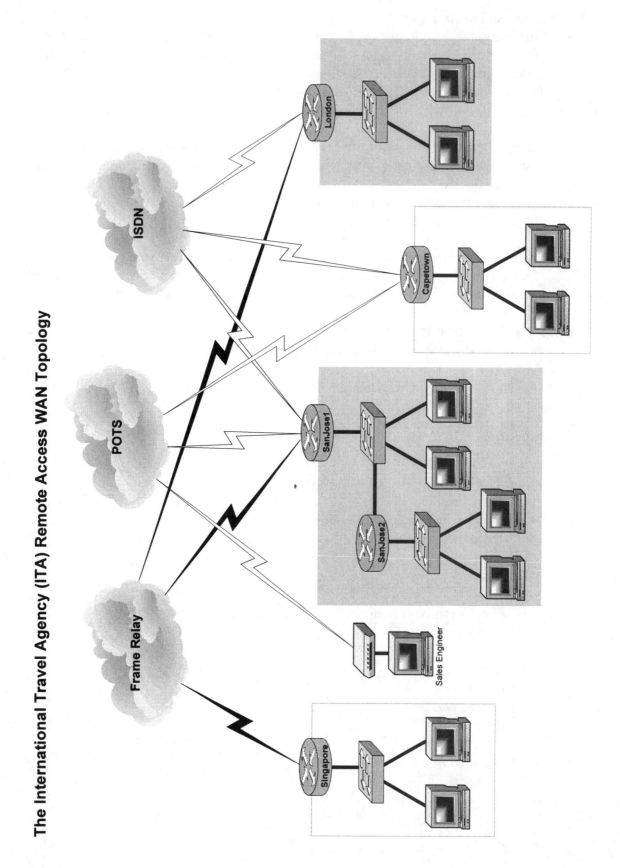

Introductory Lab 1: Getting Started and Building Start.TXT

Objective

This lab introduces the CCNP lab equipment and certain IOS features that might be new to you. This introductory activity also describes how to use a simple text editor to create all (or part) of a router configuration file. After you create a text-configuration file, you can apply that configuration to a router quickly and easily by using the techniques described in this lab.

Equipment Requirements

- A single router, preferably a 2600 series router, and a workstation running a Windows operating system
- One 3 1/2-inch floppy disk with label

Preliminary

Modular interfaces. Cisco routers can come with a variety of interface configurations. Some models have only fixed interfaces, meaning that the interfaces can't be changed or replaced by the user. Other models have one or more modular interfaces, allowing the user to add, remove, or replace interfaces as needed.

You might already be familiar with fixed interface identification, such as Serial 0, S0, Ethernet 0, and E0. Modular routers use notation such as Serial 0/0 or S0/1, where the first number refers to the module and the second number refers to the interface. Both notations use 0 as their starting reference, so S0/1 indicates that there is another serial interface S0/0.

Fast Ethernet. Many routers today are equipped with Fast Ethernet (10/100 Mbps autosensing) interfaces. You must use Fast Ethernet 0/0 or Fa0/0 on routers with Fast Ethernet interfaces.

The ip subnet-zero command. The **ip subnet-zero** command is enabled by default in IOS 12. This command allows you to assign IP addresses in the first subnet, called subnet 0. Because subnet 0 uses only binary zeros in the subnet field, its subnet address can potentially be confused with the major network address. With the advent of classless IP, the use of subnet 0 has become more common. The labs in this manual assume that you can assign addresses to the router's interfaces using subnet 0. If you use any routers that have an IOS earlier than 12.0, you must add the global configuration command, **ip subnet-zero**, to your router's configuration.

No shutdown. Interfaces are shut down by default. Remember to explicitly issue a **no shutdown** command in interface configuration mode when you are ready to bring up the interface.

Passwords. The **login** command is applied to virtual terminals by default. This means that, in order for your router to accept Telnet connections, you must configure a password. Otherwise, your router will not allow a Telnet connection, replying with the error message "password required, but none set."

Step 1

Take a few moments to examine your router. Familiarize yourself with any serial, BRI (ISDN), PRI (ISDN), and DSU/CSU interfaces on the router. Pay particular attention to any connectors or cables that are new to you.

Step 2

Establish a HyperTerminal session to the router.

Enter privileged EXEC mode.

Step 3

To clear the configuration, issue the **erase start** command.

Confirm your intentions when prompted, and answer "no" if you're asked to save changes. The result should look something like this:

```
Router#erase start
Erasing the nvram filesystem will remove all files! Continue?
[confirm]
[OK]
Erase of nvram: complete
Router#
```

When the prompt returns, issue the **reload** command.

Confirm your intentions when prompted. After the router finishes the boot process, choose not to use the AutoInstall feature, as shown:

```
Would you like to enter the initial configuration dialog? [yes/no]:
    no
Would you like to terminate autoinstall? [yes]: ← Press Enter to
    accept default.
Press RETURN to get started!
```

Step 4

In privileged mode, issue the **show run** command.

Note the following default configurations as you scroll through the running configuration:

- The version number of the IOS
- The **ip subnet-zero** command, which allows you to use subnet 0
- Each available interface and its name (*Note:* Each interface has the **shutdown** command applied to its configuration.)
- The **no ip http server** command, which prevents the router from being accessed by a Web browser

- No passwords are set for CON, AUX, and VTY sessions, as shown here:

```
line con 0
 transport input none
line aux 0
line vty 0 4
```

Using Copy and Paste with Notepad

In the next steps, you use the copy and paste feature to edit router configurations. You need to create a text file that can be pasted into your labs and used as a starting point for your router configuration. Specifically, you must build a login configuration that you can use with every lab included in this manual.

Step 5

If necessary, issue the **show run** command again so that **line con** and **line vty** are showing on your screen:

```
line con 0
 transport input none
line aux 0
line vty 0 4
!
end
```

Select the text as shown in the previous code and choose the Copy command from HyperTerminal's Edit menu.

Next, open Notepad, which is typically found on the Start menu under Programs, Accessories. After Notepad opens, select Paste from the Notepad Edit menu.

Edit the lines in Notepad to look like the following lines (the one-space indent is optional):

```
enable secret class
line con 0
 transport input none
 password cisco
 login
line aux 0
 password cisco
 login
line vty 0 4
 password cisco
 login
```

This configuration sets the enable secret to **class** and requires a login for all console, AUX port (usually a modem), and virtual terminal (Telnet) connections. The password for these connections is set to cisco. *Note:* Each of the passwords can be set to something else if you desire.

Step 6

Save the open file in Notepad to a floppy disk as start.txt.

Select all the lines in your Notepad document and choose Edit, Copy.

Step 7

Use the Windows taskbar to return to your HyperTerminal session, and enter global configuration mode.

From HyperTerminal's Edit menu, choose Paste to Host.

Issue the **show run** command to see if your configuration looks okay.

As a shortcut, you can now paste the contents of your start.txt file to any router before getting started with a lab.

Other Useful Commands

To enhance your **start.txt** file, you might consider adding one of the following commands:

- **ip subnet-zero** ensures that an older IOS allows IP addresses from subnet 0.
- **ip http server** allows you to access your routers using a Web browser. Although this configuration might not be desirable on a production router, it does give you an HTTP server for testing purposes in the lab.
- **no ip domain-lookup** prevents the router from attempting to query a DNS when you input a word that is not recognized as a command or a host table entry. This saves you time if you make a typo or misspell a command.
- **logging synchronous** in the **line con 0** configuration returns you to a fresh line when your input is interrupted by a console logging message.
- **configure terminal (conf f)** can be used in your file so that you don't have to type that command before pasting the contents of the file to the router.

Step 8

Use the Windows taskbar to return to Notepad and edit the lines so that they read as shown here:

```
config t
!
enable secret class
ip subnet-zero
ip http server
no ip domain-lookup
line con 0
 logging synchronous
 password cisco
 login
 transport input none
line aux 0
password cisco
 login
```

```
line vty 0 4
password cisco
 login
!
end
copy run start
```

Save your file to the floppy disk so that you do not lose your work.

Select and copy all the lines, and return to your HyperTerminal session.

Normally, you would enter global configuration mode before pasting, but because you included the **conf t** command in your script, you don't have to.

If necessary, return to privileged EXEC mode. From the Edit menu, select Paste to Host.

After the paste is complete, you must confirm the copy operation.

Use **show run** to see if your configuration looks okay.

Using Notepad to Assist in Editing

Understanding how to use Notepad can save you from typing and typos during editing sessions. Another major benefit is that you can do an entire router configuration in Notepad when you're at home or at the office and then paste it to the router's console when you have access. In the next steps, you look at a simple editing example.

Step 9

Configure the router with the following commands:

```
Router#config t
Router(config)#router rip
Router(config)#network 192.168.1.0
Router(config)#network 192.168.2.0
Router(config)#network 192.168.3.0
Router(config)#network 192.168.4.0
Router(config)#network 192.168.5.0
```

Press Ctrl+Z, and verify your configuration with **show run**. You just set up RIP to advertise a series of networks. But what if you want to change your routing protocol to IGRP? With the **no router rip** command, you easily get rid of RIP, but you still have to retype the **network** commands. The next steps show you an alternative.

Step 10

Issue the **show run** command and hold the output so that the **router rip** commands are displayed. Using the keyboard or mouse, select the **router rip** command and all **network** statements.

Copy the selection.

Use the taskbar to return to Notepad.

Open a new document and paste the selection onto the blank page.

Step 11

In the new document, type the word no and a space in front of the word router.

Press the End key, and press Enter.

Type **router igrp 100** (but do not press Enter). The result should look like this:

```
no router rip
router igrp 100
 network 192.168.1.0
 network 192.168.2.0
 network 192.168.3.0
 network 192.168.4.0
 network 192.168.5.0
```

Step 12

Select your results and copy them.

Use the taskbar to return to your HyperTerminal session.

While in global configuration mode, paste the results.

Use the **show run** command to verify your configuration.

Reflection

How could using copy and paste with Notepad be helpful in other editing situations?

_____

_____

_____

_____

_____

_____

_____

_____

_____

_____

Introductory Lab 2: Capturing HyperTerminal and Telnet Sessions

Objective

This activity describes how to capture HyperTerminal and Telnet sessions.

Note: Be sure to master these techniques. They will save you a tremendous amount of typing in later labs and while working in the field.

Step 1

Log in to a router using HyperTerminal.

It is possible to capture the results of your HyperTerminal session in a text file, which can be viewed and/or printed using Notepad, WordPad, or Microsoft Word.

Note: This feature captures future screens, not what is currently onscreen. In essence, you are turning on a recording session.

To start a capture session, choose the menu option Transfer, Capture Text. The Capture Text dialog box appears, as shown in the following figure.

The default filename for a HyperTerminal capture is **CAPTURE.TXT**, and the default location of this file is C:\Program Files\Accessories\HyperTerminal.

Note: When you are using Telnet, the command to begin a capture (or log) is Terminal, Start Logging. The document you create has LOG as the extension. Other than the name and path of the capture file, the logging procedures are the same for both Telnet and HyperTerminal.

Make sure that your floppy disk is in the A: drive. When the Capture Text dialog box appears, change the File path to A:\TestRun.txt.

Click the Start button. Anything that appears onscreen after this point is copied to the file.

Step 2

Issue the **show run** command again, and view the entire configuration file.

From the Transfer menu, choose Capture Text, Stop.

Telnet users should select Stop Logging from the Terminal menu to end the session.

Step 3

Using the Start menu, launch Windows Explorer. You might find Windows Explorer under Programs or Accessories, depending on which version of Windows you use.

In the left pane, select the 3 1/2 floppy (A:) drive. On the right side, you should see the file you just created.

Double-click the TestRun.txt document's icon. The result should look something like this:

```
Router#show run
Building configuration...

Current configuration:
!
version 12.0
service timestamps debug uptime
service timestamps log uptime
no service password-encryption
!
hostname Router
!
enable secret 5 $1$HD2B$6iXb.h6QEJJjtn/NnwUHO.
!
!
ip subnet-zero
no ip domain-lookup
!
interface FastEthernet0/0
 --More-- ▢▢▢▢▢▢ ▢▢▢▢▢▢ no ip address
 no ip directed-broadcast
 shutdown
```

You might see gibberish that appears near the word "More." This is where you have to press the spacebar to see the rest of the list. You can use basic word-processing techniques to clean that up.

Suggestion

You should consider capturing each router configuration for every lab that you do. Capture files can be valuable as you review configuration features and prepare for certification exams.

Reflection

Could the capture techniques be useful if a member of your lab team misses a lab session? Can you use capture techniques to configure an off-site lab?

_____
_____
_____
_____

Introductory Lab 3: Access Control List Basics and Extended Ping

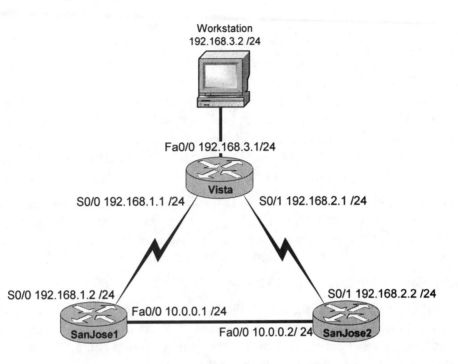

Workstation
192.168.3.2 /24

Fa0/0 192.168.3.1/24

Vista

S0/0 192.168.1.1 /24   S0/1 192.168.2.1 /24

S0/0 192.168.1.2 /24   S0/1 192.168.2.2 /24
Fa0/0 10.0.0.1 /24
SanJose1   Fa0/0 10.0.0.2/ 24   SanJose2

Objective

This lab activity reviews the basics of standard and extended access lists, which are used extensively in the CCNP curriculum.

Scenario

The LAN users connected to the Vista router are concerned about access to their network from hosts on network 10.0.0.0. You must use a standard access list to block all access to Vista's LAN from network 10.0.0.0/24.

You must also use an extended ACL to block network 192.168.3.0 host access to Web servers on the 10.0.0.0/24 network.

Step 1

Build and configure the network according to the diagram. Use RIPv1, and enable updates on all active interfaces with the appropriate **network** commands. The commands necessary to configure SanJose1 are shown here as an example:

```
SanJose1(config)#router rip
SanJose1(config-router)#network 192.168.1.0
SanJose1(config-router)#network 10.0.0.0
```

Use the **ping** command to verify your work and test connectivity among all interfaces.

Step 2

Check the routing table on Vista using the **show ip route** command. Vista should have all four networks in its table. Troubleshoot if necessary.

Access Control List Basics

Access Control Lists (ACLs) are simple but powerful tools. When the access list is configured, each statement in the list is processed by the router in the order in which it was created. If an individual packet meets a statement's criteria, the permit or deny is applied to that packet, and no further list entries are checked. The next packet to be checked starts again at the top of the list.

It is not possible to reorder an access list, skip statements, edit statements, or delete statements from a numbered access list. With numbered access lists, any attempt to delete a single statement results in the entire list's deletion. *Note*: Named ACLs (NACLs) do allow for the deletion of individual statements.

The following concepts apply to both standard and extended access lists:

Two-step process. First, the access list is created with one or more **access-list** commands while in global configuration mode. Second, the access list is applied to or referenced by other commands, such as the **access-group** command, to apply an ACL to an interface. An example would be the following:

```
Vista#config t
Vista(config)#access-list 50 deny 10.0.0.0 0.0.0.255
Vista(config)#access-list 50 permit any
Vista(config)#interface fastethernet 0/0
Vista(config-if)#ip access-group 50 out
Vista(config-if)#^Z
```

Syntax and Keywords

The basic syntax for creating an access list entry is as follows:

```
router(config)#access-list acl-number {permit | deny}...
```

The **permit** command allows packets matching the specified criteria to be accepted for whatever application the access list is being used for. The **deny** command discards packets matching the criteria on that line.

Two important keywords that can be used with IP addresses and the **access list** command are **any** and **host**. The keyword **any** matches all hosts on all networks (equivalent to **0.0.0.0 255.255.255.255**). The keyword **host** can be used with an IP address to indicate a single host address. The syntax is **host** *ip-address*, such as **host 192.168.1.10**. This is treated exactly the same as 192.168.1.10 0.0.0.0.

Implicit deny statement. Every access list contains a final "deny" statement that matches all packets. This is called the implicit deny. Because the implicit **deny**

statement is not visible in **show** command output, it is often overlooked, with dire consequences. As an example, consider the following single-line access list:

```
Router(config)#access-list 75 deny host 192.168.1.10
```

Access-list 75 clearly denies all traffic sourced from the host, 192.168.1.10. What might not be obvious is that all other traffic will be discarded as well, because the implicit **deny any** is the final statement in any access list.

At least one permit statement is required. There is no requirement that an ACL contain a **deny** statement. If nothing else, the implicit **deny any** statement takes care of that. But if there are no **permit** statements, the effect will be the same as if there were only a single **deny any** statement.

Wildcard mask. In identifying IP addresses, ACLs use a wildcard mask instead of a subnet mask. Initially, they might look like the same thing, but closer observation reveals that they are very different. Remember that a binary 0 in a wildcard bitmask instructs the router to match the corresponding bit in the IP address.

In/out. When you are deciding whether an ACL should be applied to inbound or outbound traffic, always view things from the router's perspective. In other words, determine whether traffic is coming into the router (inbound) or leaving the router (outbound).

Applying ACLs. Extended ACLs should be applied as close to the source as possible, thereby conserving network resources. Standard ACLs (by necessity) must be applied as close to the destination as possible, because the standard ACL can match only at the source address of a packet.

Step 3

On the Vista router, create the following standard ACL and apply it to the LAN interface:

```
Vista#config t
Vista(config)#access-list 50 deny 10.0.0.0 0.0.0.255
Vista(config)#access-list 50 permit any
Vista(config)#interface fastethernet 0/0
Vista(config-if)#ip access-group 50 out
Vista(config-if)#^Z
```

Try pinging 192.168.3.2 from SanJose1.

The ping should be successful. This result might be surprising, because you just blocked all traffic from the 10.0.0.0/8 network. The ping is successful because, even though it came from SanJose1, it is not sourced from the 10.0.0.0/8 network. A ping or traceroute from a router uses the closest interface to the destination as the source address. Thus, the ping is coming from the 192.168.1.0/24 (SanJose1's Serial 0/0).

In order to test the ACL from SanJose1, you must use the extended ping command to specify a specific source interface.

Step 4

On SanJose1, issue the following commands. Remember that the extended ping works only in privileged mode:

```
SanJose1#ping 192.168.3.2
Sending 5, 100-byte ICMP Echos to 192.168.3.2, timeout is 2 seconds:
!!!!!
Success rate is 100 percent (5/5), round-trip min/avg/max = 4/4/4 ms
SanJose1#
SanJose1#ping
Protocol [ip]:
Target IP address: 192.168.3.2
Repeat count [5]:
Datagram size [100]:
Timeout in seconds [2]:
Extended commands [n]: y
Source address or interface: 10.0.0.1
Type of service [0]:
Set DF bit in IP header? [no]:
Validate reply data? [no]:
Data pattern [0xABCD]:
Loose, Strict, Record, Timestamp, Verbose[none]:
Sweep range of sizes [n]:
Type escape sequence to abort.
Sending 5, 100-byte ICMP Echos to 192.168.3.2, timeout is 2 seconds:
.....
Success rate is 0 percent (0/5)
```

Step 5

Standard ACLs are numbered 1-99 (IOS 12 also allows standard lists to be numbered 1300–1699). Extended ACLs are numbered (IOS 12 allows 2000-2699). Extended ACLs can be used to enforce highly specific criteria for filtering packets. In this step, you will configure an extended ACL to block access to a Web server. Before you proceed, issue the **no access-list 50** and **no ip access-group 50** commands on the Vista router to remove the ACL configured previously.

First, you must configure both SanJose1 and SanJose2 to act as Web servers by using the **ip http server** command, as shown here:

```
SanJose1(config)#ip http server
SanJose2(config)#ip http server
```

From the workstation at 192.168.3.2, use a Web browser to view both routers' Web servers at 10.0.0.1 and 10.0.0.2. The Web login requires that you enter the router's enable secret password as the password.

After you verify Web connectivity between the workstation and the routers, proceed to Step 6.

Step 6

On the Vista router, enter the following commands:

```
Vista(config)#access-list 101 deny tcp 192.168.3.0 0.0.0.255 10.0.0.0
      0.0.0.255 eq www
Vista(config)#access-list 101 deny tcp 192.168.3.0 0.0.0.255 any eq
      ftp
Vista(config)#access-list 101 permit ip any any
Vista(config)#interface fastetherent 0/0
Vista(config)#ip access-group 101 in
```

From the workstation at 192.168.3.2, again attempt to view the Web servers at 10.0.0.1 and 10.0.0.2. Both attempts should fail.

Next, browse SanJose1 at 192.168.1.2. Why isn't this blocked?

_____

Lab 2-1: Configuring an Asynchronous Connection

Objective

In this lab, you configure a serial interface on a Cisco router to enable an asynchronous connection via a modem. You also use a workstation to remotely dial in to the router.

Scenario

The International Travel Agency wants you to configure their SanJose1 core router's serial interface to accept dialup connections so it can be managed remotely in the event of a network failure. As the network administrator, you must configure the modem to allow management sessions only. You won't set up dial-on-demand routing (DDR).

Step 1

Before you begin this lab, it is recommended that you reload the router after erasing its startup configuration. This prevents you from having problems caused by residual configurations. Build the network according to the previous diagram, but do not configure the router's interface. Use the Adtran Atlas 550 or a similar device to simulate the Public Switched Telephone Network (PSTN). If you are using the Atlas 550, the line cables from both modems must be plugged into the octal FXS voice module ports of the Atlas 550 as labeled in the diagram. (The diagram assumes the octal FXS voice module is installed in slot 3.)

Cable Connection Notes: Be sure to use the appropriate cable to connect the modem to the router's serial interface. The specific cable used will depend on the router model and type of physical serial interface. For example, different cables are used for a Smart Serial interface and a DB-60 serial interface.

Step 2

Configure SanJose1's serial interface for an asynchronous connection:

```
SanJose1(config)#interface s0/1
SanJose1(config-if)#physical-layer async
```

After entering these commands, issue the **show interface s0/1** command, as shown:

```
SanJose1#show int s0/1
Serial0/1 is down, line protocol is down
  Hardware is PQUICC Serial in async mode
  MTU 1500 bytes, BW 9 Kbit, DLY 100000 usec,
      reliability 255/255, txload 1/255, rxload 1/255
  Encapsulation SLIP, loopback not set
  DTR is pulsed for 5 seconds on reset
  Last input never, output never, output hang never
  Last clearing of "show interface" counters never
  Input queue: 0/75/0 (size/max/drops); Total output drops: 0
  Queuing strategy: weighted fair
  Output queue: 0/1000/64/0 (size/max total/threshold/drops)
     Conversations   0/0/16 (active/max active/max total)
     Reserved Conversations 0/0 (allocated/max allocated)
<output omitted>
```

1. According to the output of the **show** command, what is the default encapsulation type for an interface in physical-layer async mode?

_____

After the serial interface is configured as asynchronous, you need to figure out what line number the router is using for that interface. If you are unfamiliar with your router model's numbering scheme, you can use the **show line** command to determine the line number, as shown in this example:

```
SanJose1#show line
 Tty   Typ    Tx/Rx  A Modem    Roty  AccO  AccI  Uses  Noise
        Overruns  Int
    *  0     CTY            -     -     -     -     -    0     1
        0/0      -
    2    TTY  9600/9600  -     -     -     -     -    0     0    0/0
        Se0/1
   65    AUX  9600/9600  -     -     -     -     -    0     0    0/0
         -
   66    VTY            -     -     -     -     -    0     1    0/0
         -
   67    VTY            -     -     -     -     -    0     1    0/0
         -
   68    VTY            -     -     -     -     -    0     1    0/0
         -
   69    VTY            -     -     -     -     -    0     1    0/0
         -
   70    VTY            -     -     -     -     -    0     1    0/0
         -

Line(s) not in async mode -or- with no hardware support: 1, 3-64
```

The shaded portion of the sample **show line** command output above shows that Serial 0/1 is TTY 2.

Use your router's **show line** output to obtain the correct line number, then enter the line configuration mode, as shown in this example:

```
SanJose1(config)#line 2
```

Step 3

From the line configuration mode, configure the router to authenticate connections with the password cisco, as shown:

```
SanJose1(config-line)#login
SanJose1(config-line)#password cisco
```

Set the line speed and flow control type:

```
SanJose1(config-line)#speed 115200
SanJose1(config-line)#flowcontrol hardware
```

Next, configure the line for both incoming and outgoing calls and allow incoming calls using all available protocols. These commands allow you to reverse Telnet to the modem:

```
SanJose1(config-line)#modem inout
SanJose1(config-line)#transport input all
```

The default number of stopbits used by the router's asynchronous line is 2. Configure the line to use only 1 stopbit:

```
SanJose1(config-line)#stopbits 1
```

Reducing the number of stopbits from 2 to 1 improves throughput by reducing asynchronous framing overhead.

This completes the line configuration.

Step 4

In this step, you configure a router interface for TCP/IP. The router must have an operational interface with a valid IP address in order to establish a reverse Telnet connection to the modem. Although a physical interface could be configured with an IP address, you must configure SanJose1 with a loopback interface. A loopback interface is the best way to assign an IP address to the router because loopbacks are immune to link failure. Use the following commands to configure the loopback interface:

```
SanJose1(config-line)#interface loopback0
SanJose1(config-if)#ip address 192.168.0.1 255.255.255.255
```

Note: A 32-bit mask is used when configuring a loopback IP address. If you do not use a 32-bit mask, you are configuring your router as if it were connected to an entire subnet or network.

Step 5

After the loopback has an IP address, you can configure the modem using reverse Telnet. Before you establish a Telnet session, first secure virtual terminal access with the following commands:

```
SanJose1(config-if)#line vty 0 4
SanJose1(config-line)#login
SanJose1(config-line)#password cisco
SanJose1(config-line)#exit
```

Use the command below to open the reverse Telnet session to line 2. (If your router is not using line2, you have to change the last number to the line number appropriate to your router.)

```
SanJose1#telnet 192.168.0.1 2002
```

At this point, you are prompted for a login password. Type the password cisco and press the Enter key; this should begin a session with the modem. Although there is no prompt, issue the following command:

```
AT
```

If the modem responds with an OK, you have successfully established a reverse Telnet connection. If you do not receive an OK, troubleshoot your configuration.

Step 6

View the modem's current configuration by issuing the following command (a sample output is shown here):

```
OK
AT&V

    Option              Selection       AT Cmd
    ---------------     ------------    --------
    Comm Standard       Bell            B
    CommandCharEcho     Enabled         E
    Speaker Volume      Medium          L
    Speaker Control     OnUntilCarrier  M
    Result Codes        Enabled         Q
    Dialer Type         Tone            T/P
    ResultCode Form     Text            V
    ExtendResultCode    Enabled         X
    DialTone Detect     Enabled         X
    BusyTone Detect     Enabled         X
    LSD Action          Standard RS232  &C
    DTR Action          Standard RS232  &D
Press any key to continue; ESC to quit.

    Option              Selection       AT Cmd
    ---------------     ------------    --------
    V22b Guard Tone     Disabled        &G
    Flow Control        Hardware        &K
    Error Control Mode  V42,MNP,Buffer  \N
    Data Compression    V42bis/MNP5     %C
    AutoAnswerRing#     0            S0
    AT Escape Char      43              S2
```

```
          CarriageReturn Char   13                S3
          Linefeed Char         10                S4
          Backspace Char        8                 S5
          Blind Dial Pause      2 sec             S6
          NoAnswer Timeout      50 sec            S7
          "," Pause Time        2 sec             S8
     Press any key to continue; ESC to quit.

          Option                Selection         AT Cmd
          ---------------       ------------      --------
          No Carrier Disc       2000 msec         S10
          DTMF Dial Speed       95 msec           S11
          Escape GuardTime      1000 msec         S12
          Data Calling Tone     Disabled          S35
          Line Rate             33600             S37
     Press any key to continue; ESC to quit.

          Stored Phone Numbers
          --------------------
           &Z0=
           &Z1=
           &Z2=
```

The modem outputs its configuration information, which is stored in NVRAM.
Reset the modem to its factory defaults by entering the following command:

AT&F

After the modem is reset, issue the AT&V command again. A sample output is shown
here:

AT&V

```
          Option                Selection         AT Cmd
          ---------------       ------------      --------
          Comm Standard         Bell              B
          CommandCharEcho       Enabled           E
          Speaker Volume        Medium            L
          Speaker Control       OnUntilCarrier    M
          Result Codes          Enabled           Q
          Dialer Type           Tone              T/P
          ResultCode Form       Text              V
          ExtendResultCode      Enabled           X
          DialTone Detect       Enabled           X
          BusyTone Detect       Enabled           X
          LSD Action            Standard RS232    &C
          DTR Action            Standard RS232    &D
     Press any key to continue; ESC to quit.

          Option                Selection         AT Cmd
          ---------------       ------------      --------
          V22b Guard Tone       Disabled          &G
          Flow Control          Hardware          &K
          Error Control Mode    V42,MNP,Buffer    \N
          Data Compression      V42bis/MNP5       %C
          AutoAnswerRing#       0                 S0
          AT Escape Char        43                S2
          CarriageReturn Char   13                S3
          Linefeed Char         10                S4
          Backspace Char        8                 S5
          Blind Dial Pause      2 sec             S6
```

```
        NoAnswer Timeout       50 sec            S7
        "," Pause Time         2 sec             S8
Press any key to continue; ESC to quit.

        Option                 Selection         AT Cmd
        ---------------        ------------      --------
        No Carrier Disc        2000 msec         S10
        DTMF Dial Speed        95 msec           S11
        Escape GuardTime       1000 msec         S12
        Data Calling Tone      Disabled          S35
        Line Rate              33600             S37
Press any key to continue; ESC to quit.

        Stored Phone Numbers
        --------------------
          &Z0=
          &Z1=
          &Z2=
```

2. To what is the speaker volume set?

   _____

3. According to the output of the **AT&V** command, what is the AT command used to configure the speaker volume?

   _____

4. To what is the AutoAnswerRing# set?

   _____

5. What is the AT command used to configure the AutoAnswerRing#?

   _____

6. To what is the flow control set?

   _____

7. What is the AT command used to configure the flow control?

   _____

   Note: The ampersand (&) character, which denotes an advanced command, must be included in certain AT commands.

   Configure the modem to answer on the second ring using the following command:

   ATS0=2

   Adjust the modem's speaker volume, using this command:

   ATL3

   Use the appropriate command (**AT&V**) to view the modem's current settings and verify that your configurations have taken effect.

Finally, write (save) your configurations to NVRAM with this command:

```
AT&W
```

Step 7

Now that your modem is configured, suspend the reverse Telnet session by pressing Control+Shift+6 at the same time, release, then press X. You are returned to the router prompt. From the router prompt, disconnect the reverse Telnet session from the modem:

```
SanJose1#disconnect
```

If you do not disconnect this session, you will not be able connect to the router via the dialup.

One way to check if the Telnet session is active or not is to issue the **show line** command. The highlighted sections of the sample outputs below show the differences between an active and an idle connection.

Here's the output before establishing a reverse Telnet connection:

```
SanJose1#show line 2
   Tty Typ     Tx/Rx      A Modem  Roty AccO AccI  Uses   Noise
       Overruns   Int
     2 TTY 115200/115200- inout    -    -    -      1        0
       0/0      Se0/1

Line 2, Location: "", Type: ""
Length: 24 lines, Width: 80 columns
Baud rate (TX/RX) is 115200/115200, no parity, 1 stopbits, 8 databits
Status: No Exit Banner
Capabilities: Hardware Flowcontrol In, Hardware Flowcontrol Out
  Modem Callout, Modem RI is CD
Modem state: Idle
Modem hardware state: CTS noDSR  DTR RTS
Special Chars: Escape  Hold  Stop  Start  Disconnect  Activation
               ^^x     none   -     -       none
Timeouts:      Idle EXEC    Idle Session    Modem Answer  Session
      Dispatch
               00:10:00        never                         none
          not set
                               Idle Session Disconnect Warning
                                 never
                               Login-sequence User Response
                                 00:00:30
                         Autoselect Initial Wait
                               not set
Modem type is unknown.
Session limit is not set.
Time since activation: never
Editing is enabled.
History is enabled, history size is 10.
DNS resolution in show commands is enabled
Full user help is disabled
Allowed transports are pad v120 telnet rlogin mop.  Preferred is
telnet.
```

```
No output characters are padded
No special data dispatching characters
Router#
```

Here's the output during a reverse Telnet session:

```
SanJose1#show line 2
    Tty Typ    Tx/Rx      A Modem  Roty AccO AccI   Uses   Noise
        Overruns   Int
*    2 TTY 115200/115200- inout       -    -    -      2       0
        0/0    Se0/1

Line 2, Location: "", Type: "synch"
Length: 24 lines, Width: 80 columns
Baud rate (TX/RX) is 115200/115200, no parity, 1 stopbits, 8 databits
Status: Ready, Connected, Active, No Exit Banner
Capabilities: Hardware Flowcontrol In, Hardware Flowcontrol Out
  Modem Callout, Modem RI is CD
Modem state: Ready
Modem hardware state: CTS noDSR  DTR RTS
Special Chars: Escape  Hold  Stop  Start  Disconnect  Activation
              ^^x    none   -     -      none
Timeouts:       Idle EXEC    Idle Session   Modem Answer  Session
        Dispatch
                00:10:00       never                         none
        not set
                                Idle Session Disconnect Warning
                                  never
                                Login-sequence User Response
                                 00:00:30
                                Autoselect Initial Wait
                                  not set
Modem type is unknown.
Session limit is not set.
Time since activation: 00:00:50
Editing is enabled.
History is enabled, history size is 10.
DNS resolution in show commands is enabled
Full user help is disabled
Allowed transports are pad v120 telnet rlogin mop.  Preferred is
telnet.
No output characters are padded
No special data dispatching characters
```

On Host A, use the modem control panel to check that the modem is properly installed and working. Run HyperTerminal and select the modem from the Connect To window. Then configure HyperTerminal to dial the appropriate number. If you are using the Adtran Atlas 550, this number will be 555-6001.

At the password prompt, enter the cisco password. Next, you should see SanJose1's user mode prompt. Issue the **who** command, as shown:

```
SanJose>who

    Line      User       Host(s)              Idle Location
    0 con 0              idle                 00:26:49
*   2 tty 2              idle                 00:00:00

    Interface User      Mode                 Idle Peer Address
```

8. According to the output of this command, what TTY are you using to communicate with the router?

_____

9. Because you cannot use this connection to route TCP/IP traffic, what is the benefit of configuring a serial interface to accept calls this way?

_____

Lab 2-2: Configuring an Asynchronous Connection on the AUX Port

Objective

In this lab, you configure an AUX port on a Cisco router to accept dial-in connections from a workstation.

Scenario

The International Travel Agency wants you to configure their SanJose1 core router to accept dialup connections on its AUX port so it can be managed remotely in the event of a network failure. As the network administrator, you are to configure the modem to allow management sessions only. You won't set up DDR.

Step 1

Before beginning this lab, it is recommended that you reload each router after erasing its startup configuration. This prevents you from having problems caused by residual configurations.

Build (cable) the network according to the previous diagram. Use the Adtran Atlas 550 or a similar device to simulate the PSTN. If you are using the Atlas 550, make sure the line cables from both modems are plugged into the octal FXS voice module ports of the Atlas 550 as labeled in the diagram.

Use a rollover cable and a DCE modem adapter to connect the external modem to the router's AUX port.

Step 2

Configure SanJose1's AUX port for an asynchronous connection that will use authentication:

```
SanJose1(config)#line aux 0
SanJose1(config-line)#login
SanJose1(config-line)#password cisco
```

Set the line speed, flow control type, and number of stopbits:

```
SanJose1(config-line)#speed 115200
SanJose1(config-line)#flowcontrol hardware
SanJose1(config-line)#stopbits 1
```

The maximum speed supported by the AUX port varies depending on the router model that you are using. On the 2600 and 3600 series routers, 115200 is the maximum while other platforms might only support up to 38400. Typically, you should lock the modem speed at the maximum bit rate supported by both the router and the modem.

Next, configure the line for both incoming and outgoing calls, and allow incoming calls using all available protocols and set an enable secret password:

```
SanJose1(config-line)#modem inout
SanJose1(config-line)#transport input all
SanJose1(config-line)#exit
SanJose1(config)#enable secret cisco
SanJose1(config)#exit
```

Step 3

On SanJose1, issue the **show line** command. A sample output is shown here:

```
SanJose1>show line
   Tty Typ      Tx/Rx     A Modem  Roty AccO AccI   Uses   Noise
        Overruns    Int
*    0 CTY                 -   -      -    -    -      1       0
       0/0        -
*   65 AUX 115200/115200-  inout     -    -    -      1       1
      24/0        -
    66 VTY                 -   -      -    -    -      0       0
       0/0        -
    67 VTY                 -   -      -    -    -      0       0
       0/0        -
    68 VTY                 -   -      -    -    -      0       0
       0/0        -
    69 VTY                 -   -      -    -    -      0       0
       0/0        -
    70 VTY                 -   -      -    -    -      0       0
       0/0        -

Line(s) not in async mode -or- with no hardware support:
1-64
```

1. According to the output of this command, what is the line number for your router's AUX port?

_____

At this point, have the router automatically configure the modem without establishing a reverse Telnet connection. Instead of using reverse Telnet to configure the modem, you must use the Cisco IOS autoconfiguration feature. The **debug confmodem** command can be used to monitor the autoconfiguration process.

Enter the following commands on SanJose1, beginning in privileged mode, as shown here:

```
SanJose1#debug confmodem
SanJose1#configure terminal
SanJose1(config)#line 65
SanJose1(config-line)#modem autoconfigure discovery
```

After you type the modem autoconfigure discovery command, you should see debug output as the router queries and configures the modem (a sample **debug confmodem** output is shown here). The entire process can take approximately 30 seconds or more.

```
SanJose1#debug modem
Modem control/process activation debugging is on
SanJose1#
02:47:20: TTY65: DSR came up
02:47:20: tty65: Modem: IDLE->(unknown)
02:47:20: TTY65: EXEC creation
02:47:20: TTY65: set timer type 10, 30 seconds
SanJose1#
02:47:35: TTY65: create timer type 1, 600 seconds
SanJose1#
02:49:52: TTY65: Line reset by "Exec"
02:49:52: TTY65: Modem: (unknown)->HANGUP
02:49:52: TTY65: destroy timer type 0
02:49:52: TTY65: destroy timer type 1 (OK)
02:49:52: TTY65: destroy timer type 3
02:49:52: TTY65: destroy timer type 4
02:49:52: TTY65: destroy timer type 2
02:49:53: TTY65: dropping DTR, hanging up
02:49:53: TTY65: Set DTR to 0
02:49:53: tty65: Modem: HANGUP->IDLE
SanJose1#
02:49:55: TTY65: restoring DTR
02:49:55: TTY65: Set DTR to 1
02:49:56: TTY65: autoconfigure probe started
```

Note: Whenever possible, you should manually configure a modem or use a specific modem configuration script. The IOS modem discovery feature is unlikely to provide an optimal modem configuration.

Although you used the modem autoconfiguration feature, you might also want to establish a reverse Telnet session to the modem via the AUX port.

2. What port number would you Telnet to in order to connect to the modem on the AUX port?

_____

Step 4

Enter the following commands to enable a Telnet session with password authentication and an active interface:

```
SanJose1(config)#line vty 0 4
SanJose1(config-line)#login
SanJose1(config-line)#password cisco
SanJose1(config-line)#interface loopback 0
SanJose1(config-if)#ip address 192.168.0.1 255.255.255.255
```

3. Why should you assign a password to the virtual terminals?

_____

_____

4. Why did you need to assign an IP address to a loopback interface?

_____

_____

5. Why is a 32-bit mask used with the loopback address?

_____

_____

Finally, you might want to take advantage of the router's host table to make starting a reverse Telnet session easier. Enter the following command to create a host table mapping that will include both the IP address and the reverse Telnet port number:

```
SanJose1(config)#ip host modem 2065 192.168.0.1
```

The port number 2065 used in the previous command example might not work with your router. Use the output of the **show line** command to determine the correct number for the model you are using. A sample output is shown here:

```
SanJose1#show line
   Tty Typ    Tx/Rx     A Modem  Roty AccO AccI  Uses  Noise
       Overruns   Int
*    0 CTY               -   -     -    -    -     1      0
       0/0       -
    65 AUX 115200/115200- inout   -    -    -     1      1
      24/0       -
    66 VTY               -   -     -    -    -     0      0
       0/0       -
    67 VTY               -   -     -    -    -     0      0
       0/0       -
    68 VTY               -   -     -    -    -     0      0
       0/0       -
    69 VTY               -   -     -    -    -     0      0
       0/0       -
    70 VTY               -   -     -    -    -     0      0
       0/0       -

Line(s) not in async mode -or- with no hardware support:
1-64
```

After you configure the host table mapping, you only need to type the host name to start a Telnet session. Enter the host name at the prompt, as shown here:

```
SanJose1#modem
```

This opens a reverse Telnet session with the modem. Issue the **AT&V** command to verify that you are talking to the modem. Troubleshoot as necessary.

To disconnect the reverse Telnet session, do the following:

```
CTRL-SHIFT-6 then X
SanJose1#disconnect
```

Step 5

On Host A, use the modem control panel to check that the modem is properly installed and working. Run HyperTerminal and select the modem from the Connect To window. Then configure HyperTerminal to dial the appropriate number. If you are using the Adtran Atlas 550, this number will be 555-6001.

If Host A successfully connects to SanJose1, you will see a password prompt. At the password prompt, enter the "cisco" password to access the router. Troubleshoot as necessary.

Lab 2-3: Configuring Asynchronous PPP

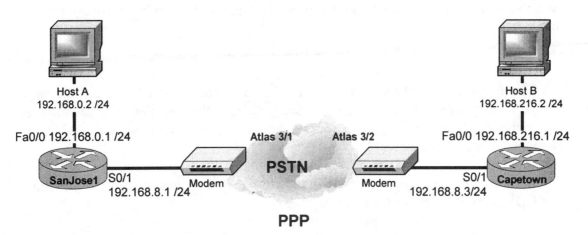

PPP

Objective

In this lab, you configure two Cisco routers to connect to each other asynchronously using PPP.

Scenario

The International Travel Agency wants to give a remote site, Capetown, access to the company's headquarters, SanJose1. Capetown needs only occasional access to company e-mail. As the network administrator, you are asked to configure a dialup PPP connection between the two sites. When you are finished, Capetown will be able to establish a DDR connection to SanJose1. You will verify this configuration by sending a ping from Capetown's Host B to SanJose1 Host A.

Step 1

Before beginning this lab, it is recommended that you reload each router after erasing its startup configuration. This prevents you from having problems caused by residual configurations. Build and configure the network according to the above diagram, but do not configure either router's serial interfaces yet. Use the Adtran Atlas 550 or similar device to simulate the PSTN. If you are using the Atlas 550, be sure the line cables from both modems are plugged into the octal FXS voice module ports of the Atlas 550 as labeled in the diagram. Also, be sure to configure both workstations with the correct IP address and default gateway (router Fa0/0 IP address).

Step 2

Configure Capetown's serial interface for an asynchronous connection:

```
Capetown(config)#interface s0/1
Capetown(config-if)#physical-layer async
Capetown(config-if)#ip address 192.168.8.3 255.255.255.0
Capetown(config-if)#encapsulation ppp
Capetown(config-if)#async mode dedicated
```

The command, **ppp encapsulation**, configures the serial interface to use PPP encapsulation.

1. What is the default encapsulation type for a serial interface when in physical-layer async mode?

The **async mode dedicated** command puts the interface in dedicated asynchronous network mode. In this mode, the interface only uses the specified encapsulation (PPP, in this case). An EXEC prompt does not appear, and the router is not available for normal interactive use.

Because you are configuring a low-bandwidth dialup connection, you should turn off CDP updates to reduce bandwidth usage.

```
Capetown(config-if)#no cdp enable
```

You must also enter additional commands so that Capetown can dial up SanJose1:

```
Capetown(config-if)#dialer in-band
```

The **dialer in-band** command specifies that the interface will support DDR.

```
Capetown(config-if)#dialer idle-timeout 300
```

The **dialer idle-timeout** command specifies the number of seconds the router will allow the connection to remain idle before disconnecting. The default is 120 seconds.

```
Capetown(config-if)#dialer wait-for-carrier-time 60
```

The **dialer wait-for-carrier-time** command specifies the length of time the interface waits for a carrier when trying to establish a connection. The default wait time is 30 seconds. The routers in this lab use a chat script to initialize the modem and cause it to dial (you will configure a chat script later in this step). On asynchronous interfaces, the **dialer wait-for-carrier-time** command essentially sets the total time allowed for the chat script to run.

```
Capetown(config-if)#dialer hold-queue 50
```

The **dialer hold-queue** command is used to allow outgoing packets to be queued until a modem connection is established. If no hold queue is configured, packets are dropped during the time required to establish a connection. The 50 in this command specifies 50 packets.

```
Capetown(config-if)#dialer-group 1
```

The **dialer-group** command controls access by configuring an interface to belong to a specific dialing group. In Step 3, you specify what kind of traffic will trigger DDR for interfaces belonging to group 1 (using the **dialer-list** command).

```
Capetown(config-if)#dialer map ip 192.168.8.1 name SanJose1 modem-
    script
    hayes56k broadcast 5556001
```

This **dialer map** command creates a mapping between an IP address and the phone number that should be dialed to reach that address. It also tells the router to use the appropriate chat script. Chat scripts are used in DDR to give commands to dial a modem and commands to log on to remote systems.

This completes the interface configuration. Enter global configuration mode to define the chat script. The following command should be used with Hayes 56 K Accura modems:

```
Capetown(config)#chat-script hayes56k ABORT ERROR "" "AT Z" OK "ATDT
    \T"
    TIMEOUT 30 CONNECT\c
```

Step 3

After the serial interface and chat script are configured for asynchronous PPP, configure the line parameters as shown here:

```
Capetown(config)#line 2
Capetown(config-line)#speed 115200
Capetown(config-line)#flowcontrol hardware
Capetown(config-line)#modem inout
Capetown(config-line)#transport input all
Capetown(config-line)#stopbits 1
```

2. What is the default number of stopbits on a line?

_____

Step 4

Finally, configure Capetown to establish a dialup connection for IP traffic:

```
Capetown(config)#dialer-list 1 protocol ip permit
```

Because this dialer list is numbered 1, it is linked to dialer group 1. The **dialer-list** command specifies the traffic that is to be permitted on interfaces that belong to the corresponding dialer group.

In order for Capetown to route traffic via the Serial 0/1 interface, configure this default route to the central site:

```
Capetown(config)#ip route 0.0.0.0 0.0.0.0 192.168.8.1
```

This completes the remote Capetown router configuration.

Step 5

Configure the company headquarters router, SanJose1. Enter the following commands:

```
SanJose1(config)#interface s0/1
SanJose1(config-if)#physical-layer async
SanJose1(config-if)#ip address 192.168.8.1 255.255.255.0
SanJose1(config-if)#encapsulation ppp
SanJose1(config-if)#async mode dedicated
SanJose1(config-if)#no cdp enable
SanJose1(config)#line 2
SanJose1(config-line)#speed 115200
SanJose1(config-line)#flowcontrol hardware
SanJose1(config-line)#modem inout
SanJose1(config-line)#transport input all
SanJose1(config-line)#stopbits 1
SanJose1(config-line)#modem autoconfigure discovery
SanJose1(config)#ip route 192.168.216.0 255.255.255.0 192.168.8.3
```

Step 6

At this point, you might want to reboot all of the lab equipment in order to prevent potential problems with residual configurations. Write both SanJose1's and Capetown's configuration to NVRAM and reload the router, power cycle the modem, and power cycle the Adtran Atlas 550.

Step 7

From Capetown Host B, ping SanJose1 Host A (192.168.0.2). The first set of pings might fail. If they do, issue the **ping** command a second or third time. Eventually, the ping should be successful, which means Capetown Host B has dialed SanJose1 Host A and your configuration is working. Troubleshoot as necessary.

After you verify successful pings, issue the **show dialer** command on Capetown. A sample output is shown here:

```
Capetown#show dialer

Serial0/1 - dialer type = IN-BAND ASYNC NO-PARITY
Idle timer (300 secs), Fast idle timer (20 secs)
Wait for carrier (60 secs), Re-enable (15 secs)
Dialer state is data link layer up
Dial reason: ip (s=192.168.216.2, d=192.168.0.2)
Time until disconnect 217 secs
Connected to 5556001

Dial String      Successes    Failures    Last DNIS    Last status
5556001                  1           0    00:04:19        successful
```

3. What is the dialer type of S0/1?

_____

4. What is the dialer state?

_____

5. What is the dial reason?

_____

6. How much longer will this connection remain up if it is idle?

_____

Lab 3-1: Configuring PPP Interactive Mode

Objective

In this lab, you configure a Cisco router to connect asynchronously to a modem and use a workstation (Host A) to remotely dial in to the router. You also configure PPP interactive mode, so that Host A's user can select between a PPP session and a router management EXEC session.

Scenario

The International Travel Agency wants you to configure dialup access to the central router SanJose1. The company wants you to set up access so that the remote user at Host A can dial up the router for either an EXEC management session on the router, or a PPP connection to the corporate LAN. This configuration will allow the dialup user to choose between configuring the router remotely and accessing the central site's network. Because the user might choose to access International Travel Agency's TCP/IP-based network, your configuration must account for assigning an IP address to Host A.

Step 1

Before beginning this lab, it is recommended that you reload the router after erasing its startup configuration. This prevents you from having problems caused by residual configurations. Build and configure the network according to the above diagram, but do not configure SanJose1's serial interface yet. Configure SanJose1 with the appropriate hostname and loopback 0 IP address. Use the Adtran Atlas 550, or a similar device, to simulate the PSTN. If you are using the Atlas 550, be sure the line cables from both modems are plugged into the octal FXS voice module ports of the Atlas 550 as labeled in the diagram.

Step 2

Configure SanJose1's serial interface for an asynchronous connection:

```
SanJose1(config)#interface s0/1
SanJose1(config-if)#physical-layer async
SanJose1(config-if)#ip address 192.168.8.1 255.255.255.0
SanJose1(config-if)#async mode interactive
SanJose1(config-if)#peer default ip address 192.168.8.5
```

The **async mode interactive** command allows the remote user to select between a PPP session and an EXEC session with the router. The **peer default ip address** command configures the router to assign an IP address to the dial-in host. An IP address is required in order for the remote host to access the International Travel Agency's TCP/IP corporate network.

Because you will use Telnet and reverse Telnet in this exercise, configure SanJose1's virtual terminals with the following commands:

```
SanJose1(config)#line vty 0 4
SanJose1(config-line)#login
SanJose1(config-line)#password cisco
```

Step 3

Configure the appropriate line so that it can communicate with the modem (line 2 is used here as an example; use **show line** to verify your router's number):

```
SanJose1(config-line)#line 2
SanJose1(config-line)#login
SanJose1(config-line)#password cisco
SanJose1(config-line)#speed 115200
SanJose1(config-line)#flowcontrol hardware
SanJose1(config-line)#modem inout
SanJose1(config-line)#transport input all
SanJose1(config-line)#stopbits 1
```

For this scenario, you also configure this line to select PPP automatically:

```
SanJose1(config-line)#autoselect ppp
```

The **autoselect** command configures the Cisco IOS software to identify the type of connection being requested. This command is used on lines making different types of connections.

Finally, reverse Telnet to the modem, restore the modem's factory default settings (AT&F), and configure the modem to answer on the second ring (ATS0=2).

```
SanJose1#telnet 192.168.0.1 2002

Password: cisco
(no prompt) AT
OK
AT&F
ATS0=2
```

1. What port number will you use to establish a reverse Telnet session with the modem?

_____

Now that your modem is configured, suspend the reverse Telnet session by pressing Control+Shift+6 at the same time, releasing, then pressing X. You should be returned to the router prompt. From the router prompt, disconnect the reverse Telnet session to the modem as shown here:

```
SanJose1#disconnect
```

Step 4

In this step, you must verify that SanJose1 is accepting dialup PPP connections from Host A.

First, change the TCP/IP properties of the network card to obtain an IP address automatically.

Next, configure dial-up networking (DUN) on Host A. The exact configuration steps for DUN will vary depending on the operating system used by Host A. If you are using Windows 9x/2000/Me, open the Dial-Up Networking folder and click the Make New Connection icon. In Windows 2000, this folder is called Network and Dial-Up Connections. If you are using the standard Adtran Atlas configuration, configure the connection to dial 555-6001 (port 1). Because you have not configured PPP authentication, no username or password for this connection is required.

When you have named and completed the DUN configuration, double-click your connection's icon and establish a dial-up connection with SanJose1. If the connection fails, troubleshoot as necessary.

After your connection is established, check Host A's IP address. Remember that this address will be bound to the dial-up adapter (modem), and not a network interface card.

2. What IP address has been assigned to the dialup adapter?

_____

Verify that Host A has TCP/IP connectivity to the corporate network by pinging San-Jose1's loopback interface of 192.168.0.1. If Host A does not receive a reply, troubleshoot as necessary.

From Host A, Telnet to SanJose1 at 192.168.8.1 and enter the appropriate password. On SanJose1, issue the **show interface s0/1** command. A partial sample output is shown here:

```
SanJose1#show interface s0/1
Serial0/1 is up, line protocol is up
  Hardware is PQUICC Serial in async mode
  Internet address is 192.168.8.1/24
  MTU 1500 bytes, BW 115 Kbit, DLY 100000 usec,
    reliability 255/255, txload 1/255, rxload 1/255
  Encapsulation PPP, loopback not set
  Keepalive not set
<output omitted>
```

3. According to the output of the **show interface** command, what is the encapsulation set to?

_____

Now that you have verified TCP/IP connectivity, exit the Telnet session and disconnect the dialup link.

Step 5

In this step, you must verify that SanJose1 is accepting dialup management (EXEC) sessions from Host A.

First, right-click on your connection's icon in the Dial-Up Networking window and select Properties. If you are using Windows 95/98, click the Configure button on the General tab, which will open the modem configuration window. In this window, select the Options tab, and check the box that says Bring up terminal window after dialing. If you are using Windows 2000, check the Show terminal window box on the Security tab.

Now establish the dialup connection, as you did in Step 4. When the router answers the call, a terminal window should appear. Press the Enter key to trigger the router password prompt and then enter the appropriate password.

While you are still connected, issue the **show interface s0/1** command on SanJose1.

4. According to the output of the **show interface** command, what is the line encapsulation set to?

_____

5. The interface isn't in an up-and-up state even though you have an established connection. Why is this so?

_____

6. Has Host A's dialup adapter been assigned an IP address?

_____

Finally, in asynchronous interactive mode, you can begin a PPP session with the router by entering the appropriate command while in the management session. In your dialup terminal window, type the following command:

```
RTA>ppp
```

You will see strings of character output, which are representations of PPP frames. Click on the Continue button at the bottom of the Dial-Up Networking terminal window. After a few seconds, check Host A's IP address. The dialup adapter should now have the address 192.168.8.5.

Verify that you have TCP/IP connectivity by Telnetting from Host A to SanJose1 via 192.168.8.1.

Lab 3-2: Configuring PPP Options: Authentication and Compression

Objective

In this lab, you configure a Cisco router to accept PPP dialup connections from a workstation using key PPP options: authentication and compression.

Scenario

The International Travel Agency wants you to configure dialup access to the central router SanJose1 using PPP. In order to secure dialup access, you are to configure authentication. Also, you have been asked to configure compression in order to maximize the amount of data that can be transferred across the link.

Step 1

Before beginning this lab, it is recommended that you reload the router after erasing its startup configuration. This prevents you from having problems caused by residual configurations. Build and configure the network according to the above diagram, but do not configure SanJose1's serial interface yet. Configure SanJose1 with the appropriate hostname and IP addresses. Use the Adtran Atlas 550, or a similar device, to simulate the PSTN. If you are using the Atlas 550, be sure the line cables from both modems are plugged into the respective octal FXS voice module ports of the Atlas 550 as labeled in the diagram.

Step 2

Configure SanJose1's serial interface for an asynchronous connection:

```
SanJose1(config)#interface s0/1
SanJose1(config-if)#physical-layer async
SanJose1(config-if)#async mode dedicated
SanJose1(config-if)#ip address 192.168.8.1 255.255.255.0
SanJose1(config-if)#peer default ip address 192.168.8.5
```

Remember: The **peer default ip address** command is used to automatically assign an IP address to the dialup host.

```
SanJose1(config-if)#line 2
SanJose1(config-line)#login
SanJose1(config-line)#password cisco
SanJose1(config-line)#speed 115200
SanJose1(config-line)#flowcontrol hardware
SanJose1(config-line)#modem inout
SanJose1(config-line)#transport input all
SanJose1(config-line)#stopbits 1
```

Because you will be using Telnet and reverse Telnet during this exercise, configure the virtual terminals, as shown here:

```
SanJose1(config-line)#line vty 0 4
SanJose1(config-line)#login
SanJose1(config-line)#password cisco
```

Step 3

Configure PPP to use PAP authentication using the following commands:

```
SanJose1(config-line)#interface s0/1
SanJose1(config-if)#encapsulation ppp
SanJose1(config-if)#ppp authentication pap
SanJose1(config-if)#exit
SanJose1(config)#username hosta password itsasecret
```

Recall that PPP supports two different authentication protocols, PAP and CHAP.

1. Which protocol, PAP or CHAP, is considered the most secure? Why?

_____

_____

When using PPP authentication, the router checks received username and password combinations against a database. In this exercise, the username and password database are stored locally on the router. The **username** *name* **password** *password* command is used to enter this local authentication information. In Lab 12, you will configure the router to use a non-local password/username database stored on a security server.

Step 4

Configure PPP to use compression, using the following commands:

```
SanJose1(config)#interface s0/1
SanJose1(config-if)#ppp compression stacker
```

The **ppp compression** command specifies the compression algorithm to use with PPP. Both link partners must be configured to use the same compression algorithm. In this case, you will configure PPP to use the stacker algorithm (sometimes called the Lempel-Ziv algorithm, or LZS). Stacker is CPU-intensive.

2. What other methods of PPP compression are available?

_____

You can also compress the headers of your TCP/IP packets in order to reduce their size, thereby increasing performance. Header compression is particularly useful on networks with a large percentage of small packets, such as those supporting many Telnet connections. This feature only compresses the TCP header, so it has no effect on UDP packets or other protocol headers. Enable TCP header compression with the following command:

```
SanJose1(config-if)#ip tcp header-compression
```

Note: TCP header compression is often referred to as Van Jacobsen (VJ) compression, after its inventor's name.

This completes the PPP configuration.

Step 5

Reverse Telnet to the modem, restore the modem's factory default settings (AT&F), configure the modem to answer on the second ring (ATS0=2), then disconnect the session. (Refer to Lab 3-1 for the procedure if necessary.)

At this point, you might want to reboot all of the lab equipment in order to prevent potential problems with residual configurations. Write SanJose1's configuration to NVRAM and reload the router, power cycle the modem, and power cycle the Adtran Atlas 550.

Step 6

Before configuring Host A's DUN, enable PPP debug on SanJose1's console using the following commands:

```
SanJose1#debug ppp negotiation
SanJose1#debug ppp authentication
```

After enabling debug, configure DUN on Host A to dial SanJose1. If you are using the standard Adtran Atlas 550 configuration, configure DUN to dial 555-6001, with the username hosta, and password itsasecret.

Be sure this connection is not configured to bring up a terminal window. From Host A, dial SanJose1. If the connection attempt fails, troubleshoot as necessary (you might have to repeat Step 5). After you have connected successfully, examine the debug output, SanJose1's output should include the following:

```
Se0/1 LCP: State is Open
Se0/1 PPP: Phase is AUTHENTICATING, by this end
Se0/1 PAP: I AUTH-REQ id 1 len 16 from "hosta"
Se0/1 PAP: Authenticating peer hosta
Se0/1 PAP: O AUTH-ACK id 1 len 5
Se0/1 PPP: Phase is UP
Se0/1 IPCP: O CONFREQ [Closed] id 8 len 16
Se0/1 IPCP: CompressType VJ 15 slots (0x0206002D0F00)
Se0/1 IPCP: Address 192.168.8.1 (0x03060A010101)
Se0/1 CCP: O CONFREQ [Closed] id 4 len 10
Se0/1 CCP: LZSDCP history 1 check mode SEQ process UNCOMPRESSSED
(0x170600010201)
```

3. According to the debug output, who is the authenticating peer?

_____

4. During the authenticating phase, does the debug indicate the authentication protocol used?

_____

5. The CompressType VJ refers to what?

_____

6. LZSDCP refers to what?

_____

7. According to the debug output on your screen, during which PPP phase(s) are LCP frames exchanged?

_____

8. According to the debug output on your screen, which kinds of NCPs were exchanged between Host A and SanJose1?

_____

While Host A is still connected to SanJose1 (reconnect if necessary), issue the **show compress** command. A sample output is shown here:

```
SanJose1#show compress
 Serial0/1
        Software compression enabled
        uncompressed bytes xmt/rcv 0/2357
        1  min avg ratio xmt/rcv 0.000/0.000
        5  min avg ratio xmt/rcv 0.000/0.000
        10 min avg ratio xmt/rcv 0.000/2.419
        no bufs xmt 0 no bufs rcv 0
        resyncs 0
        Additional Stacker Stats:
        Transmit bytes:  Uncompressed = 0 Compressed = 0
        Received bytes:  Compressed = 564 Uncompressed = 0
```

9. According to the output of this command, is the compression method hardware- or software-based?

_____

Disconnect your dialup session and redial using the wrong password. Leave the PPP debug running on SanJose1. The connection should fail.

10. What indications as to why the connection failed are included in the debug ouput's authenticating phase?

_____

_____

Lab 3-3: Configuring PPP Callback

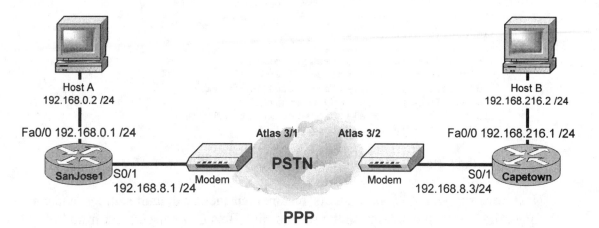

Objective

In this lab, you configure a Cisco router for PPP callback.

Scenario

You are to configure PPP callback so the International Travel Agency's remote router (Capetown) can dial the central router (SanJose1), hang up, and then accept an incoming call from SanJose1. By configuring SanJose1 to call back, you prevent Capetown from incurring excessive toll charges. Assume the International Travel Agency's central site (SanJose1) has secured lower call rates.

Step 1

Before beginning this lab, it is recommended that you reload the routers after erasing their startup configuration. This prevents you from having problems caused by residual configurations. Build and configure the network according to the previous diagram, but do not configure either router's serial interfaces yet. Use the Adtran Atlas 550 or a similar device to simulate the PSTN. If you are using the Atlas 550, be sure the line cables from both modems are plugged into the octal FXS voice module ports of the Atlas 550 as labeled in the diagram. Also, be sure to configure both workstations with the correct IP address and default gateway (router Fa0/0 IP address).

Step 2

Configure both routers' serial interfaces for asynchronous connections. Be sure that you have set the correct IP addresses for each router. The following are the commands for SanJose1 as an example:

```
SanJose1(config)#interface s0/1
SanJose1(config-if)#physical-layer async
SanJose1(config-if)#async mode dedicated
SanJose1(config-if)#ip address 192.168.8.1 255.255.255.0
```

Configure the following line parameters for *both* routers. The following are the commands for SanJose1 as an example:

```
SanJose1(config-if)#line 2
SanJose1(config-line)#login
SanJose1(config-line)#password cisco
SanJose1(config-line)#speed 115200
SanJose1(config-line)#flowcontrol hardware
SanJose1(config-line)#modem inout
SanJose1(config-line)#transport input all
SanJose1(config-line)#stopbits 1
```

Configure the virtual terminals on *both* routers with passwords.

Next, reverse Telnet to *both* modems, restore their factory default settings, and configure the modems to answer on the second ring. Be sure to disconnect from the reverse Telnet session after changing the setting by pressing Ctrl+Shift+6 at the same time, releasing, then pressing X. Then type the **disconnect** command.

Step 3

Configure both routers to use their modems to initiate dialup connections. On both routers, enter the **dialer** commands that you used in Lab 2-3. The following are the commands for SanJose1 as an example:

```
SanJose1(config)#interface serial 0/1
SanJose1(config-if)#no cdp enable
SanJose1(config-if)#dialer in-band
SanJose1(config-if)#dialer idle-timeout 300
SanJose1(config-if)#dialer wait-for-carrier-time 60
SanJose1(config-if)#dialer hold-queue 50
SanJose1(config-if)#dialer-group 1
SanJose1(config)#chat-script hayes56k ABORT ERROR "" "AT Z" OK "ATDT
\T"
TIMEOUT 30 CONNECT \c
SanJose1(config)#dialer-list 1 protocol ip permit
```

After you enter the previous commands on both routers, you can configure the dialer map on Capetown by using the same command required in Lab 2-3.

```
Capetown(config)#interface s0/1
Capetown(config-if)#dialer map ip 192.168.8.1 name SanJose1
        modem-script
hayes56k broadcast 5556001
```

This command maps SanJose1's IP address to its phone number, and specifies the chat script that should be used to initialize the modem. Because SanJose1 will be the callback server, its dialer map configuration will require additional keywords. You will enter SanJose1's dialer map configuration in the next step.

Step 4

Configure SanJose1's serial interface to act as a PPP callback server. First, you must configure PPP for PAP authentication, as shown here:

```
SanJose1(config)interface s0/1
SanJose1(config-if)#encapsulation ppp
SanJose1(config-if)#ppp authentication pap
SanJose1(config-if)#ppp pap sent-username SanJose1 password alpha
```

The **ppp pap sent-username** command configures SanJose1 to send the specified username and password combination if prompted during the PPP authentication phase. Next, enter the PPP commands required to configure SanJose1 as a PPP callback server, as shown here:

```
SanJose1(config-if)#ppp callback accept
SanJose1(config-if)#dialer callback-secure
SanJose1(config-if)#exit
SanJose1(config)#username Capetown password bravo
```

The **ppp callback accept** command configured SanJose1 to accept callback requests from clients. The **dialer callback-secure** command affects those users not authorized to be called back with the **dialer callback-server** command. If the username is not authorized for callback, the call will be disconnected. Next, configure authorization for callback service on SanJose1:

```
SanJose1(config)#map-class dialer dialback
SanJose1(config-map-class)#dialer callback-server username
SanJose1(config-map-class)#exit
SanJose1(config)#interface s0/1
SanJose1(config-if)#dialer map ip 192.168.8.3 name Capetown class
    dialback modem-script hayes56k broadcast 5556002
```

Step 5

Configure Capetown for PPP with PAP authentication and callback request by using the **ppp callback request** command, as shown here:

```
Capetown(config)#interface s0/1
Capetown(config-if)#encapsulation ppp
Capetown(config-if)#ppp authentication pap
Capetown(config-if)#ppp pap sent-username Capetown password bravo
Capetown(config-if)#ppp callback request
Capetown(config-if)#exit
Capetown(config)#username SanJose1 password alpha
```

Step 6

Set up static routes on both routers. For SanJose1, configure a static route to Capetown's LAN as shown here:

```
SanJose1(config)#ip route 192.168.216.0 255.255.255.0 192.168.8.3
```

On Capetown, configure a default route to the central router like this:

```
Capetown(config)#ip route 0.0.0.0 0.0.0.0 192.168.8.1
```

Step 7

At this point, you might want to reboot all of the lab equipment in order to prevent potential problems with residual configurations. Write both SanJose1's and Capetown's configuration to NVRAM and reload the router, power cycle the modem, and power cycle the Adtran Atlas 550.

After all the lab equipment has rebooted, enable debug on SanJose1's console:

```
SanJose1#debug dialer
```

The **debug dialer** command outputs dialup related information to the console. Now bring up the asynchronous connection by pinging from Host B to Host A (192.168.0.2).

1. Which of Capetown's routing table entries will be used to route Host B's ping packet to 192.168.0.2?

   _____

2. What is the next-hop IP address mapped to that route?

   _____

3. What is the phone number mapped to that address in Capetown's configuration?

   _____

Capetown should call SanJose1, SanJose1 should disconnect the call, then SanJose1 should call back Capetown. Troubleshoot as necessary. The **debug dialer** output should reflect this process, as shown in this example:

```
SanJose1#
01:07:06: %LINK-3-UPDOWN: Interface Serial0/1, changed state to up
SanJose1#Dialer statechange to up Serial0/1
01:07:06: Serial0/1 DDR: Dialer received incoming call from <unknown>
01:07:08: Serial0/1 DDR: PPP callback Callback server starting to
         Capetown 5556002
01:07:08: Serial0/1 DDR: disconnecting call
01:07:10: %LINK-5-CHANGED: Interface Serial0/1, changed state to
         reset
01:07:15: %LINK-3-UPDOWN: Interface Serial0/1, changed state to down
01:07:30: Serial0/1 DDR: re-enable timeout
01:07:30: DDR: callback triggered by dialer_timers
01:07:30: Serial0/1 DDR: beginning callback to Capetown 5556002
01:07:30: Serial0/1 DDR: Attempting to dial 5556002
01:07:30: CHAT2: Attempting async line dialer script
01:07:30: CHAT2: Dialing using Modem script: hayes56k & System
         script: none
01:07:30: DDR: Freeing callback to Capetown 5556002
01:07:30: CHAT2: process started
01:07:30: CHAT2: Asserting DTR
01:07:30: CHAT2: Chat script hayes56k started
01:07:58: CHAT2: Chat script hayes56k finished, status = Success
01:08:00: %LINK-3-UPDOWN: Interface Serial0/1, changed state to up
SanJose1#Dialer statechange to up Serial0/1Dialer call has been
         placed Serial0/1
```

4. According to the debug output, what happens on SanJose1 immediately after it attempts to dial 555-6002?

Finally, test your connection by attempting to Telnet from Host B to 192.168.0.1 (SanJose1's Ethernet interface). After the dialup connection is established from SanJose1 to Capetown, the Telnet should be successful. Troubleshoot as necessary.

Asynchronous PPP Challenge Lab

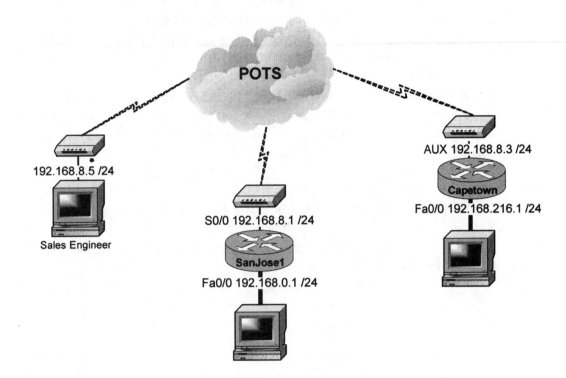

Objective

In this challenge lab, you configure two routers and a host for PPP over asynchronous plain old telephone service.

Scenario

As the enterprise network administrator for the International Travel Agency, you are responsible for designing and implementing internetwork connectivity. You are tasked with configuring an asynchronous PPP remote access solution for the Capetown office. In addition, you must also configure dialup access for a remote host, used by a mobile sales engineer to gain access to the central site in San Jose. Company policy is to use CHAP authentication on all circuit-switched connections.

Design Considerations

Because SanJose1 has a single external modem, it can only handle one call at a time, so this lab can actually be completed with only two modems (if you split time between the host and Capetown). ITA's primary concern is that Capetown and the sales engineer can dial in using CHAP, not that SanJose1 can dial out. Routing will have to be configured between Capetown and SanJose1 in order for the hosts on each LAN to communicate.

Implementation Requirements

- SanJose1 uses its serial interface to connect to an external modem.
- As the central site, SanJose1 will accept only dedicated PPP connections.
- Capetown uses its AUX port to connect to an external modem, and can make DDR calls to SanJose1, using stacker compression.
- CHAP authentication is used by all hosts.
- A remote sales engineer uses a laptop or PC to connect to an external modem and dial in to SanJose1, from which the laptop automatically receives it's IP address.
- Configure SanJose1 as a callback server, with Capetown as a callback client (optional).

Implementation Completion Tests

- Successful pings from a host on the Capetown LAN to a host on the SanJose1 LAN.
- Sales engineer host successfully dials in, receives an IP address, and can ping hosts on the SanJose1 LAN.

Lab 4-1: Configuring ISDN BRI

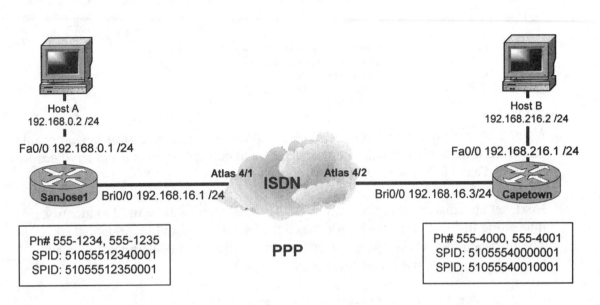

Host A
192.168.0.2 /24

Fa0/0 192.168.0.1 /24

SanJose1 Bri0/0 192.168.16.1 /24

Atlas 4/1 **ISDN** Atlas 4/2

PPP

Host B
192.168.216.2 /24

Fa0/0 192.168.216.1 /24

Bri0/0 192.168.16.3/24 Capetown

Ph# 555-1234, 555-1235
SPID: 51055512340001
SPID: 51055512350001

Ph# 555-4000, 555-4001
SPID: 51055540000001
SPID: 51055540010001

Objective

In this lab, you configure two Cisco routers for DDR using ISDN BRI.

Scenario

The International Travel Agency wants you to configure an ISDN DDR connection between a remote office (Capetown) and its corporate network core router (SanJose1). They have asked that you configure PPP encapsulation and CHAP authentication over this link. You are asked to configure DDR so that the only following mission-critical applications qualify as designated interesting traffic: Web, DNS, FTP, Telnet, and mail.

Step 1

Before beginning this lab, it is recommended that you reload the routers after erasing their startup configuration. This prevents you from having problems caused by residual configurations. Build and configure the network according to the above diagram, but do not configure either router's BRI interfaces yet. Use the Adtran Atlas 550 or a similar device to simulate the ISDN cloud. If you are using the Atlas 550, be sure to use straight-through cables and connect both routers to their respective BRI module ports of the Atlas 550 as labeled in the diagram. Also, be sure to configure both workstations with the correct IP address and default gateway (router Fa0/0 IP address). You should read Appendix B before you proceed to Step 2.

Step 2

Configure SanJose1 to use the appropriate ISDN switch type. Your ISP will provide you with this information and in this case, the International Travel Agency has been told their provider is using the National switch type. Enter the following command:

```
SanJose1(config)#isdn switch-type basic-ni
```

Because you will be using PPP encapsulation and CHAP on the B channels, enter username and password information for the remote router and an enable password for SanJose1 as shown here. SanJose1 will use the enable password when responding to CHAP challenges.

```
SanJose1(config)#username Capetown password cisco
SanJose1(config)#enable password cisco
SanJose1(config)#line vty 0 4
SanJose1(config-line)#password cisco
SanJose1(config-line)#exit
```

Note: You could use the enable secret here, but for the purposes of this lab, an enable password is all that's needed. The virtual terminal configuration is necessary because you will Telnet to SanJose1 in Step 7.

Next, set up a dialer list to use with DDR. This dialer list will be used to identify interesting traffic, that is, traffic for which the ISDN link should be established. The International Travel Agency wants you to restrict what constitutes "interesting" traffic, but for now, use the following command:

```
SanJose1(config)#dialer-list 1 protocol ip permit
```

This permissive command will establish the link in the event that *any* IP traffic needs to be routed out the BRI. In Step 7, you will reconfigure this dialer list.

Step 3

Configure the BRI on SanJose1 as shown here:

```
SanJose1(config)#interface bri0/0
SanJose1(config-if)#ip address 192.168.16.1 255.255.255.0
SanJose1(config-if)#encapsulation ppp
SanJose1(config-if)#ppp authentication chap
SanJose1(config-if)#dialer-group 1
```

The dialer-group 1 command associates this interface with dialer list 1. In order for this BRI to establish a connection with the ISP's ISDN switch, you must configure at least one SPID (service profile identifier). With two B channels, you will configure two SPIDs. Enter the following commands on SanJose1:

```
SanJose1(config-if)#isdn spid1 51055512340001 5551234
SanJose1(config-if)#isdn spid2 51055512350001 5551235
SanJose1(config-if)#no shutdown
```

After the SPIDs and ISDN switch type are configured, the router sends the SPID to the switch. If you have made a configuration error, you might receive the following output:

```
%ISDN-4-INVALID_SPID: Interface BR0/0, Spid1 was rejected
```

If you don't receive an error message, use the **show isdn status** command to verify that SanJose1 has established communication with the ISDN switch. A sample output is shown here:

```
SanJose1#show isdn status
Global ISDN Switchtype = basic-ni
ISDN BRI0/0 interface
        dsl 0, interface ISDN Switchtype = basic-ni
    Layer 1 Status:
      ACTIVE
    Layer 2 Status:
        TEI = 64, Ces = 1, SAPI = 0, State = MULTIPLE_FRAME_ESTABLISHED
        TEI = 65, Ces = 2, SAPI = 0, State = MULTIPLE_FRAME_ESTABLISHED
    Spid Status:
        TEI 64, ces = 1, state = 8(established)
            spid1 configured, spid1 sent, spid1 valid
            Endpoint ID Info: epsf = 0, usid = 70, tid = 1
        TEI 65, ces = 2, state = 8(established)
            spid2 configured, spid2 sent, spid2 valid
            Endpoint ID Info: epsf = 0, usid = 70, tid = 2
    Layer 3 Status:
        0 Active Layer 3 Call(s)
    Activated dsl 0 CCBs = 0
    The Free Channel Mask:   0x80000003
    Total Allocated ISDN CCBs = 0
```

Note that the highlighted lines of the above output show that the Layer 2 state between the switch and the router is established and that SPID1 and SPID2 were accepted. If the SPID status is not established, or if you change your router's SPID configuration, issue the command below to force the router to resend the SPID to the switch. Although executing the command once should be sufficient, when using the Atlas 550 with the Cisco IOS, it might be necessary to repeat the command a second or third time (see Appendix B):

```
SanJose1#clear interface bri0/0
```

You can also use the **debug isdn q921** command to troubleshoot Layer 2 issues between the router and the ISDN switch. Once you have verified connectivity to the ISDN switch, issue the **show interface bri0/0** command, as shown here:

```
SanJose1#show interface bri0/0
BRI0/0 is up, line protocol is up (spoofing)
Hardware is PQUICC BRI with U interface
Internet address is 10.1.1.1/24
MTU 1500 bytes, BW 64 Kbit, DLY 20000 usec,
    reliability 255/255, txload 1/255, rxload 1/255
Encapsulation PPP, loopback not set
<output omitted>
```

The highlighted portion of the above output shows that the BRI0/0 interface is up and the line protocol is up (spoofing).

1. Because no ISDN call has been made yet, why do you think the BRI shows "up and up (spoofing)"?

Now issue the **show ip interface brief** command, as shown here:

```
SanJose1#show ip interface brief
Interface          IP-Address      OK?   Method    Status      Protocol
FastEthernet0/0    192.168.0.1     YES   manual    up          up
Serial0/0          unassigned      YES   unset     down        down
BRI0/0             192.168.16.1    YES   manual    up          up
BRI0/0:1           unassigned      YES   unset     down        down
BRI0/0:2           unassigned      YES   unset     down        down
Serial0/1          unassigned      YES   unset     down        down
```

2. To what does BRI0/0:1 and BRI0/0:2 refer?

_____

3. Why is BRI0/0 up, and BRI0/0:1 down?

_____

Issue the **show dialer** command. A sample output is shown here:

```
SanJose1#show dialer
BRI0/0 - dialer type = ISDN

Dial String      Successes    Failures    Last DNIS    Last status
0 incoming call(s) have been screened.
0 incoming call(s) rejected for callback.

BRI0/0:1 - dialer type = ISDN
Idle timer (120 secs), Fast idle timer (20 secs)
Wait for carrier (30 secs), Re-enable (15 secs)
Dialer state is idle

BRI0/0:2 - dialer type = ISDN
Idle timer (120 secs), Fast idle timer (20 secs)
Wait for carrier (30 secs), Re-enable (15 secs)
Dialer state is idle
```

4. What is the idle timer set to for both BRI0/0:1 and BRI0/0:2?

_____

Because organizations are typically charged by the minute when making a DDR call, it is very important that you consider the dialer idle timeout. If the connection is idle, the router will wait for this configurable period of time before closing the connection. The International Travel Agency would like you to set an aggressive idle timeout in order to reduce costs. Use the following command to change the timer:

```
SanJose1(config)#interface bri0/0
SanJose1(config-if)#dialer idle-timeout 60
```

Finally, you must configure a dialer map for this interface, as shown here:

```
SanJose1(config-if)#dialer map ip 192.168.16.3 name Capetown 5554000
```

Notice that this **dialer map** command is similar to the dialer maps you created in previous labs, but because a modem is not used, no modem script is required.

Step 4

Configure Capetown using the following, which are essentially the same procedures outlined in Steps 2 - 4:

```
Capetown(config)#isdn switch-type basic-ni
Capetown(config)#username SanJose1 password cisco
Capetown(config)#enable password cisco
Capetown(config)#line vty 0 4
Capetown(config-line)#password cisco
Capetown(config-line)#exit
Capetown(config)#dialer-list 1 protocol ip permit
Capetown(config)#interface bri0/0
Capetown(config-if)#ip address 192.168.16.3 255.255.255.0
Capetown(config-if)#encapsulation ppp
Capetown(config-if)#ppp authentication chap
Capetown(config-if)#dialer-group 1
Capetown(config-if)#isdn spid1 51055540000001 5554000
Capetown(config-if)#isdn spid2 51055540010001 5554001
Capetown(config-if)#dialer idle-timeout 60
Capetown(config-if)#dialer map ip 192.168.16.1 name SanJose1 5551234
Capetown(config-if)#no shutdown
```

Issue a **show isdn status** to check Layer 2 and see if the SPIDs have been accepted. If not, execute a **clear interface bri0/0** until the SPIDs are accepted.

Step 5

Configure a static route to 192.168.216.0/24 on SanJose1. Set up a static default route on Capetown, as shown here:

```
SanJose1(config)#ip route 192.168.216.0 255.255.255.0 192.168.16.3
Capetown(config)#ip route 0.0.0.0 0.0.0.0 192.168.16.1
```

Step 6

Test your ISDN connection. Before you bring up the ISDN link, enable debugging on *both* routers. This will allow you to troubleshoot more efficiently in the event you encounter problems. Issue the following command to view dialer information on both routers:

```
SanJose1#debug dialer
```

You might also want to debug ISDN with this command:

```
SanJose1#debug isdn events
```

Finally, because you are using PPP with CHAP authentication, you should also debug PPP:

```
SanJose1#debug ppp authentication
SanJose1#debug ppp negotiation
```

Now, ping Host A from Host B. There will be a number of debug outputs—including a dialer debug on Capetown—that should report the following:

```
00:56:00: BRI0/0 DDR: Dialing cause ip (s=192.168.216.2,
         d=192.168.0.2)
00:56:00: BRI0/0 DDR: Attempting to dial 5551234
```

Also, Capetown should report that channel B1 is now up, as shown here:

```
00:56:01:%LINEPROTO-5-UPDOWN:Line protocol on Interface
         BRI0/0:1,changed state to up
00:56:06: %ISDN-6-CONNECT: Interface BRI0/0:1 is now connected to
         5551234 SanJose1
```

Troubleshoot this connection as necessary. Use the debug output for clues. You may have to use the **clear interface bri0/0** command several times on both routers to reset the interfaces.

Note: To manually disconnect an ISDN call on BRI0/0, use the following command:

```
SanJose1#isdn disconnect interface bri0/0 [all, b1, b2]
```

Continue testing your ISDN connection; you should be able to **ping** Host A from Host B and vice versa. You can also issue a **show isdn history** command to view all active and prior ISDN connections. A **show isdn active** will output information about the current active connection. The following are sample outputs of both commands:

```
SanJose1#show isdn history
-------------------------------------------------------------------------------
                          ISDN CALL HISTORY
-------------------------------------------------------------------------------
History table has a maximum of 100 entries.
History table data is retained for a maximum of 15 Minutes.
-------------------------------------------------------------------------------
Call    Calling      Called     Remote  Seconds Seconds Seconds Charges
Type    Number       Number     Name    Used    Left    Idle    Units/Currency
-------------------------------------------------------------------------------
In                                       Failed
Out +ilable----    5551234    Capetown    60
Out +ilable----    5551234    Capetown    40      19      40
-------------------------------------------------------------------------------


Capetown#show isdn active
-------------------------------------------------------------------------------
                          ISDN ACTIVE CALLS
-------------------------------------------------------------------------------
History table has a maximum of 100 entries.
History table data is retained for a maximum of 15 Minutes.
-------------------------------------------------------------------------------
    Call    Calling     Called     Remote  Seconds Seconds Seconds Charges
    Type    Number      Number     Name    Used    Left    Idle
            Units/Currency
-------------------------------------------------------------------------------
    Out                5551234    SanJose1   18      44      15      0
-------------------------------------------------------------------------------
```

Step 7

Now that you have a working ISDN connection, you will return to your router configurations to configure a more restrictive dialer list on the Capetown remote router. The International Travel Agency has asked that only the following mission-critical applications be designated as interesting traffic: Web, DNS, FTP, Telnet, and mail. To do this, you must reconfigure dialer list 1 on Capetown (the remote router). The central site router, SanJose1, will continue to be allowed to build DDR connections for any IP traffic.

Create an access list on Capetown that will permit the mission critical services:

```
Capetown(config)#access-list 101 permit tcp any any eq www
Capetown(config)#access-list 101 permit udp any any eq domain
Capetown(config)#access-list 101 permit tcp any any eq ftp
Capetown(config)#access-list 101 permit tcp any any eq telnet
Capetown(config)#access-list 101 permit tcp any any eq pop3
Capetown(config)#access-list 101 permit tcp any any eq smtp
```

Now enter a new **dialer-list** command that references this access list. The new **dialer-list** command will automatically replace the old one, as seen here:

```
Capetown(config)#dialer-list 1 protocol ip list 101
```

After you configure the new dialer list, ping Host A from Host B.

5. The ping should fail. Why?

_____

_____

Now Telnet from Host B to SanJose1.

6. The Telnet request should bring up the ISDN connection. Why?

_____

_____

With the connection still up, **ping** Host A from Host B again.

7. Instead of failing as before, this ping should work. Why?

_____

_____

You should also be able to **ping** Host B from Host A. While connected, issue the **show dialer** command on both SanJose1 and Capetown.

8. According to the output of this command, what was SanJose1's time until disconnect?

_____

Lab 4-2: Configuring Snapshot Routing

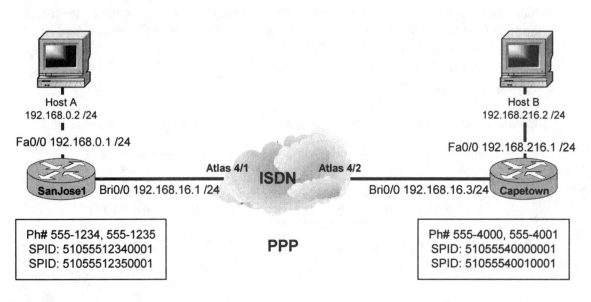

Objective

In this lab, you configure two Cisco routers for DDR and snapshot routing using ISDN BRI.

Scenario

The International Travel Agency wants you to configure an ISDN DDR connection between its Capetown regional headquarters and the corporate network's SanJose1 core router. You must configure snapshot routing so routing updates are exchanged between the routers without keeping the link up continuously. The company also asks that you configure PPP encapsulation and CHAP authentication over this link.

Step 1

Before beginning this lab, it is recommended that you reload the routers after erasing their startup configuration. This prevents you from having problems caused by residual configurations. Build and configure the network according to the above diagram, but do not configure either router's BRI interfaces yet. Use the Adtran Atlas 550 or a similar device to simulate the ISDN cloud. If you are using the Atlas 550, be sure to use straight-through cables and connect both routers to their respective BRI module ports of the Atlas 550 as labeled in the diagram. Also, be sure to configure both workstations with the correct IP address and default gateway (router Fa0/0 IP address).

Step 2

Configure SanJose1 *and* Capetown for ISDN. Refer to the following commands to guide your configuration:

```
SanJose1(config)#isdn switch-type basic-ni
SanJose1(config)#dialer-list 1 protocol ip permit
SanJose1(config)#interface bri0/0
```

```
SanJose1(config-if)#ip address 192.168.16.1 255.255.255.0
SanJose1(config-if)#encapsulation ppp
SanJose1(config-if)#ppp authentication chap
SanJose1(config-if)#isdn spid1 51055512340001 5551234
SanJose1(config-if)#isdn spid2 51055512350001 5551235
SanJose1(config-if)#dialer-group 1
SanJose1(config-if)#dialer map ip 192.168.16.3 name Capetown
     broadcast 5554000
SanJose1(config-if)#no shutdown

Capetown(config)#isdn switch-type basic-ni
Capetown(config)#dialer-list 1 protocol ip permit
Capetown(config)#interface bri0/0
Capetown(config-if)#ip address 192.168.16.3 255.255.255.0
Capetown(config-if)#encapsulation ppp
Capetown(config-if)#ppp authentication chap
Capetown(config-if)#isdn spid1 51055540000001 5554000
Capetown(config-if)#isdn spid2 51055540010001 5554001
Capetown(config-if)#dialer-group 1
Capetown(config-if)#dialer map ip 192.168.16.1 name SanJose1
     broadcast 5551234
Capetown(config-if)#no shutdown
```

1. What does the keyword **broadcast** do when used with the **dialer map** command?

_____

_____

Use the **show isdn status** command to verify that the routers have established communication with the ISDN switch. Use the **clear interface bri0/0** command multiple times if necessary to enable a valid and established SPID status. Also, remember the random timer of up to five minutes.

Step 3

Configure both routers with the appropriate password and username information, as shown for SanJose1 below. Be sure to substitute the appropriate username on the Capetown router as shown here:

```
SanJose1(config)#username Capetown password cisco
SanJose1(config)#enable password cisco
SanJose1(config)#line vty 0 4
SanJose1(config-line)#password cisco
SanJose1(config-line)#^z
```

After both routers are configured, issue the **debug dialer** command on both SanJose1 and Capetown. Then verify that DDR works by pinging SanJose1 (192.168.16.1) from Capetown. The **show isdn active** command can also verify an active connection. Troubleshoot as necessary.

Leave **debug dialer** enabled; you will use the output of this command in Step 5.

Step 4

In this lab, you will not use static routes. The International Travel Agency has asked you to configure dynamic routing, so that as new networks are added, routing table updates will occur automatically.

2. How often does IGRP send updates by default?

_____

3. Are IGRP updates unicast, multicast, or broadcast?

_____

4. What is the default setting of the dialer idle timeout?

_____

Starting with SanJose1, configure IGRP for AS 100 on **both** SanJose1 and Capetown. The commands for SanJose1 are shown here:

```
SanJose1(config)#router igrp 100
SanJose1(config-router)#network 192.168.0.0
SanJose1(config-router)#network 192.168.16.0
```

After you configure the routing process on Capetown, the **debug dialer** output should show the following:

```
BRI0/0 DDR: Dialing cause ip (s=192.168.16.3, d=255.255.255.255)
BRI0/0 DDR: Attempting to dial 5551234
```

5. According to the debug output, what is the destination of the packet that caused the attempt to dial?

_____

6. What process on the router is causing this broadcast packet to be generated?

_____

7. Under the current configuration, this DDR link should never go down. Why?

_____

_____

Step 5

Configure snapshot routing. The core router, SanJose1 will act as the server and Capetown will be the client. Issue the following commands on SanJose1:

```
SanJose1(config)#interface bri0/0
SanJose1(config-if)#snapshot server 5
```

The **snapshot server 5** command tells the server that the active period is five minutes long.

8. What is the maximum interval that you can assign using the snapshot server command (use the help feature to find this)?

___

Now configure Capetown as a snapshot routing client as shown here:

```
Capetown(config)#interface bri0/0
Capetown(config-if)#dialer map snapshot 1 name SanJose1 broadcast
    5551234
Capetown(config-if)#snapshot client 5 10 suppress-statechange-updates
    dialer
```

The **dialer map snapshot** command establishes a map that Capetown uses to connect for the exchange of routing updates with SanJose1. The **snapshot client** command configures the length of the active and quiet periods. In the command above, the active period is set to five minutes (this value must match the value set in the snapshot server's configuration) and sets the length of the quiet period to 10 minutes.

The **suppress-statechange-updates** keyword prevents the routers from exchanging updates during connections that are established to transfer user data. The **dialer** keyword allows the client router to dial up the server router in the absence of regular traffic and is required when you use the **suppress-statechange-updates** keyword.

Observe the result of your configuration. If the routers are still connected, use the **show dialer** command to determine how long the routers will wait until disconnecting an idle link.

Let the link remain idle for 120 seconds; the routers should disconnect.

Check the routing tables of SanJose1 and Capetown. Verify that routing is working in your network by pinging SanJose1 (192.168.16.1) from Capetown.

Issue the **show snapshot** command on both routers. Notice that SanJose1's output differs significantly from Capetown's output, as shown here:

```
SanJose1#show snapshot
BRIO/0 is up, line protocol is upSnapshot server line state down
   Length of active period:        5 minutes
     For ip address: 192.168.16.3
       Current state: active, remaining time: 5 minutes

Capetown#show snapshot
BRIO/0 is up, line protocol is upSnapshot client
   Options: dialer support, stay asleep on carrier up
   Length of active period:        5 minutes
   Length of quiet period:        10 minutes
   Length of retry period:         8 minutes
     For dialer address 1
       Current state: active, remaining/exchange time: 5/0 minutes
       Connected dialer interface:
         BRIO/0:1
```

9. According to the output of this command, what is the retry period set to?

_____

> After allowing the connection to time out, wait five minutes with **debug dialer** running on each router. Below are sample outputs for SanJose1 and Capetown when snapshot routing is activated:

```
SanJose1#debug dialer
01:21:49: %LINK-3-UPDOWN: Interface BRI0/0:1, changed state to up
01:21:49: %ISDN-6-CONNECT: Interface BRI0/0:1 is now connected to
          unknown
01:21:49: isdn_call_connect: Calling lineaction of BRI0/0:1
01:21:49: BRI0/0:1 DDR: Authenticated host Capetown with no matching
          dialer map
01:21:49: BR0/0:1 DDR: Dialer protocol up
01:21:49: BRI0/0:1 DDR: dialer protocol up
01:21:49: BRI0/0: dialer_ckt_swt_client_connect: incoming circuit
          switched call
01:21:50: %LINEPROTO-5-UPDOWN: Line protocol on Interface BRI0/0:1,
          changed state to up
01:21:55: %ISDN-6-CONNECT: Interface BRI0/0:1 is now connected to
          Capetown


Capetown#debug dialer
00:29:27282767: isdn_call_connect: Calling lineaction of BRI0/0:1
00:29:00: BRI0/0:1 DDR: Authenticated host SanJose1 with no matching
          dialer map
00:29:00: BR0/0:1 DDR: Dialer protocol up
00:29:00: BRI0/0:1 DDR: dialer protocol up
00:29:00: BRI0/0: dialer_ckt_swt_client_connect: incoming circuit
          switched call
00:29:01: %LINEPROTO-5-UPDOWN: Line protocol on Interface BRI0/0:1,
          changed state to up
00:29:06: %ISDN-6-CONNECT: Interface BRI0/0:1 is now connected to
          5551234 SanJose1
```

10. Which router dials the other to receive snapshot routing information?

_____

Lab 4-3: Using PPP Multilink for ISDN B Channel Aggregation

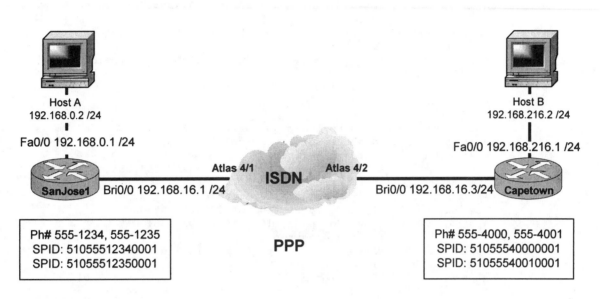

Host A
192.168.0.2 /24

Fa0/0 192.168.0.1 /24

SanJose1   Bri0/0 192.168.16.1 /24

Atlas 4/1   **ISDN**   Atlas 4/2

PPP

Ph# 555-1234, 555-1235
SPID: 51055512340001
SPID: 51055512350001

Host B
192.168.216.2 /24

Fa0/0 192.168.216.1 /24

Bri0/0 192.168.16.3/24   Capetown

Ph# 555-4000, 555-4001
SPID: 51055540000001
SPID: 51055540010001

Objective

In this lab, you configure two Cisco routers for DDR using PPP multilink so that both B channels are used as 128-kbps bundles.

Scenario

The International Travel Agency wants you to configure an ISDN DDR connection between a remote office (Capetown) and its corporate network core router (San-Jose1). To maximize bandwidth, you are to configure PPP multilink so that both B channels are used for the data link.

Step 1

Before beginning this lab, it is recommended that you reload the routers after erasing their startup configuration. This will prevent you from having problems caused by residual configurations. Build and configure the network according to the previous diagram, but do not configure either router's BRI interfaces yet. Use the Adtran Atlas 550 or a similar device to simulate the ISDN cloud. If you are using the Atlas 550, be sure to use straight-through cables and connect both routers to their respective BRI module ports of the Atlas 550 as labeled in the diagram. Also, be sure to configure both workstations with the correct IP address and default gateway (router Fa0/0 IP address).

Step 2

Configure SanJose1 *and* Capetown for ISDN. Refer to the following commands to guide your configuration:

```
SanJose1(config)#isdn switch-type basic-ni
SanJose1(config)#dialer-list 1 protocol ip permit
SanJose1(config)#interface bri0/0
```

```
SanJose1(config-if)#ip address 192.168.16.1 255.255.255.0
SanJose1(config-if)#encapsulation ppp
SanJose1(config-if)#ppp authentication chap
SanJose1(config-if)#isdn spid1 51055512340001 5551234
SanJose1(config-if)#isdn spid2 51055512350001 5551235
SanJose1(config-if)#dialer-group 1
SanJose1(config-if)#dialer map ip 192.168.16.3 name Capetown
     broadcast 5554000
SanJose1(config-if)#dialer map ip 192.168.16.3 name Capetown
     broadcast 5554001
SanJose1(config-if)#dialer idle-timeout 60
SanJose1(config-if)#no shutdown

Capetown(config)#isdn switch-type basic-ni
Capetown(config)#dialer-list 1 protocol ip permit
Capetown(config)#intereface bri0/0
Capetown(config-if)#ip address 192.168.16.3 255.255.255.0
Capetown(config-if)#encapsulation ppp
Capetown(config-if)#ppp authentication chap
Capetown(config-if)#isdn spid1 51055540000001 5554000
Capetown(config-if)#isdn spid2 51055540010001 5554001
Capetown(config-if)#dialer-group 1
Capetown(config-if)#dialer map ip 192.168.16.1 name SanJose1
     broadcast 5551234
Capetown(config-if)#dialer map ip 192.168.16.1 name SanJose1
     broadcast 5551235
Capetown(config-if)#dialer idle-timeout 60
Capetown(config-if)#no shutdown
```

Note: The above configurations include two **dialer map** statements. The second **dialer map** command is needed for PPP multilink to work in this particular configuration.

Use the **show isdn status** command to verify that the routers have established communication with the ISDN switch. Use the **clear interface bri0/0** command multiple times if necessary to enable a valid and established SPID status.

On *both* SanJose1 and Capetown, issue the following commands for PPP multilink:

```
SanJose1(config)#interface bri0/0
SanJose1(config-if)#ppp multilink
SanJose1(config-if)#dialer load-threshold 1 either
```

The **ppp multilink** command is used on ISDN interfaces to bundle both 64-kbps B channels so that they function together as a 128-kbps pipe.

The **dialer load-threshold** command specifies how much traffic on the first B channel will force the second channel to be brought up. This command takes a numerical argument from 1–255. The number 1 is the minimum load, and the number 255 is a full load. Using this system, 128 would be approximately a 50 percent load.

If you set the threshold to 255, the second B channel will not be brought up until the first channel is completely loaded. The keyword **either** is used to specify that the load threshold applies to both inbound and outbound traffic. You have the option of specifying **inbound** or **outbound** instead.

Step 3

Configure *both* routers with the appropriate password and username information, as shown here:

```
SanJose1(config)#username Capetown password cisco
SanJose1(config)#enable password cisco
SanJose1(config)#line vty 0 4
SanJose1(config-line)#password cisco
SanJose1(config-line)#exit
```

Step 4

Configure a static route to 192.168.216.0/24 on SanJose1. Set up a static default route on Capetown as shown here

```
SanJose1(config)#ip route 192.168.216.0 255.255.255.0 192.168.16.3
Capetown(config)#ip route 0.0.0.0 0.0.0.0 192.168.16.1
```

Step 5

Ping Host A from Host B. This ping should bring up the DDR connection. Troubleshoot as necessary.

After the connection is up, issue the **show ip interface brief** command on *both* routers. You should see that both B channels are up. If only channel 1 is up, send more pings to Host A from Host B. Below are sample outputs:

```
SanJose1#show ip interface brief
Interface               IP-Address      OK? Method Status                Protocol
FastEthernet0/0         192.168.0.1     YES NVRAM  up                    up
Serial0/0               unassigned      YES NVRAM  administratively down  down
BRI0/0                  192.168.16.1    YES NVRAM  up                    up
BRI0/0:1                unassigned      YES unset  up                    up
BRI0/0:2                unassigned      YES unset  up                    up
Serial0/1               unassigned      YES NVRAM  administratively down  down
Virtual-Access1         unassigned      YES TFTP   up                    up

Capetown#show ip interface brief
Interface               IP-Address      OK? Method Status                Protocol
FastEthernet0/0         192.168.216.1   YES NVRAM  up                    up
Serial0/0               unassigned      YES NVRAM  administratively down  down
BRI0/0                  192.168.16.3    YES NVRAM  up                    up
BRI0/0:1                unassigned      YES unset  up                    up
BRI0/0:2                unassigned      YES unset  up                    up
Serial0/1               unassigned      YES NVRAM  administratively down  down
Virtual-Access1         unassigned      YES TFTP   up                    up
```

Both B channels show "up and up."

1. A new interface has appeared in the output of the **show ip interface brief** command. What is it called?

With the ISDN connection still active, issue the **show dialer** command on *both* routers. The following are sample outputs:

```
SanJose1#show dialer

BRI0/0 - dialer type = ISDN

Dial String      Successes    Failures    Last DNIS   Last status
0 incoming call(s) have been screened.
0 incoming call(s) rejected for callback.

BRI0/0:1 - dialer type = ISDN
Idle timer (60 secs), Fast idle timer (20 secs)
Wait for carrier (30 secs), Re-enable (15 secs)
Dialer state is multilink member (Capetown)

BRI0/0:2 - dialer type = ISDN
Idle timer (60 secs), Fast idle timer (20 secs)
Wait for carrier (30 secs), Re-enable (15 secs)
Dialer state is multilink member
Connected to <unknown phone number> (Capetown)

Capetown#show dialer

BRI0/0 - dialer type = ISDN

Dial String      Successes    Failures    Last DNIS   Last status
5551235               0           0       never                 -
5551234              21           0       00:00:31    successful
0 incoming call(s) have been screened.
0 incoming call(s) rejected for callback.

BRI0/0:1 - dialer type = ISDN
Idle timer (60 secs), Fast idle timer (20 secs)
Wait for carrier (30 secs), Re-enable (15 secs)
Dialer state is multilink member
Dial reason: ip (s=192.168.216.2, d=192.168.0.2)
Connected to 5551234 (SanJose1)

BRI0/0:2 - dialer type = ISDN
Idle timer (60 secs), Fast idle timer (20 secs)
Wait for carrier (30 secs), Re-enable (15 secs)
Dialer state is multilink member
Dial reason: Multilink bundle overloaded
Connected to 5551234 (SanJose1)
```

2. Which part of the **show dialer** command output indicated that PPP multilink is functioning?

_____

3. What was the dial reason for the first B channel? What was the dial reason for the second B channel?

_____

Issue the **show ppp multilink** command on SanJose1 and Capetown. The following are sample outputs:

```
SanJose1#show ppp multilink

Virtual-Access1, bundle name is Capetown
  Dialer interface is BRI0/0
  0 lost fragments, 0 reordered, 0 unassigned, sequence 0x3/0x0
      rcvd/sent
  0 discarded, 0 lost received, 1/255 load
  Member links: 2 (max not set, min not set)
    BRI0/0:1
    BRI0/0:2


Capetown#show ppp multilink

Virtual-Access1, bundle name is SanJose1
  Dialer interface is BRI0/0
  0 lost fragments, 0 reordered, 0 unassigned, sequence 0x0/0x6
      rcvd/sent
  0 discarded, 0 lost received, 1/255 load
  Member links: 2 (max not set, min not set)
    BRI0/0:1
    BRI0/0:2
```

4. According to the output of this command, how many channels are participating in the bundle?

_____

Lab 4-4: Configuring ISDN PRI

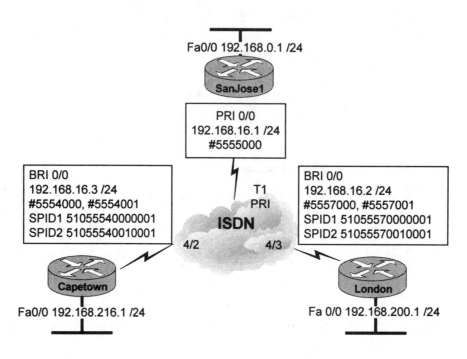

Objective

In this lab, you configure ISDN BRI and ISDN PRI on the remote and central site routers.

Scenario

The International Travel Agency wants you to configure a connection between the remote offices (Capetown and London) and its corporate network router (SanJose1). The corporate office has just had an ISDN PRI provisioned so that SanJose1 can handle 23 ISDN BRI and/or V.90 asynchronous dialup calls simultaneously. Your job is to configure the BRIs on the remote routers, and configure the T1 controller and PRI D channel on SanJose1. When configuration is complete, each router should be able to dial the other two routers; SanJose1 should be able to receive calls from both London and Capetown.

Step 1

Note: This lab assumes that SanJose1 has a T1 controller module installed.

Before beginning this lab, it is recommended that you reload the routers after erasing their startup configuration. This prevents you from having problems caused by residual configurations. Build and configure the network according to the above diagram, but do not configure the routers' PRI and BRI interfaces yet. Use the Adtran Atlas 550 or a similar device to simulate the ISDN cloud. If you are using the Atlas 550, be sure to use straight-through cables and connect both routers to the BRI module ports of the Atlas 550, as labeled in the diagram. Connect SanJose's T1 controller to the T1

PRI port on the Atlas 550. This connection may require a DB-15-to-RJ45 adapter on the T1 controller module and the appropriate cable supplied with the Atlas 550.

Step 2

Configure the ISDN PRI connection. You must specify the ISDN PRI switch type, which is determined by the carrier. For this lab, the switch type is National. The command to configure the switch type is shown here:

```
SanJose1(config)#isdn switch-type primary-ni
```

Next, configure the local username and password database, as shown here, so that SanJose1 can authenticate the remote routers with CHAP:

```
SanJose1(config)#username Capetown password cisco
SanJose1(config)#username London password cisco
```

Specify what types of traffic will generate a call to the remote router. Configure a dialer list to specify any IP traffic as interesting with the following command:

```
SanJose1(config)#dialer-list 1 protocol ip permit
```

The SanJose1 router must have a route to both the Capetown and London Ethernet networks. Using the appropriate commands, configure two static routes to the LAN interfaces of these routers.

1. What are the commands to do this?

Step 3

In this step, you configure the T1 controller. The controller must be configured according to your provider's framing and line coding. In this case, use extended super frame and the binary 8-zero substitution linecode. Also, set the T1 controller to use all timeslots (remember that a T1 has twenty-four 64-kbps channels). To configure the PRI controller, issue the following commands:

```
SanJose1(config)#controller t1 1/0
SanJose1(config-controller)#framing esf
SanJose1(config-controller)#linecode b8zs
SanJose1(config-controller)#pri-group timeslots 1-24
```

The final part of the configuration is to configure the PRI D channel, which is responsible for call setup and signaling. The D channel uses channel 23 (which is the 24th channel, since they are numbered beginning with 0). Issue the following commands:

```
SanJose1(config)#interface serial 1/0:23
SanJose1(config-if)#ip address 192.168.16.1 255.255.255.0
SanJose1(config-if)#dialer-group 1
SanJose1(config-if)#dialer load-threshold 1 outbound
SanJose1(config-if)#dialer idle-timeout 60
SanJose1(config-if)#encapsulation ppp
```

```
SanJose1(config-if)#ppp multilink
SanJose1(config-if)#ppp authentication chap
```

Configure dialer maps statements as shown here, so the router knows which numbers to dial to reach specific next-hop IP addresses:

```
SanJose1(config-if)#dialer map ip 192.168.16.3 name Capetown 5554000
SanJose1(config-if)#dialer map ip 192.168.16.3 name Capetown 5554001
SanJose1(config-if)#dialer map ip 192.168.16.2 name London 5557000
SanJose1(config-if)#dialer map ip 192.168.16.2 name London 5557001
```

Finally, use the **show isdn status** command to verify that communication between the router and the ISDN switch has been successfully established, as shown here:

```
SanJose1#show isdn status
Global ISDN Switchtype = primary-ni
ISDN Serial1/0:23 interface
        dsl 0, interface ISDN Switchtype = primary-ni
    Layer 1 Status:
        ACTIVE
    Layer 2 Status:
        TEI = 0, Ces = 1, SAPI = 0, State =
        MULTIPLE_FRAME_ESTABLISHED
    Layer 3 Status:
        0 Active Layer 3 Call(s)
    Activated dsl 0 CCBs = 0
    The Free Channel Mask:  0x801FFFFF
    Total Allocated ISDN CCBs = 2
```

2. How is the **show isdn status** output for Layer 2 of a PRI different from a BRI?

_____

Step 4

Configure the remote routers to use the appropriate ISDN switch type, National ISDN-1. Because you will be using PPP encapsulation and CHAP on the B channels, enter the username and password information on both routers (as shown here) for London. When configuring Capetown, substitute the appropriate information:

```
London(config)#enable password cisco
London(config)#line vty 0 4
London(config-line)#password cisco
London(config-line)#exit

London(config)#isdn switch-type basic-ni
London(config)#username SanJose1 password cisco
London(config)#username Capetown password cisco
London(config)#interface  bri0/0
London(config)#ip address 192.168.16.2 255.255.255.0
London(config-if)#encapsulation ppp
London(config-if)#ppp authenticate chap
London(config-if)#isdn spid1 51055570000001 5557000
London(config-if)#isdn spid2 51055570010001 5557001
London(config-if)#dialer group-group 1
London(config-if)#dialer idle-timeout 60
London(config-if)#no shutdown
```

3. PPP is the line encapsulation on the B channels; what is the encapsulation protocol used on the D channel?

Configure **dialer-list 1** to identify all IP traffic as "interesting" on *both* routers:

```
London(config)#dialer-list 1 protocol ip permit
```

Configure both routers with the username and password of SanJose1, so that they will each authenticate SanJose1 using CHAP. You must also configure a static route to the central office LAN on both routers. Example commands for Capetown are shown here:

```
Capetown(config)#username SanJose1 password cisco
Capetown(config)#username London password cisco
Capetown(config)#ip route 192.168.0.0 255.255.255.0 192.168.16.1
Capetown(config)#ip route 192.168.200.0 255.255.255.0 192.168.16.2
```

Finally, configure the remote routers' BRI interfaces with the appropriate **dialer map** commands. The commands required for Capetown are shown here:

```
Capetown(config)#interface bri 0/0
Capetown(config-if)#dialer map ip 192.168.16.1 name SanJose1 5555000
Capetown(config-if)#dialer map ip 192.168.16.2 name London 5557000
Capetown(config-if)#dialer map ip 192.168.16.2 name London 5557001
```

Step 5

Test your configuration by sending pings to SanJose1's FastEthernet interface from both Capetown and London. These pings to 192.168.0.1 should be successful; troubleshoot as necessary.

After the pings, both Capetown and London will be connected to SanJose1 simultaneously. With multilink configured, Capetown and London should be using both of their B channels.

If either link is disconnected, ping SanJose1's FastEthernet interface again. After both the Capetown and London links are up, issue the **show ip interface brief** command on SanJose1, as shown here:

```
SanJose1#show ip interface brief
Interface              IP-Address      OK? Method Status                Protocol
FastEthernet0/0        192.168.0.1     YES NVRAM  up                    up
Serial0/0              unassigned      YES NVRAM  administratively down  down
Serial0/1              unassigned      YES NVRAM  administratively down  down
Serial1/0:0            unassigned      YES unset  down                   down
Serial1/0:1            unassigned      YES unset  down                   down
Serial1/0:2            unassigned      YES unset  down                   down
Serial1/0:3            unassigned      YES unset  down                   down
Serial1/0:4            unassigned      YES unset  down                   down
Serial1/0:5            unassigned      YES unset  down                   down
Serial1/0:6            unassigned      YES unset  down                   down
Serial1/0:7            unassigned      YES unset  down                   down
```

```
Serial1/0:8            unassigned     YES unset  down            down
Serial1/0:9            unassigned     YES unset  down            down
Serial1/0:10           unassigned     YES unset  down            down
Serial1/0:11           unassigned     YES unset  down            down
Serial1/0:12           unassigned     YES unset  down            down
Serial1/0:13           unassigned     YES unset  down            down
Serial1/0:14           unassigned     YES unset  down            down
Serial1/0:15           unassigned     YES unset  down            down
Serial1/0:16           unassigned     YES unset  down            down
Serial1/0:17           unassigned     YES unset  down            down
Serial1/0:18           unassigned     YES unset  down            down
Serial1/0:19           unassigned     YES unset  up              up
Serial1/0:20           unassigned     YES unset  up              up
Serial1/0:21           unassigned     YES unset  up              up
Serial1/0:22           unassigned     YES unset  up              up
Serial1/0:23           192.168.16.1   YES NVRAM  up              up
Virtual-Access1        unassigned     YES TFTP   up              up
```

4. According to the output of this command, which channels of the PRI are connected?

    _____

5. Why does Serial1/0:23 have an IP address, but not Serial1/0:22 or Serial1/0:20?

    _____

    With both connections active, issue the **show dialer** command on SanJose1.

6. What is the dialer reason for Serial1/0:19?

    _____

7. What is the dialer reason for Serial1/0:20?

    _____

8. What is the dialer reason for Serial1/0:21?

    _____

9. What is the dialer reason for Serial1/0:22?

    _____

Lab 5-1: Configuring ISDN Using Dialer Profiles

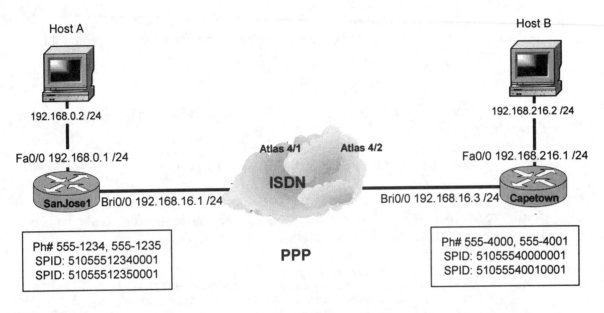

Objective

In this lab, you configure two Cisco routers for ISDN BRI using dialer profiles.

Scenario

The International Travel Agency wants you to configure an ISDN DDR connection between a remote office (Capetown) and its corporate network core router (San-Jose1). They asked that you configure PPP encapsulation and CHAP authentication over this link. Because the company plans to increase the number of ISDN connections at the central and remote sites, you will use dialer profiles to simplify future configurations.

Step 1

Before beginning this lab, it is recommended that you reload the router after erasing its startup configuration. This prevents you from having problems caused by residual configurations. Build and configure the network according to the above diagram, but do not configure either router's BRI interfaces yet. Use the Adtran Atlas 550 or a similar device to simulate the ISDN cloud. If you are using the Atlas 550, be sure to use straight-through cables and connect both routers to the BRI module ports of the Atlas 550 as labeled in the diagram. Also, be sure to configure both workstations with the correct IP address and default gateway (router Fa0/0 IP address).

Step 2

Configure both routers to use the appropriate ISDN switch type, National ISDN-1. Because you will be using PPP encapsulation and CHAP on the B channels, enter username and password information on both routers as shown below for SanJose1:

```
SanJose1(config)#isdn switch-type basic-ni
SanJose1(config)#username Capetown password cisco
```

```
SanJose1(config)#enable password cisco
SanJose1(config)#line vty 0 4
SanJose1(config-line)#password cisco
SanJose1(config-line)#exit
```

1. PPP is the line encapsulation on the B channels. What is the encapsulation protocol used on the D channel?

Configure **dialer-list 1** to identify all IP traffic as "interesting" on both routers, as shown here:

```
SanJose1(config)#dialer-list 1 protocol ip permit
```

Step 3

Configure the BRI on SanJose1 and Capetown to use a dialer profile, as shown here; do not assign an IP address to these interfaces:

```
SanJose1(config)#interface bri0/0
SanJose1(config-if)#isdn spid1 51055512340001 5551234
SanJose1(config-if)#isdn spid2 51055512350001 5551235
SanJose1(config-if)#encapsulation ppp
SanJose1(config-if)#ppp authentication chap
SanJose1(config-if)#dialer pool-member 1
SanJose1(config-if)#no shutdown

Capetown(config)#interface bri0/0
Capetown(config-if)#isdn spid1 51055540000001 5554000
Capetown(config-if)#isdn spid2 51055540010001 5554001
Capetown(config-if)#encapsulation ppp
Capetown(config-if)#ppp authentication chap
Capetown(config-if)#dialer pool-member 1
Capetown(config-if)#no shutdown
```

Dialer profiles were introduced in IOS version 11.2 and are the preferred way to configure DDR in complex environments. The dialer profile concept is based on a separation between logical and physical interface configuration. The use of dialer profiles allows the logical and physical configurations to be bound together dynamically on a per-call basis. When using a dialer profile, you assign an interface to a dialer pool or pools. In this case, you have assigned BRI0/0 to be in dialer pool 1. All the other logical configurations (IP address, dialer string, and dialer group) will be assigned by the dialer interface. Depending on the IOS version, you might have to specify the line encapsulation on both the physical interface and the logical interface.

In Cisco IOS software releases prior to IOS 12.0(7)T, dialer profiles in the same dialer pool need encapsulation configuration information entered under both the dialer profile interface and the ISDN interface. If any conflict arises between the logical and the physical interfaces, the dialer profile will not work. That's why this configuration has **encapsulation ppp** configured on BRI0/0 and dialer interface 0.

In the new dialer profile model introduced by the dynamic multiple encapsulations feature (IOS 12.0(7)T and later), the configuration on the ISDN interface is ignored and only the configuration on the profile interface is used, unless PPP name binding is used. Before a successful bind by calling line identification (CLID) occurs, no encapsulation type and configuration are assumed or taken from the physical interfaces.

Step 4

Configure the dialer interfaces for both routers, starting with SanJose1. The dialer interface receives the logical configuration that is applied to a physical interface. Issue the following commands on SanJose1:

```
SanJose1(config)#interface dialer 0
SanJose1(config-if)#dialer pool 1
SanJose1(config-if)#ip address 192.168.16.1 255.255.255.0
SanJose1(config-if)#encapsulation ppp
SanJose1(config-if)#ppp authentication chap
SanJose1(config-if)#ppp multilink
SanJose1(config-if)#dialer load-threshold 1 either
SanJose1(config-if)#dialer-group 1
SanJose1(config-if)#dialer remote-name Capetown
SanJose1(config-if)#dialer string 5554000
SanJose1(config-if)#dialer string 5554001
```

Now create a dialer profile on Capetown, as shown here:

```
Capetown(config)#interface dialer 0
Capetown(config-if)#dialer pool 1
Capetown(config-if)#ip address 192.168.16.3 255.255.255.0
Capetown(config-if)#encapsulation ppp
Capetown(config-if)#ppp authentication chap
Capetown(config-if)#ppp multilink
Capetown(config-if)#dialer load-threshold 1 either
Capetown(config-if)#dialer-group 1
Capetown(config-if)#dialer remote-name SanJose1
Capetown(config-if)#dialer string 5551234
Capetown(config-if)#dialer string 5551235
```

Note: With a dialer interface, you use the **dialer remote-name** and **dialer string** commands in place of a dialer map.

Use the **show isdn status** command to check ISDN Layer 2 and SPID status. Use the **clear interface bri0/0** command, multiple times if necessary, to enable a SPID status of established and valid.

2. How will SanJose1 know to use Capetown at 5554000 when it receives interesting traffic that must be routed to 192.168.16.3? In other words, is there anything in the dialer interface configuration that SanJose1 can use to determine that this dialer profile should be used to reach 192.168.16.3?

_____

_____

_____

Step 5

Configure static routing on both routers so that nodes on the remote network can reach nodes at the central site. Use a default route on the Capetown router (because it is a remote site stub network):

```
SanJose1(config)#ip route 192.168.216.0 255.255.255.0 192.168.16.3

Capetown(config)#ip route 0.0.0.0 0.0.0.0 192.168.16.1
```

Step 6

Enable **debug dialer** on both SanJose1 and Capetown.

Test your ISDN connection by pinging Host B from Host A. This ping should eventually be successful. Once you are connected, issue the **show dialer** command.

3. According to the output from **show dialer**, what logical interface has been bound to interface BRI0/0:1?

_____

Issue the **show ip interface brief** command. Since you configured PPP multilink, both B Channels should show "up and up." Troubleshoot as necessary.

Allow the ISDN connection to time out, or manually disconnect both B channels by issuing the **isdn disconnect interface bri0/0 all** command at either router.

With both B Channels disconnected on each router, issue the **show ip interface brief** command a second time.

4. According to this command, interface dialer 0 is still "up and up." Why?

_____

_____

Lab 5-2: Using a Dialer Map-Class with Dialer Profiles

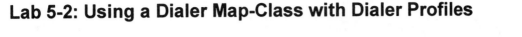

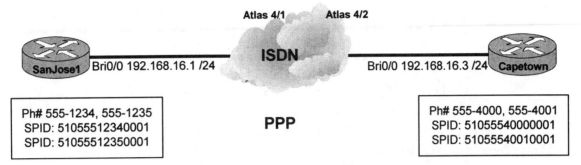

Objective

In this lab, you configure two Cisco routers for ISDN BRI using dialer profiles and a dialer map-class.

Scenario

The International Travel Agency wants you to configure an ISDN DDR connection between a remote office (Capetown) and its corporate network core router (San-Jose1). They asked that you configure PPP encapsulation and CHAP authentication over this link. Because the company plans to increase the number of ISDN connections at the central and remote sites, you will use dialer profiles to simplify future configurations.

Although the company has only one remote site connection at this time, you have been instructed to configure two dialer profiles in order to test its operation. Because you will be testing router-to-router connectivity, you do not need to configure the workstations in this exercise.

Step 1

Before beginning this lab, it is recommended that you reload the router after erasing its startup configuration. This prevents you from having problems caused by residual configurations. Build (cable) the network according to the above diagram, but do not configure either router's BRI interfaces yet. Use the Adtran Atlas 550 or a similar device to simulate the ISDN cloud. If you are using the Atlas 550, be sure to use straight-through cables and connect both routers to the BRI module ports of the Atlas 550, as labeled in the diagram.

Step 2

Configure both routers to use the appropriate ISDN switch type, National ISDN-1. Because you will be using PPP encapsulation and CHAP on the B channels, enter password information on both routers. Note that this lab uses different passwords and username combinations than previous labs.

```
SanJose1(config)#isdn switch-type basic-ni
SanJose1(config)#username Capetown password cisco
SanJose1(config)#username JULIET password cisco
SanJose1(config)#enable password cisco
```

```
SanJose1(config)#line vty 0 4
SanJose1(config-line)#password cisco
SanJose1(config-line)#exit

Capetown(config)#isdn switch-type basic-ni
Capetown(config)#username SanJose1 password cisco
Capetown(config)#username ROMEO password cisco
Capetown(config)#enable password cisco
Capetown(config)#line vty 0 4
Capetown(config-line)#password cisco
Capetown(config-line)#exit
```

On both routers, configure **dialer-list 5** to identify all IP traffic as "interesting" as shown below for SanJose1:

```
SanJose1(config)#dialer-list 5 protocol ip permit
```

Step 3

Configure the BRI on SanJose1 and Capetown to use dialer profiles. In this lab, you configure both BRIs to be members of two dialer pools. Remember, you must enter encapsulation configuration commands for both the physical interface (BRI 0/0) and the logical (dialer0, etc.).

```
SanJose1(config)#interface bri0/0
SanJose1(config-if)#isdn spid1 51055512340001 5551234
SanJose1(config-if)#isdn spid2 51055512350001 5551235
SanJose1(config-if)#encapsulation ppp
SanJose1(config-if)#ppp authentication chap
SanJose1(config-if)#ppp chap hostname ROMEO
SanJose1(config-if)#dialer pool-member 1
SanJose1(config-if)#no shutdown

Capetown(config)#interface bri0/0
Capetown(config-if)#isdn spid1 51055540000001 5554000
Capetown(config-if)#isdn spid2 51055540010001 5554001
Capetown(config-if)#encapsulation ppp
Capetown(config-if)#ppp authentication chap
Capetown(config-if)#ppp chap hostname JULIET
Capetown(config-if)#dialer pool-member 1
Capetown(config-if)#no shutdown
```

Note: The **ppp chap hostname** command configures an alternate CHAP username for each router. For example, using the previous configuration, SanJose1 can authenticate as both SanJose1 and ROMEO.

Step 4

On both routers, create a **map-class** called AGGRESSIVE that can be used to apply multiple dialer configurations to a dialer string easily. Issue the following commands on both routers as shown below for SanJose1:

```
SanJose1(config)#map-class dialer AGGRESSIVE
SanJose1(config-map-class)#dialer idle-timeout 30
SanJose1(config-map-class)#dialer fast-idle 10
SanJose1(config-map-class)#dialer wait-for-carrier-time 25
SanJose1(config-map-class)#exit
```

1. In addition to dialer, what other types of map-class can you configure? (Use the Help feature to find the answer.)

_____

_____

Step 5

Configure the dialer interfaces for both routers, starting with SanJose1. The dialer interface receives the logical configuration that is applied to a physical interface.

```
SanJose1(config)#interface dialer 0
SanJose1(config-if)#ip address 192.168.16.1 255.255.255.0
SanJose1(config-if)#dialer pool 1
SanJose1(config-if)#encapsulation ppp
SanJose1(config-if)#ppp authentication chap
SanJose1(config-if)#dialer remote-name Capetown
SanJose1(config-if)#dialer-group 5
SanJose1(config-if)#dialer string 5554000 class AGGRESSIVE
SanJose1(config-if)#dialer string 5554001 class AGGRESSIVE
```

2. By applying the map-class, AGGRESSIVE, to each dialer string, which timers are you configuring?

_____

_____

```
SanJose1(config)#interface dialer 1
SanJose1(config-if)#ip address 172.16.0.1 255.255.255.0
SanJose1(config-if)#dialer pool 1
SanJose1(config-if)#encapsulation ppp
SanJose1(config-if)#ppp authentication chap
SanJose1(config-if)#ppp chap hostname ROMEO
SanJose1(config-if)#dialer remote-name JULIET
SanJose1(config-if)#dialer-group 5
SanJose1(config-if)#dialer string 5554000 class AGGRESSIVE
SanJose1(config-if)#dialer string 5554001 class AGGRESSIVE
```

3. What does the command **ppp chap hostname ROMEO** do?

_____

Now create a dialer profile on Capetown, as shown here:

```
Capetown(config)#interface dialer 0
Capetown(config-if)#ip address 192.168.16.3 255.255.255.0
Capetown(config-if)#dialer pool 1
Capetown(config-if)#encapsulation ppp
Capetown(config-if)#ppp authentication chap
Capetown(config-if)#dialer remote-name SanJose1
Capetown(config-if)#dialer-group 5
Capetown(config-if)#dialer string 5551234 class AGGRESSIVE
Capetown(config-if)#dialer string 5551235 class AGGRESSIVE
Capetown(config)#interface dialer 1
Capetown(config-if)#ip address 172.16.0.3 255.255.255.0
Capetown(config-if)#dialer pool 1
Capetown(config-if)#encapsulation ppp
Capetown(config-if)#ppp authentication chap
```

```
Capetown(config-if)#ppp chap hostname JULIET
Capetown(config-if)#dialer remote-name ROMEO
Capetown(config-if)#dialer-group 5
Capetown(config-if)#dialer string 5551234 class AGGRESSIVE
Capetown(config-if)#dialer string 5551235 class AGGRESSIVE
```

Step 6

To simplify testing, create hostname mappings on both routers, as shown here:

```
SanJose1(config)#ip host Capetown 192.168.16.3
SanJose1(config)#ip host JULIET 172.16.0.3

Capetown(config)#ip host SanJose1 192.168.16.1
Capetown(config)#ip host ROMEO 172.16.0.1
```

Step 7

Before connecting, issue the **show dialer** command.

4. According to the output of this command, to what is BRI0/0:1's dialer idle timeout set?

_____

5. To what is BRI0/0:1's fast idle timer set?

_____

Use the **show isdn status** command on both routers to check the ISDN Layer 2 and SPID status. Use the **clear interface bri0/0** command, multiple times if necessary, to enable a SPID status of established and valid.

Now test the dialer profile operation. In addition to **debug dialer**, you may also want to enable debugging for PPP authentication. Ping Capetown (192.168.16.3) from SanJose1 using the following command:

```
SanJose1#ping Capetown
```

SanJose1 should dial Capetown and connect. The pings should eventually be successful, as shown here:

```
Sending 5, 100-byte ICMP Echos to 192.168.16.3, timeout is 2 seconds:
00:49:26: BRI0/0 DDR: rotor dialout [priority]
00:49:26: BRI0/0 DDR: Dialing cause ip (s=192.168.16.1,
     d=192.168.16.3)
00:49:26: BRI0/0 DDR: Attempting to dial 5554000
00:49:111669149728: %LINK-3-UPDOWN: Interface BRI0/0:1, changed state
     to up
00:49:113835732748: BRI0/0:1: interface must be fifo queue, force
     fifo
00:49:113835732564: %DIALER-6-BIND: Interface BRI0/0:1 bound to
     profile Dialer0
00:49:115964116991: %ISDN-6-CONNECT: Interface BRI0/0:1 is now
     connected to 5554000
00:49:111698112601: isdn_call_connect: Calling lineaction of
     BRI0/0:1.
00:49:28: BR0/0:1 DDR: Dialer protocol up
00:49:28: BRI0/0:1 DDR: dialer protocol up
```

```
00:49:28: Dialer0: dialer_ckt_swt_client_connect: incoming circuit
        switched call.!!!
Success rate is 60 percent (3/5), round-trip min/avg/max =
        32/32/32 ms
```

6. According to the output of **debug dialer**, what logical interface has been bound to interface BRI0/0:1?

_____

Troubleshoot as necessary.

With SanJose1 still connected to Capetown (reconnect if necessary), **ping** JULIET from SanJose1 using the following command:

```
SanJose1#ping JULIET
```

Again, the connection and pings should eventually be successful by using the second B Channel, BRI0/0:2. Troubleshoot as necessary.

7. According to the output of **debug dialer**, what logical interface has been bound to interface BRI0/0:2?

_____

With both connections still active, issue the **show dialer** command on SanJose1. A partial sample output is shown here:

```
SanJose1# show dialer
<output omitted>
BRI0/0:1 - dialer type = ISDN
Idle timer (30 secs), Fast idle timer (10 secs)
Wait for carrier (25 secs), Re-enable (15 secs)
Dialer state is data link layer up
Dial reason: ip (s=192.168.16.1, d=192.168.16.3)
Interface bound to profile Dialer0
Time until disconnect 4 secs
Current call connected 00:00:29
Connected to 5554000 (Capetown)

BRI0/0:2 - dialer type = ISDN
Idle timer (30 secs), Fast idle timer (10 secs)
Wait for carrier (25 secs), Re-enable (15 secs)
Dialer state is data link layer up
Dial reason: ip (s=172.16.0.1, d=172.16.0.3)
Interface bound to profile Dialer1
Time until disconnect 19 secs
Current call connected 00:00:13
Connected to 5554001 (JULIET)

Dialer0 - dialer type = DIALER PROFILE
Idle timer (120 secs), Fast idle timer (20 secs)
Wait for carrier (30 secs), Re-enable (15 secs)
Dialer state is data link layer up
Number of active calls = 0
Number of active circuit switched calls = 0
<output omitted>
```

8. According to the output of the **show dialer** command, to what phone number is BRI0/0:1 connected? What is the hostname of that router?

_____

_____

9. To what phone number is BRI0/0:2 connected? What is the hostname of that router?

_____

_____

10. According to the output of the **show dialer** command, to what is BRI0/0:1's idle timer set?

_____

11. To what is BRI0/0:1's fast idle timer set?

_____

12. Why did these values change when SanJose1 connected to Capetown?

_____

_____

_____

13. What is one advantage of using a dialer profile instead of a dedicated configuration on the BRI?

_____

_____

_____

_____

14. What is one advantage of using a dialer map-class?

_____

_____

_____

_____

Lab 6-1: Configuring X.25 SVCs

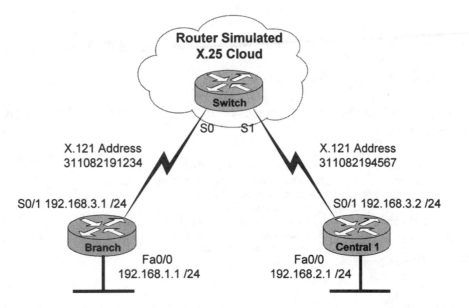

Objective

Configure X.25 SVCs to connect a central office router to a branch location using a third router as a simulated X.25 switch.

Scenario

International Travel Agency (ITA) has a small branch office in an area that is not served by either Frame Relay or ISDN technology. You are asked to put together an X.25 prototype to see if the technology will meet ITA's requirements. In this first trial, you will try using switched virtual circuits (SVCs).

Because an X.25 test network is not available, you must first configure a router to act as an X.25 switch. After the switch is configured, you configure two routers to interface with the X.25 network. Use X.25 SVCs to create a functional link between the two routers. The branch router (Branch) connects a stub network, so configure a default route on the branch router side and a static route on the central router (Central_1) side.

Step 1

Before beginning this lab, it is recommended that you reload the routers after erasing their startup configuration. This prevents you from having problems caused by residual configurations. Cable the lab as shown in the diagram.

Step 2

The first router to be configured is the X.25 switch router, which will simulate the X.25 network. Configure the following information on the router.

Set the hostname to Switch on the router:

```
Router(config)#hostname Switch
```

Turn on the X.25 switching feature with the following command:

```
Switch(config)#x25 routing
```

Configure each of the serial interfaces on the X.25 switch (Switch) router to use X.25 encapsulation:

```
Switch(config)#interface serial 0/0
Switch(config-if)#encapsulation x25 dce
Switch(config-if)#clockrate 56000
Switch(config-if)#no shutdown
Switch(config-if)#interface serial 0/1
Switch(config-if)#encapsulation x25 dce
Switch(config-if)#clockrate 56000
Switch(config-if)#no shutdown
Switch(config-if)#^Z
```

Use the following commands to set up the static X.121 address for each connection. The X.25 switch uses this information to determine which interface to use to switch a packet to the appropriate destination.

```
Switch(config)#x25 route 311082191234 interface serial 0/0
Switch(config)#x25 route 311082194567 interface serial 0/1
```

Step 3

Configure the Branch router using the following steps.

Set the hostname to Branch on the router:

```
router(config)#hostname Branch
```

Configure the interfaces and assign the IP addresses:

```
Branch(config)#interface fastethernet 0/0
Branch(config-if)#ip address 192.168.1.1 255.255.255.0
Branch(config-if)#no shutdown
Branch(config)#interface serial 0/0
Branch(config-if)#encapsulation x25
Branch(config-if)#ip address 192.168.3.1 255.255.255.0
Branch(config-if)#no shutdown
```

Assign the X.121 address to this interface:

```
Branch(config-if)#x25 address 311082191234
```

Set up the X.25 mapping to the other side:

```
Branch(config-if)#x25 map ip 192.168.3.2 311082194567 broadcast
```

Add the necessary default route to facilitate successful routing:

```
Branch(config)#ip route 0.0.0.0 0.0.0.0 192.168.3.2
```

Step 4

Configure the central office (Central_1) router using the following steps.

Set the hostname to Central_1 on the router:

```
router(config)#hostname Central_1
```

Configure the interfaces and assign the IP addresses:

```
Central_1(config)#interface fastethernet 0/0
Central_1(config-if)#ip address 192.168.2.1 255.255.255.0
Central_1(config-if)#no shutdown
Central_1(config)#interface serial 0/0
Central_1(config-if)#encapsulation x25
Central_1(config-if)#ip address 192.168.3.2 255.255.255.0
Central_1(config-if)#no shutdown
```

Assign the X.121 address to this interface:

```
Central_1(config-if)#x25 address 311082194567
```

Set up the X.25 mapping to the other side:

```
Central_1(config-if)#x25 map ip 192.168.3.1 311082191234 broadcast
```

Add the necessary static route to facilitate successful routing:

```
Central_1(config)#ip route 192.168.1.0 255.255.255.0 192.168.3.1
```

Step 5

Verify end-to-end connectivity.

From either Branch or Central_1, ping the other's FastEthernet interface.

If it doesn't work, you have a problem with your configuration. Make sure that the Ethernet interfaces are up and connected at least to a hub or switch.

Remember: Connectivity is between Branch and Central_1. The other router is working as a switch.

Step 6

On all three routers, use the appropriate **show interfaces** command and see what X.25 information is available. The following is an example of what the output for Central_1 might look like:

```
Central_1#show interfaces serial 0/0
serial 0/0 is up, line protocol is up
```

```
Hardware is HD64570 with 5-in-1 module
Internet address is 192.168.3.2/24
MTU 1500 bytes, BW 1544 Kbit, DLY 20000 usec,
    reliability 255/255, txload 1/255, rxload 1/255
Encapsulation X25, loopback not set
X.25 DTE, address 311082194567, state R1, modulo 8, timer 0
    Defaults: idle VC timeout 0
        cisco encapsulation
        input/output window sizes 2/2, packet sizes 128/128
    Timers: T20 180, T21 200, T22 180, T23 180
    Channels: Incoming-only none, Two-way 1-1024, Outgoing-only
     none
    RESTARTs 0/0 CALLs 0+0/0+0/0+0 DIAGs 0/0
LAPB DTE, state CONNECT, modulo 8, k 7, N1 12056, N2 20
    T1 3000, T2 0, interface outage (partial T3) 0, T4 0
    VS 3, VR 1, tx NR 1, Remote VR 3, Retransmissions 0
    Queues: U/S frames 0, I frames 0, unack. 0, reTx 0
    IFRAMEs 27/17 RNRs 0/0 REJs 0/0 SABM/Es 0/1 FRMRs 0/0 DISCs 0/0
Last input 00:01:05, output 00:00:49, output hang never
Last clearing of "show interface" counters 00:01:41
Queueing strategy: fifo
Output queue 0/40, 0 drops; input queue 0/75, 0 drops
5 minute input rate 0 bits/sec, 0 packets/sec
5 minute output rate 0 bits/sec, 0 packets/sec
    45 packets input, 645 bytes, 0 no buffer
    Received 0 broadcasts, 0 runts, 0 giants, 0 throttles
    0 input errors, 0 CRC, 0 frame, 0 overrun, 0 ignored, 0 abort
    36 packets output, 3087 bytes, 0 underruns
    0 output errors, 0 collisions, 0 interface resets
    0 output buffer failures, 0 output buffers swapped out
    0 carrier transitions
    DCD=up  DSR=up  DTR=up  RTS=up  CTS=up
Central_1#
```

Note the encapsulation and the DTE/DCE designation.

1. In the previous output, what is the LAPB state?

_____

2. In the previous output, what is the X.25 address of the interface?

_____

On any of the three routers, use the **show x25 ?** command to see the show x25 options, as shown here:

```
Central_1#show x25 ?
  context     Show X.25 state for one or more interfaces
  hunt-group  Show X.25 hunt group(s)
  interface   Show X.25, CMNS, or Annex-G VCs on one interface
  map         Show x25 map table
  profile     Show X.25 profile(s)
  route       Show x25 routing table
  services    Show X.25 services information (default)
  vc          Show specific X.25/CMNS/ANNEXG virtual circuit(s)
  xot         Show XOT (X.25-Over-TCP) VCs
  |           Output modifiers
  <cr>
  pad         X25 pad connection status
  remote-red  X25 REMOTE-RED table
Central_1#show x25
```

Try the **context** option and compare the results to the show interfaces result. Try **map**, **services** and any others that interest you. *Note*: Not all the commands will display results, depending on which router you are using. The **map** option works on either end router but not on the switch, for example.

On the Switch router, try the **show X25 route** command. This command shows nothing on the other two routers because they are not serving as an X.25 switch:

```
Switch#show x25 route
  #  Match                          Substitute              Route to
  1  dest 311082191234                                      serial 0/0
  2  dest 311082194567                                      serial 0/1
Switch#
```

Lab 6-2: Configuring X.25 PVCs

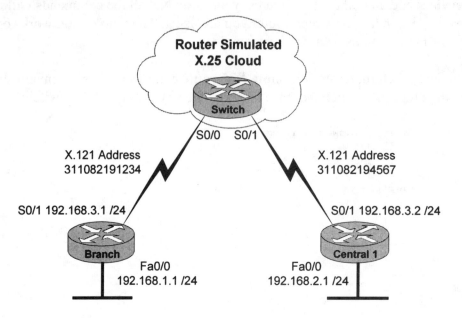

Objective

Configure X.25 PVCs to connect a central office router to a branch location by using a third router as a simulated X.25 switch.

Scenario

International Travel Agency (ITA) has a small branch office (Branch) in an area that is not served by either Frame Relay or ISDN technology. You are asked to put together an X.25 prototype to see if the technology will meet ITA's requirements. In this second trial, you must try using permanent virtual circuits (PVCs).

Because an X.25 network is not available, you will first configure a router to act as an X.25 switch. After the switch is configured, you need to configure two routers to interface with the X.25 network. Use X.25 PVCs to create a functional link between the two routers. The branch router (Branch) connects a stub network, so configure a default route on the branch router side and a static route on the central router (Central_1) side.

Step 1

Before beginning this lab, it is recommended that you reload the routers after erasing their startup configuration. This prevents you from having problems caused by residual configurations. Cable the lab as shown in the previous diagram.

Step 2

The first router to be configured is the Switch router, which will simulate the X.25 network. Log into the Switch router and enter global configuration mode.
Configure the following information into the router.

Set the hostname to Switch on the router, as shown here:

```
router(config)#hostname Switch
```

Turn on the X.25 switching feature with the following command:

```
Switch(config)#x25 routing
```

Configure each of the serial interfaces on the X.25 switch router so that they use X.25 encapsulation and set up the PVC mappings, as shown here:

```
Switch(config)#interface serial 0/0
Switch(config-if)#encapsulation x25 dce
Switch(config-if)#x25 ltc 25
Switch(config-if)#x25 htc 128
Switch(config-if)#x25 pvc 1 interface serial1 pvc 4
Switch(config-if)#clockrate 56000
Switch(config-if)#no shutdown
Switch(config-if)#interface serial 0/1
Switch(config-if)#encapsulation x25 dce
Switch(config-if)#x25 ltc 25
Switch(config-if)#x25 htc 128
Switch(config-if)#x25 pvc 4 interface serial0 pvc 1
Switch(config-if)#clockrate 56000
Switch(config-if)#no shutdown
```

Set up the static X.121 address. The X.25 switch uses this information to determine which interface to use to switch a packet to the appropriate destination:

```
Switch(config)#x25 route 311082191234 interface serial 0/0
Switch(config)#x25 route 311082194567 interface serial 0/1
```

Step 3

Configure the Branch router using the following steps.

Set the router hostname to Branch:

```
router(config)#hostname Branch
```

Configure the interfaces and assign the IP addresses:

```
Branch(config)#interface fastethernet 0/0
Branch(config-if)#ip address 192.168.1.1 255.255.255.0
Branch(config-if)#no shutdown
Branch(config-if)#interface serial 0/0
Branch(config-if)#encapsulation x25
Branch(config-if)#ip address 192.168.3.1 255.255.255.0
Branch(config-if)#no shutdown
```

Assign the X.121 address to this interface:

```
Branch(config-if)#x25 address 311082191234
```

To set the highest and lowest two-way virtual circuit number, use the **x25 htc** and **x25 ltc** commands:

```
Branch(config-if)#x25 ltc 25
Branch(config-if)#x25 htc 128
```

Instead of using the **x25 map** command to establish an SVC, use the **x25 pvc** command to create a PVC. These PVCs are the X.25 equivalent of leased lines. Set up the PVC in interface configuration mode:

```
Branch(config-if)#x25 pvc 1 ip 192.168.3.2 311082194567 broadcast
```

Add the necessary default route to facilitate successful routing:

```
Branch(config)#ip route 0.0.0.0 0.0.0.0 192.168.3.2
```

Step 4

Configure the central office (Central_1) router using the following steps.

Set the hostname to Central_1 on the router:

```
router(config)#hostname Central_1
```

Configure the interfaces and assign the IP addresses:

```
Central_1(config)#interface fastethernet 0/0
Central_1(config-if)#ip address 192.168.2.1 255.255.255.0
Central_1(config-if)#no shutdown
Central_1(config-if)#interface serial 0/0
Central_1(config-if)#encapsulation x25
Central_1(config-if)#ip address 192.168.3.2 255.255.255.0
Central_1(config-if)#no shutdown
```

Assign the X.121 address to this interface:

```
Central_1(config-if)#x25 address 311082194567
```

Set up the X.25 PVC to the other side:

```
Central_1(config-if)#x25 ltc 25
Central_1(config-if)#x25 htc 128
Central_1(config-if)#x25 pvc 4 ip 192.168.3.1 311082191234 broadcast
```

Add the necessary static route to facilitate successful routing:

```
Central_1(config)#ip route 192.168.1.0 255.255.255.0 192.168.3.1
```

Step 5

Verify end-to-end connectivity.

From either Branch or Central_1, ping the other's FastEthernet interface.

If it doesn't work, you have a problem with your configuration. Make sure that the FastEthernet interfaces are up; troubleshoot as necessary.

Remember: Connectivity is between Branch and Central_1. The other router is working as a switch.

Step 6

On all three routers, use the appropriate **show interfaces** command and see what X.25 information is available.

Use the **show x25 vc** command to display information about the X.25 PVC. On all three routers, use the appropriate **show interfaces** command and see what X.25 information is available. The following is an example of what Switch might look like:

```
Switch#show interfaces
serial 0/0 is up, line protocol is up
  Hardware is HD64570 with 5-in-1 module
  MTU 1500 bytes, BW 1544 Kbit, DLY 20000 usec,
     reliability 255/255, txload 1/255, rxload 1/255
  Encapsulation X25, loopback not set
  X.25 DCE, address <none>, state R1, modulo 8, timer 0
     Defaults: idle VC timeout 0
       cisco encapsulation
       input/output window sizes 2/2, packet sizes 128/128
     Timers: T10 60, T11 180, T12 60, T13 60
     Channels: Incoming-only none, Two-way 25-128, Outgoing-only
     none
     RESTARTs 1/0 CALLs 0+0/0+0/0+0 DIAGs 0/0
  LAPB DCE, state CONNECT, modulo 8, k 7, N1 12056, N2 20
     T1 3000, T2 0, interface outage (partial T3) 0, T4 0
     VS 0, VR 0, tx NR 0, Remote VR 0, Retransmissions 0
     Queues: U/S frames 0, I frames 0, unack. 0, reTx 0
     IFRAMEs 8/8 RNRs 0/0 REJs 0/0 SABM/Es 24/1 FRMRs 0/0 DISCs 0/0
  Last input never, output 00:05:29, output hang never

  serial 0/1 is up, line protocol is up
  Hardware is HD64570 with 5-in-1 module
  MTU 1500 bytes, BW 1544 Kbit, DLY 20000 usec,
     reliability 255/255, txload 1/255, rxload 1/255
  Encapsulation X25, loopback not set
  X.25 DCE, address <none>, state R1, modulo 8, timer 0
     Defaults: idle VC timeout 0
       cisco encapsulation
       input/output window sizes 2/2, packet sizes 128/128
     Timers: T10 60, T11 180, T12 60, T13 60
     Channels: Incoming-only none, Two-way 25-128, Outgoing-only
     none
     RESTARTs 1/0 CALLs 0+0/0+0/0+0 DIAGs 0/0
  LAPB DCE, state CONNECT, modulo 8, k 7, N1 12056, N2 20
     T1 3000, T2 0, interface outage (partial T3) 0, T4 0
     VS 7, VR 7, tx NR 7, Remote VR 7, Retransmissions 0
     Queues: U/S frames 0, I frames 0, unack. 0, reTx 0
     IFRAMEs 7/7 RNRs 0/0 REJs 0/0 SABM/Es 92/1 FRMRs 0/0 DISCs 0/0
  Last input never, output 00:06:54, output hang never
```

Lab 7-1: Basic Frame Relay Router and Switch Configuration

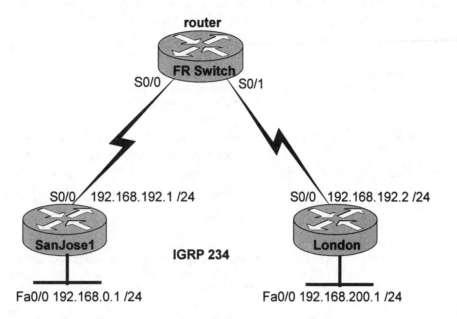

Objective

Configure a router as a Frame Relay switch, connecting two routers in a point-to-point topology.

Scenario

You are the network engineer for International Travel Agency, preparing to deploy Frame Relay as the primary connectivity for the company WAN. While waiting for the service provider to provision T1 lines, you create router configurations in advance. Because you do not have access to a Frame Relay switch, you must configure a Cisco router as a Frame Relay switch to test router configurations. Your network will use IGRP, autonomous system number 234, to advertise LANs at each location.

Step 1

Before beginning this lab, it is recommended that you reload each router after erasing its startup configuration. This prevents you from having problems caused by residual configurations. After you prepare the equipment, proceed with Step 2. This lab assumes version 11.2 or later IOS on all routers.

Step 2

Configure the Frame Relay switch with static mapping necessary to switch packets along the appropriate PVC.

Start by enabling **frame-relay switching** on the router acting as the service provider Frame Relay cloud.

```
FRswitch(config)#frame-relay switching
```

The remaining configurations on the Frame Relay switch are interface-specific. On both serial interfaces, encapsulate frames as Frame Relay, define the interface as DCE and provide a synchronization clocking rate for that link. Here's an example:

```
FRswitch(config)#interface serial 0/0
FRswitch(config-if)#encapsulation frame-relay
FRswitch(config-if)#frame-relay intf-type dce
```

Frame Relay switches identify inbound frames by their data-link connection identifier (DLCI). The DLCI is then referenced in a switching table to determine the outbound port. To statically define an end-to-end PVC between SanJose1 and London, a static route needs to be configured for each serial interface, as shown here:

```
FRswitch(config)#interface serial 0/0
FRswitch(config-if)#frame-relay route 18 interface serial 0/1 16
FRswitch(config-if)#interface serial 0/1
FRswitch(config-if)#frame-relay route 16 interface serial 0/0 18
```

Note: Don't get confused by semantics. When discussing the internal processes of a network device, switches "route" frames between interfaces, and routers "switch" packets between interfaces. If you read that phrase out loud a few hundred times, you can convince yourself it makes sense.

The switch logic says, "If frame inbound interface serial 0/0 is labeled DLCI 18, send outbound interface serial 0/1 labeled with DLCI 16." For traffic traveling in the opposite direction, "If frame inbound interface serial 0/1 is labeled DLCI 16, send outbound interface serial 0/0 labeled with DLCI 18." This can be seen with **show frame-relay route** on the switch:

```
FRswitch#show frame-relay route
Input Intf     Input Dlci     Output Intf     Output Dlci     Status
Serial0/0      18             Serial0/1       16              active
Serial0/1      16             Serial0/0       18              active
```

Step 3

Next, configure SanJose1 with IP addresses and a routing protocol as shown in the previous diagram. Because the default encapsulation for Cisco routers is HDLC, interface serial 0/0 needs to be configured for Frame Relay encapsulation, as shown here:

```
SanJose1(config)#interface serial 0/0
SanJose1(config-if)#encapsulation frame-relay
SanJose1(config-if)#ip address 192.168.192.1 255.255.255.0
SanJose1(config-if)#exit
SanJose1(config)#router igrp 234
SanJose1(config-router)#network 192.168.0.0
SanJose1(config-router)#network 192.168.192.0
```

Configure London using the same command syntax.

Step 4

Use extended pings and **show ip route** to test Frame Relay connectivity and IGRP route propagation.

```
London#show ip route

Gateway of last resort is not set

C    192.168.192.0/24 is directly connected, Serial0/0
C    192.168.200.0/24 is directly connected, FastEthernet0/0
I    192.168.0.0/24 [100/80135] via 192.168.192.1, 00:00:25,
        Serial0/0


London#ping
Protocol [ip]:
Target IP address: 192.168.0.1
Repeat count [5]: 20
Datagram size [100]:
Timeout in seconds [2]:
Extended commands [n]: y
Source address or interface: 192.168.200.1
Type of service [0]:
Set DF bit in IP header? [no]:
Validate reply data? [no]:
Data pattern [0xABCD]:
Loose, Strict, Record, Timestamp, Verbose[none]:
Sweep range of sizes [n]:
Type escape sequence to abort.
Sending 20, 100-byte ICMP Echos to 192.168.0.1, timeout is 2
        seconds:
!!!!!!!!!!!!!!!!!!!!
Success rate is 100 percent (20/20), round-trip min/avg/max =
        64/64/68 ms
London#
```

That is all it takes to configure an end-to-end Frame Relay network. This is a simple process, due to the ability of Cisco routers to dynamically learn information from the adjacent Frame Relay switch and neighboring routers. Also, realize the router is using default values for Frame Relay variables that are not explicitly configured.

Step 5

Many variables were defined through default configuration and discovery, but you can still view those default values for Frame Relay encapsulation type, DLCI mapping, and LMI on SanJose1.

Cisco routers support two Frame Relay encapsulation types: Cisco and IETF (Internet Engineering Task Force). Cisco is a proprietary encapsulation type; IETF is standards based. Use IETF whenever connecting to a non-Cisco router through a Frame Relay PVC. Since Frame Relay encapsulation type has not been defined, the default must be in use. Issue **show interface serial 0/0** on SanJose1:

```
SanJose1#show interfaces serial 0/0
Serial0/0 is up, line protocol is up
```

```
     Hardware is PowerQUICC Serial
     Internet address is 192.168.192.1/24
     MTU 1500 bytes, BW 1544 Kbit, DLY 20000 usec,
        reliability 255/255, txload 1/255, rxload 1/255
     Encapsulation FRAME-RELAY, loopback not set
     Keepalive set (10 sec)
   !
<output ommited>
```

In the previous output, there's no indication of the encapsulation type other than FRAME-RELAY. Change SanJose1 Serial 0/0 Frame Relay encapsulation type to IETF and **show interface serial 0/0** again:

```
SanJose1(config)#interface serial 0/0
SanJose1(config-if)#encapsulation frame-relay ietf
```

```
SanJose1#show interface serial 0/0
Serial0/0 is up, line protocol is up
   Hardware is PowerQUICC Serial
   Internet address is 192.168.192.1/24
   MTU 1500 bytes, BW 1544 Kbit, DLY 20000 usec,
      reliability 255/255, txload 1/255, rxload 1/255
   Encapsulation FRAME-RELAY IETF, loopback not set
   Keepalive set (10 sec)
   !
<output ommited>
```

In the previous output, the IETF encapsulation type is declared. Thus, if you see only FRAME-RELAY, the router must be using the default encapsulation type, Cisco. Change the encapsulation type back to Cisco by not specifying a type:

```
SanJose1(config)#interface serial 0/0
SanJose1(config-if)#encapsulation frame-relay
```

DLCIs identify unique permanent or switched virtual circuits (PVCs or SVCs). One device can support DLCIs ranging from 16-1007. The complete DLCI range is 0-1023, with 0-15 and 1008-1023 reserved for special purposes. For example, multicasts are identified with 1019 and 1020.

Issue the **show frame-relay map** command on SanJose1, as shown here:

```
SanJose1#show frame-relay map
Serial0/0 (up): ip 192.168.192.2 dlci 18(0x12,0x420), dynamic,
               broadcast,, status defined, active
```

Mapping is the association between a DLCI and its next-hop network address. The router logic says, "If routing to next-hop 192.168.192.2, tag frame with DLCI 18." The Frame Relay switch does not understand IP addressing, but does know where to send frames tagged as DLCI 18. Recall the switch logic from Step 2.

1. Given the minimal commands executed on SanJose1, how does the router know which DLCI to use, and the IP address of the next-hop router using that PVC?

_____

_____

_____

_____

DLCIs must be configured on the Frame Relay switch. If DLCIs are not configured on the router, they are learned dynamically from the switch through LMI (defined below). After the router has a DLCI number identifying a virtual circuit, the router sends an Inverse ARP through that circuit requesting information from whatever DTE (router) is on the other end. When the process is completed in both directions, the circuit is ready for traffic.

Link Management Interface (LMI) is the Layer 2 protocol between the DTE (the router) and a DCE (switch), exchanging keepalives every 10 seconds, with DLCI information conveyed every 60 seconds. Three different LMI types exist: Cisco, ANSI, and Q933a. DTE devices must match the LMI type of the DCE. Because you did not explicitly configure the LMI type on the switch, the network must be using the default LMI type. Execute **show frame-relay lmi** on SanJose1.

```
SanJose1#show frame-relay lmi
LMI Statistics for interface Serial0/0 (Frame Relay DTE) LMI TYPE
  = CISCO
    Invalid Unnumbered info 0          Invalid Prot Disc 0
    Invalid dummy Call Ref 0           Invalid Msg Type 0
    Invalid Status Message 0           Invalid Lock Shift 0
    Invalid Information ID 0           Invalid Report IE Len 0
    Invalid Report Request 0           Invalid Keep IE Len 0
    Num Status Enq. Sent 325           Num Status msgs Rcvd 326
    Num Update Status Rcvd 0           Num Status Timeouts 0
```

The default LMI type is Cisco. Note that LMI type is interface-specific. This same router could use a different LMI type on another serial interface; perhaps when connected to a second Frame-Relay switch for redundancy. The LMI type is also identified by a DLCI, communicated from the switch to the router.

2. Which DLCI is used by the Cisco LMI type?

_____

If you don't already know the answer, issue the **show interface serial 0/0** command on SanJose1:

```
SanJose1#show interface serial 0/0
Serial0/0 is up, line protocol is up
  Hardware is PowerQUICC Serial
  Internet address is 192.168.192.1/24
  MTU 1500 bytes, BW 1544 Kbit, DLY 20000 usec,
     reliability 255/255, txload 1/255, rxload 1/255
  Encapsulation FRAME-RELAY, loopback not set
  Keepalive set (10 sec)
```

```
        LMI enq sent  109, LMI stat recvd 109, LMI upd recvd 0, DTE
            LMI up
        LMI enq recvd 0, LMI stat sent  0, LMI upd sent  0
        LMI DLCI 1023  LMI type is CISCO  frame relay DTE
        Broadcast queue 0/64, broadcasts sent/dropped 36/0, interface
            broadcasts 17
        Last input 00:00:05, output 00:00:05, output hang never
        Last clearing of "show interface" counters 00:18:15
    !
    <output ommited>
```

The Cisco LMI type uses DLCI 1023.

Frame Relay can be implemented in four basic topologies: point-to-point, hub-and-spoke (star), full mesh, and partial mesh. Frame Relay is easy to configure in a simple topology, but it has many variations. Complication is introduced when multiple PVCs share one physical interface or when implementing a Non-Broadcast Multiple-Access Network (NBMA) over Frame Relay. Common variations are addressed in the following labs.

Lab 7-2: Configuring Full-Mesh Frame Relay

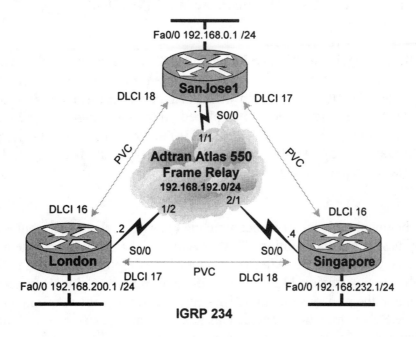

Fa0/0 192.168.0.1 /24

DLCI 18 — SanJose1 — DLCI 17

.1 S0/0

1/1

Adtran Atlas 550 Frame Relay 192.168.192.0/24

PVC

PVC

DLCI 16

1/2

2/1

DLCI 16

.2

S0/0

London

.4

S0/0

Singapore

Fa0/0 192.168.200.1 /24

DLCI 17

PVC

DLCI 18

Fa0/0 192.168.232.1/24

IGRP 234

Or

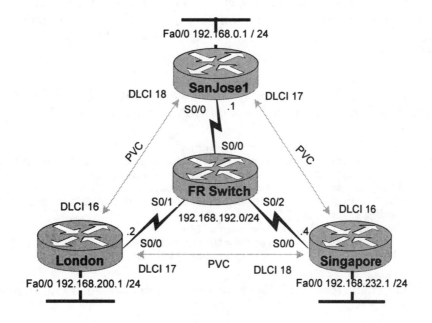

Fa0/0 192.168.0.1 / 24

DLCI 18 — SanJose1 — DLCI 17

S0/0 .1

PVC

PVC

S0/0

FR Switch

DLCI 16

S0/1

S0/2

DLCI 16

192.168.192.0/24

.2

S0/0

London

.4

S0/0

Singapore

Fa0/0 192.168.200.1 /24

DLCI 17

PVC

DLCI 18

Fa0/0 192.168.232.1 /24

IGRP 234

Objective

Configure three routers with Frame Relay in a full-mesh topology.

Scenario

Your ISP has provisioned Frame Relay PVCs for the International Travel Agency WAN. As the administrator, you are responsible for configuring Frame Relay among regional offices. You begin with North America, Asia, and Europe. The design calls for all three routers to be placed on the same logical IP network in a full-mesh topology. Also, use IGRP (AS 234) to dynamically exchange routes. The ISP Frame Relay switch uses the ANSI LMI-type, and is configured with the DLCIs shown in the previous diagram.

Step 1

Before beginning this lab, it is recommended that you reload each router after erasing its startup configuration. This prevents you from having problems caused by residual configurations. After you prepare the equipment, proceed to Step 2. This lab assumes version 11.2 or later IOS on all routers. Cable the network according to the previous diagram. This lab assumes use of an Adtran Atlas 550 for Frame Relay emulation. You can also use a router with three serial interfaces as a Frame Relay switch. If you are using the Atlas 550, be sure to connect the routers' serial interfaces to the correct port on the Atlas (labeled in the diagram) using a V.35 cable. Even if you have a WAN emulator, perform the lab both ways if possible. Being able to configure a router as a Frame Relay switch in a full-mesh topology is beneficial to understanding Frame Relay connectivity. Following this lab is a sample configuration file for a 2620 router as a Frame Relay switch.

Step 2

On SanJose1, apply IP addressing to the interfaces, configure IGRP as the routing protocol, and encapsulate the Serial 0/0 WAN link as Frame Relay:

```
SanJose1(config)#interface serial 0/0
SanJose1(config-if)#ip address 192.168.192.1 255.255.255.0
SanJose1(config-if)#encapsulation frame-relay
SanJose1(config-if)#interface fastethernet 0/0
SanJose1(config-if)#ip address 192.168.0.1 255.255.255.0
SanJose1(config-if)#exit
SanJose1(config)#router igrp 234
SanJose1(config-router)#network 192.168.0.0
SanJose1(config-router)#network 192.168.192.0
```

Configure Frame Relay on Singapore and London using the same command syntax.

Step 3

Verify complete configuration of full-mesh Frame Relay WAN.

Test with extended pings between each set of routers. For example, London to Singapore:

```
London#ping
Protocol [ip]:
Target IP address: 192.168.232.1
Repeat count [5]: 50
Datagram size [100]:
Timeout in seconds [2]:
Extended commands [n]: y
Source address or interface: 192.168.200.1
Type of service [0]:
Set DF bit in IP header? [no]:
Validate reply data? [no]:
Data pattern [0xABCD]:
Loose, Strict, Record, Timestamp, Verbose[none]:
Sweep range of sizes [n]:
Type escape sequence to abort.
Sending 50, 100-byte ICMP Echos to 192.168.232.1, timeout is 2
     seconds:
!!!!!!!!!!!!!!!!!!!!!!!!!!!!!!!!!!!!!!!!!!!!!!!!!!!!
Success rate is 100 percent (50/50), round-trip min/avg/max =
     56/60/80 ms
```

All pings should be successful. With only one physical connection to the Frame Relay cloud, two different next-hop routers can be reached.

Issue the **show frame-relay lmi** on Singapore:

```
Singapore#show frame-relay lmi

LMI Statistics for interface Serial0/0 (Frame Relay DTE) LMI TYPE
     = ANSI
    Invalid Unnumbered info 0          Invalid Prot Disc 0
    Invalid dummy Call Ref 0           Invalid Msg Type 0
    Invalid Status Message 0           Invalid Lock Shift 0
    Invalid Information ID 0           Invalid Report IE Len 0
    Invalid Report Request 0          Invalid Keep IE Len 0
    Num Status Enq. Sent 2523          Num Status msgs Rcvd 2522
    Num Update Status Rcvd 0           Num Status Timeouts 7
```

The LMI type is ANSI.

1. The default LMI type is Cisco and you did not explicitly configure another type. Why did the router select ANSI?

_____

_____

_____

_____

If a router is running Cisco IOS release 11.2 or later, it can autosense the LMI type as either Cisco, ANSI T1.617 Annex D (ANSI), or ITU-T Q.933 Annex A (q933a).

Issue the **show frame-relay pvc** command on Singapore:

```
Singapore#show frame-relay pvc

PVC Statistics for interface Serial0/0 (Frame Relay DTE)

                 Active      Inactive      Deleted      Static
    Local          2             0            0            0
    Switched       0             0            0            0
    Unused         0             0            0            0
DLCI = 16, DLCI USAGE = LOCAL, PVC STATUS = ACTIVE, INTERFACE =
        Serial0/0

    input pkts 676         output pkts 470        in bytes 92211
    out bytes 86466        dropped pkts 0         in FECN pkts 0
    in BECN pkts 0         out FECN pkts 0        out BECN pkts
        0
    in DE pkts 0           out DE pkts 0
    out bcast pkts 372      out bcast bytes 76274
    pvc create time 03:32:04, last time pvc status changed 03:32:04

DLCI = 18, DLCI USAGE = LOCAL, PVC STATUS = ACTIVE, INTERFACE =
        Serial0/0

    input pkts 433         output pkts 436        in bytes 81309
    out bytes 82942        dropped pkts 0         in FECN pkts 0
    in BECN pkts 0         out FECN pkts 0        out BECN pkts
        0
    in DE pkts 0           out DE pkts 0
    out bcast pkts 371      out bcast bytes 76182
    pvc create time 03:32:05, last time pvc status changed 03:32:05
```

Singapore S0/0 is using two DLCIs, 16 and 18, which you did not explicitly configure. The router learned about these dynamically from the Frame Relay switch. Recall that a DLCI identifies a PVC through the Frame Relay cloud.

Issue the **show frame-relay map** command on Singapore:

```
Singapore#show frame-relay map
Serial0/0 (up): ip 192.168.192.1 dlci 16 (0x10,0x400), dynamic,
                broadcast,, status defined, active
Serial0/0 (up): ip 192.168.192.2 dlci 18 (0x11,0x410), dynamic,
                broadcast,, status defined, active
```

Recall that mapping is the association between a DLCI and the next-hop DTE (router). The next hop is identified by its IP address.

2. Because mapping was not explicitly configured, how was this mapping achieved?

_____

_____

_____

_____

After a router receives a list of DLCIs, it sends an Inverse ARP through every PVC requesting information regarding the DTE at the other end. The returned IP address and status information is displayed in the map table. Note that, according to the **show frame-relay map** output above, these maps were created dynamically.

Note: Broadcasts and multicasts are supported on these PVCs, enabling routing protocols to exchange updates between regional sites.

Now issue the **show ip route** command on Singapore:

```
Singapore#show ip route

Gateway of last resort is not set

C    192.168.192.0/24 is directly connected, Serial0/0
I    192.168.200.0/24 [100/8486] via 192.168.192.2, 00:00:03,
       Serial0/0
C    192.168.232.0/24 is directly connected, FastEthernet0/0
I    192.168.0.0/24 [100/8486] via 192.168.192.1, 00:00:05,
       Serial0/0
```

Singapore should have a complete routing table, indicating that your full-mesh Frame Relay configuration is complete.

Step 4

Network engineers may not be comfortable with implicit configurations. The benefits of dynamic mapping are minor due to the static nature of most WANs. After a link is established, there might not be a change for years. Also, if variables are not explicitly defined with configuration commands, the configuration file will not yield much information about the Frame Relay network.

You can explicitly configure the routers to define elements discussed previously. Here is an example of how SanJose1 might be configured:

```
SanJose1(config)#interface fastethernet 0/0
SanJose1(config-if)#ip address 192.168.0.1 255.255.255.0
SanJose1(config-if)#interface serial 0/0
SanJose1(config-if)#encapsulation frame-relay
SanJose1(config-if)#frame-relay map ip 192.168.192.2 18 broadcast
SanJose1(config-if)#frame-relay map ip 192.168.192.2 18 broadcast
SanJose1(config-if)#frame-relay lmi-type ansi
SanJose1(config-if)#exit
SanJose1(config)#router igrp 234
SanJose1(config-router)#network 192.168.192.0
SanJose1(config-router)#network 192.168.0.0
SanJose1(config-router)#passive-interface fastethernet 0/0
```

The **frame-relay map** command associates next-hop ip addresses with local a DLCI. The **broadcast** keyword allows multicasts and broadcasts to be propagated through that PVC. The **frame-relay lmi-type** command statically defines the DTE (router) LMI protocol, which must match the DCE (switch).

Note that, in this configuration, IGRP routing updates are blocked from exiting FastEthernet 0/0. This saves bandwidth on the LAN, as there are no IGRP neighbors on that network.

Lab 7-3: Configuring Full-Mesh Frame Relay With Subinterfaces

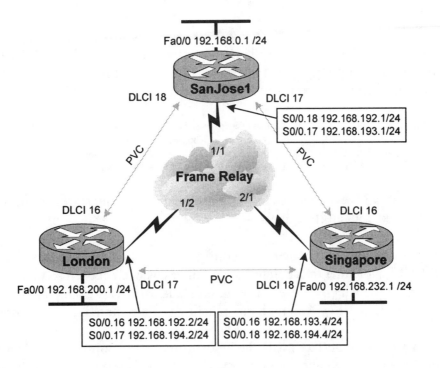

Objective

Configure three routers with Frame Relay in a full mesh using subinterfaces.

Scenario

While looking forward to fine-tuning traffic flow among regional sites connected to the International Travel Agency WAN, you realize greater control could be implemented if an individual physical leased line was between each site. Unfortunately, your managers will not approve the cost of an additional leased line.

However, you can configure separate logical connections between the sites by using subinterfaces. Each router will have one physical interface connected to the Frame Relay switch. The single physical interface (s0/0) has two logical subinterfaces configured, one for each regional site. Physical redundancy is achieved in the carrier's Frame Relay cloud, enabled by multiple PVCs per physical interface on the routers. Although your provider charges for each additional PVC, the fee is small, especially compared to the cost of a leased line.

Step 1

Before beginning this lab, it is recommended that you reload each router after erasing its startup configuration. This prevents you from having problems caused by residual configurations. After you prepare the equipment, proceed to Step 2.
Build the network according to the previous diagram. This lab assumes use of an Adtran Atlas 550 as the Frame Relay cloud. You can use other WAN emulators or a

router as a Frame Relay switch. If you are using the Atlas 550, be sure to connect each router's serial interface to the correct port on the Atlas (labeled in the diagram) using a V.35 cable.

Step 2

Configure each router's FastEthernet interface and IGRP (AS 234), as shown in the diagram. Configure serial interfaces to use Frame Relay with subinterfaces. Enter the following commands on SanJose1:

```
SanJose1(config)#interface serial 0/0
SanJose1(config-if)#no ip address
SanJose1(config-if)#encapsulation frame-relay
SanJose1(config-if)#frame-relay lmi-type ansi
```

The **no ip address** command is only necessary if the interface has already been configured with an IP address.

Issue the following commands to configure a point-to-point subinterface using DLCI 17. Note that the subinterface number has been chosen so that you can easily determine which PVC each subinterface is using (for example, subinterface 0.17 uses DLCI 17). Although this practice is not required, it is very common.

Specify the subinterfaces with the keyword **point-to-point**, not **multipoint**. Some versions of the IOS allow you to create a subinterface without specifying either type, which results in a multipoint subinterface (the default).

```
SanJose1(config)#interface s0/0.17 point-to-point
SanJose1(config-subif)#ip address 192.168.193.1 255.255.255.0
SanJose1(config-subif)#frame-relay interface-dlci 17
```

The **frame-relay interface-dlci** command is used to specify which DLCI is used by each subinterface. Point-to-point subinterfaces can each use only one DLCI. If you do not specify a subinterface for a DLCI, it will be associated with the major interface (s0/0 in this case). Now issue the commands needed to configure the subinterface that will use DLCI 18, as shown here:

```
SanJose1(config)#interface s0/0.18 point-to-point
SanJose1(config-subif)#ip address 192.168.192.1 255.255.255.0
SanJose1(config-subif)#frame-relay interface-dlci 18
```

Configure London and Singapore according to the previous diagram. Use the command **syntax** in this step as a guide.

Step 3

Verify PVC status by issuing **show frame-relay pvc** on SanJose1:

```
SanJose1#show frame-relay pvc

PVC Statistics for interface Serial0/0 (Frame Relay DTE)
```

```
                Active      Inactive      Deleted      Static
Local             2            1             0           0
Switched          0            0             0           0
Unused            0            0             0           0

DLCI = 16, DLCI USAGE = LOCAL, PVC STATUS = INACTIVE, INTERFACE =
        Serial0/0

   input pkts 0            output pkts 0          in bytes 0
   out bytes 0             dropped pkts 0         in FECN pkts 0
   in BECN pkts 0          out FECN pkts 0        out BECN pkts 0
   in DE pkts 0            out DE pkts 0
   out bcast pkts 0         out bcast bytes 0
   pvc create time 00:48:21, last time pvc status changed 00:48:21

DLCI = 17, DLCI USAGE = LOCAL, PVC STATUS = ACTIVE, INTERFACE =
        Serial0/0.17

   input pkts 167         output pkts 179         in bytes 21552
   out bytes 19871        dropped pkts 5          in FECN pkts 0
   in BECN pkts 0         out FECN pkts 0         out BECN pkts 0
   in DE pkts 0           out DE pkts 0
   out bcast pkts 59       out bcast bytes 10890
   pvc create time 00:48:34, last time pvc status changed 00:29:13

DLCI = 18, DLCI USAGE = LOCAL, PVC STATUS = ACTIVE, INTERFACE =
        Serial0/0.18

   input pkts 156         output pkts 135         in bytes 27757
   out bytes 18758        dropped pkts 5          in FECN pkts 0
   in BECN pkts 0         out FECN pkts 0         out BECN pkts 0
   in DE pkts 0           out DE pkts 0
   out bcast pkts 55       out bcast bytes 10718
   pvc create time 00:48:35, last time pvc status changed 00:07:14
```

The output of this command shows the PVC status according to the router's perspective. The different states are ACTIVE, INACTIVE, and DELETED. ACTIVE is a successful end-to-end (DTE to DTE) circuit. INACTIVE is a successful connection to the switch (DTE to DCE) without a DTE detected on the other end of the PVC. This can occur if the router dynamically learns of a DLCI not intended for its network, due to a residual or incorrect configuration on the Frame Relay switch. The DELETED state is when the DTE is configured for a DLCI the switch does not recognize as valid for that interface.

If you see INACTIVE DLCIs that you don't intend to use, check with your service provider regarding their status. In this configuration, SanJose1 detects DLCI 16, which is not used in this lab. To keep your router from dynamically creating a PVC with whatever DTE is on the other end, disable Inverse-ARP for DLCI 16, as shown here:

```
SanJose1(config)#interface serial 0/0
SanJose1(config-if)#no frame-relay inverse-arp ip 16
```

Issue the **show frame-relay map** command on SanJose1 to determine if Frame Relay has mapped the appropriate DLCIs to the correct IP address:

```
SanJose1#show frame-relay map
Serial0/0.17 (up): point-to-point dlci, dlci 17 (0x11,0x410),
        broadcast
            status defined, active
Serial0/0.18 (up): point-to-point dlci, dlci 18 (0x12,0x420),
        broadcast
            status defined, active
```

1. According to the output, are DLCI 17 and DLCI 18 mapped to next-hop IP addresses?

_____

With point-to-point subinterfaces, there is no mapping between a local DLCI and a next-hop address. Each subinterface is treated as if it were a separate physical interface and each Frame Relay PVC contains only two hosts. There is no need to explicitly identify the next-hop. Point-to-point subinterfaces can also be implemented using IP unnumbered.

Step 4

Make sure IGRP is working by issuing **show ip route** on SanJose1:

```
SanJose1#show ip route

Gateway of last resort is not set

C    192.168.192.0/24 is directly connected, Serial0/0.18
C    192.168.193.0/24 is directly connected, Serial0/0.17
I    192.168.194.0/24 [100/82125] via 192.168.192.2, 00:00:00,
        Serial0/0.18
                      [100/82125] via 192.168.193.4, 00:01:25,
        Serial0/0.17
I    192.168.200.0/24 [100/80135] via 192.168.192.2, 00:00:00,
        Serial0/0.18
I    192.168.232.0/24 [100/80135] via 192.168.193.4, 00:01:25,
        Serial0/0.17
C    192.168.0.0/24 is directly connected, FastEthernet0/0
```

Verify round-trip connectivity with an extended **ping** from SanJose1 (sourced from 192.168.0.1) to London (192.168.200.1). This ping should be successful. Troubleshoot as necessary.

Lab 7-4: Configuring Hub-and-Spoke Frame Relay

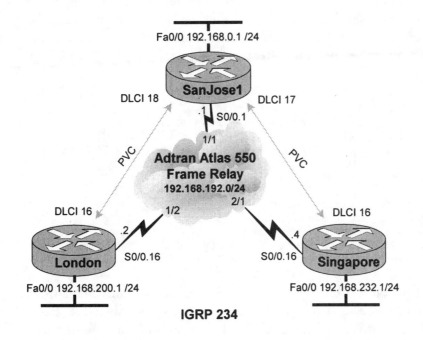

Objective

Configure Frame Relay on three routers in a hub-and-spoke topology.

Scenario

In an effort to cut costs, you monitor the International Travel Agency's internet-work traffic patters and determine that the PVC between London and Singapore is underutilized. By canceling the redundant PVC, you can save money and still provide connectivity among all regional sites with a hub-and-spoke topology. Any traffic destined for Singapore and originating in London would be relayed through SanJose1. The hub-and-spoke topology creates a single point of failure (the hub router), a risk ITA administration is willing to take.

Step 1

Before beginning this lab, it is recommended that you reload each router after erasing its startup configuration. This prevents you from having problems caused by residual configurations. After you prepare the equipment, proceed to Step 2.

Build the network according to the above diagram. This lab assumes use of an Adtran Atlas 550 as the Frame Relay cloud. You can use other WAN emulators or a router as a Frame Relay switch. If you are using the Atlas 550, be sure to connect each router's serial interfaces to the correct port on the Atlas (labeled in the previous diagram) by using a V.35 cable.

Step 2

Configure SanJose1 for IGRP (AS 234) and Frame Relay. As the hub router, SanJose1 needs to direct packets through multiple PVCs. Configuring a multi-point subinterface allows one subinterface to be associated with more than one DLCI. Use the **frame-relay interface-dlci** command to specify local DLCIs, as shown here:

```
SanJose1(config)#interface serial 0/0
SanJose1(config-if)#encapsulation frame-relay
SanJose1(config-if)#interface serial 0/0.1 multipoint
SanJose1(config-subif)#ip address 192.168.192.1 255.255.255.0
SanJose1(config-subif)#frame-relay interface-dlci 17
SanJose1(config-fr-dlci)#exit
SanJose1(config-subif)#frame-relay interface-dlci 18
SanJose1(config-fr-dlci)#exit
SanJose1(config-subif)#exit
SanJose1(config)#router igrp 234
SanJose1(config-router)#network 192.168.192.0
SanJose1(config-router)#network 192.168.0.0
```

Next, configure London for IGRP (AS 234) and Frame Relay. Only one DLCI is needed on the spoke routers, so you can use a point-to-point subinterface. Because this is a subinterface configuration, include the **frame-relay interface-dlci** command, as shown here:

```
London(config)#interface serial 0/0
London(config-if)#encapsulation frame-relay
London(config-if)#interface serial 0/0.16 point-to-point
London(config-subif)#ip add 192.168.192.2 255.255.255.0
London(config-subif)#frame-relay interface-dlci 16
London(config-fr-dlci)#exit
London(config-subif)#exit
London(config)#router igrp 234
London(config-router)#network 192.168.200.0
London(config-router)#network 192.168.192.0
```

Using the previous commands as a guide, configure Singapore according to the diagram.

Step 3

Test for connectivity with pings between routers:

```
London#ping 192.168.192.1

Type escape sequence to abort.
Sending 5, 100-byte ICMP Echos to 192.168.192.1, timeout is 2
      seconds:
!!!!!
Success rate is 100 percent (5/5), round-trip min/avg/max =
      44/44/44 ms

London#ping 192.168.192.4

Type escape sequence to abort.
Sending 5, 100-byte ICMP Echos to 192.168.192.4, timeout is 2
      seconds:
```

```
!!!!!
Success rate is 100 percent (5/5), round-trip min/avg/max =
88/90/92 ms
```

1. Do the pings demonstrate successful connectivity?

In order to have a functioning internetwork, hosts at each site must be able to communicate. You can test the complete path, from LAN to LAN, with extended pings.

First, ping from SanJose1's LAN interface (192.168.0.1) to Singapore's LAN interface (192.168.232.1). This ping should be successful. Next, ping from SanJose1's LAN interface (192.168.0.1) to London's LAN interface (192.168.200.1). This ping should also be successful.

Finally, ping from London's LAN interface to Singapore's LAN interface, and vice versa:

```
London#ping
Protocol [ip]:
Target IP address: 192.168.232.1
Repeat count [5]:
Datagram size [100]:
Timeout in seconds [2]:
Extended commands [n]: y
Source address or interface: 192.168.200.1
Type of service [0]:
Set DF bit in IP header? [no]:
Validate reply data? [no]:
Data pattern [0xABCD]:
Loose, Strict, Record, Timestamp, Verbose[none]:
Sweep range of sizes [n]:
Type escape sequence to abort.
Sending 5, 100-byte ICMP Echos to 192.168.232.1, timeout is 2
        seconds:
.....
Success rate is 0 percent (0/5)
```

These pings fail. Because users on the London LAN cannot access the Singapore LAN, your configuration is not complete.

To isolate the problem, view all three routing tables:

```
SanJose1#show ip route

Gateway of last resort is not set

C    192.168.192.0/24 is directly connected, Serial0/0.1
I    192.168.200.0/24 [100/80135] via 192.168.192.2, 00:01:19,
       Serial0/0.1
I    192.168.232.0/24 [100/80135] via 192.168.192.4, 00:00:53,
       Serial0/0.1
C    192.168.0.0/24 is directly connected, FastEthernet0/0
```

```
London#show ip route

Gateway of last resort is not set

C    192.168.192.0/24 is directly connected, Serial0/0.16
C    192.168.200.0/24 is directly connected, FastEthernet0/0
I    192.168.0.0/24 [100/80135] via 192.168.192.1, 00:00:18,
       Serial0/0.16


Singapore#show ip route

Gateway of last resort is not set

C    192.168.192.0/24 is directly connected, Serial0/0.16
C    192.168.232.0/24 is directly connected, FastEthernet0/0
I    192.168.0.0/24 [100/8486] via 192.168.192.1, 00:01:06,
       Serial0/0.16
```

London and Singapore have not received IGRP updates about each other's LANs. However, both of these networks are properly advertised via IGRP commands, and have been installed in SanJose1's routing table.

As the hub router, SanJose1 should forward information to the spoke routers, including routing advertisements. Recall that distance vector routing protocols combat routing loops with the split horizon rule, which states that a router cannot advertise a route through the same physical interface it was received on. When you configure an interface with the **encapsulation frame-relay** command, split horizon is automatically disabled on the major interface (Serial 0/0, etc). However, split horizon is enabled by default on Frame Relay subinterfaces.

Because both of the PVCs use the same multipoint subinterface on SanJose1, routes learned from one spoke router cannot be sent back through the same subinterface to the other spoke router. You must disable spilt horizon in order for SanJose1 to be able to send a route learned from one spoke to the other.

Disable split horizon on SanJose1's subinterface, Serial 0/0.1:

```
SanJose1(config)#interface serial 0/0.1 multipoint
SanJose1(config-subif)#no ip split-horizon
```

Verify your configuration by issuing the **show ip interface s0/0.1** command, as shown here:

```
SanJose1#show ip interface s0/0.1
Serial0/0.1 is up, line protocol is up
  Internet address is 192.168.192.1/24
  Broadcast address is 255.255.255.255
  Address determined by setup command
  MTU is 1500 bytes
  Helper address is not set
  Directed broadcast forwarding is disabled
  Outgoing access list is not set
  Inbound  access list is not set
  Proxy ARP is enabled
```

```
Security level is default
Split horizon is disabled
ICMP redirects are always sent
ICMP unreachables are always sent
ICMP mask replies are never sent
IP fast switching is enabled
IP fast switching on the same interface is enabled
IP Flow switching is disabled
IP Feature Fast switching turbo vector
IP multicast fast switching is enabled
IP multicast distributed fast switching is disabled
IP route-cache flags are Fast
Router Discovery is disabled
```

Now check Singapore's routing table again:

```
Singapore#show ip route

Gateway of last resort is not set

C    192.168.192.0/24 is directly connected, Serial0/0.16
I    192.168.200.0/24 [100/82135] via 192.168.192.1, 00:00:19,
        Serial0/0.16
C    192.168.232.0/24 is directly connected, FastEthernet0/0
I    192.168.0.0/24 [100/8486] via 192.168.192.1, 00:00:19,
        Serial0/0.16
```

Confirm internetwork connectivity between the Singapore and London LANs with an extended ping:

```
Singapore#ping
Protocol [ip]:
Target IP address: 192.168.200.1
Repeat count [5]: 55
Datagram size [100]:
Timeout in seconds [2]:
Extended commands [n]: y
Source address or interface: 192.168.232.1
Type of service [0]:
Set DF bit in IP header? [no]:
Validate reply data? [no]:
Data pattern [0xABCD]:
Loose, Strict, Record, Timestamp, Verbose[none]:
Sweep range of sizes [n]:
Type escape sequence to abort.
Sending 55, 100-byte ICMP Echos to 192.168.200.1, timeout is 2
        seconds:
!!!!!!!!!!!!!!!!!!!!!!!!!!!!!!!!!!!!!!!!!!!!!!!!!!!!!!!!!!!
Success rate is 100 percent (55/55), round-trip min/avg/max =
        92/93/108 ms
```

If this ping is successful, all three regional sites are communicating over a hub-and-spoke Frame Relay topology.

Lab 8-1: Frame Relay Subinterfaces and Traffic Shaping

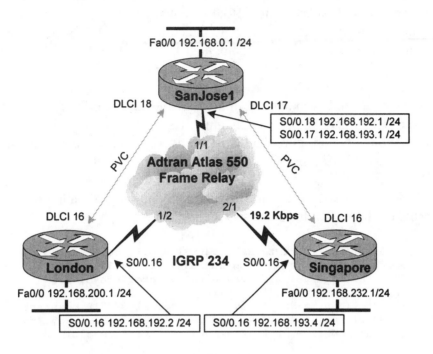

Objective

Configure Frame Relay on three routers in a hub-and-spoke topology using subinterfaces and map-classes. Configure rate enforcement to control traffic rates on a per-PVC basis.

Scenario

Each Frame Relay link in the International Travel Agency (ITA) WAN is a T1 (1.544 Mbps). After monitoring traffic patterns on ITA's WAN for one week, you notice that the PVC between SanJose1 and Singapore has a low average throughput. In an effort to cut costs, you decide to revise your contract with the service provider to reduce the Committed Information Rate (CIR) from 1.544 Mbps to 19.2 Kbps.

If SanJose1 transmits 80 times faster than Singapore can receive, either the Frame Relay switches need to buffer the frames or Singapore could be flooded with traffic. Not wanting to rely on the traffic management of the Frame Relay service provider, you decide to throttle back the rate at which SanJose1 transmits to Singapore. This will reduce congestion before it becomes an issue in the WAN.

Step 1

Before beginning this lab, it is recommended that you reload each router after erasing its startup configuration. This prevents you from having problems caused by residual configurations.

Build the network according to the above diagram. This lab assumes use of an Adtran Atlas 550 as the Frame Relay cloud. You can use other WAN emulators or a router as a Frame Relay switch. If you are using the Atlas 550, be sure to connect the routers' serial interfaces to the correct port on the Atlas (labeled in the previous diagram) using a V.35 cable.

Step 2

Using the commands you learned in the previous labs, configure the three routers for Frame Relay according to the diagram. Use Cisco Frame Relay encapsulation. You can explicitly configure the LMI-type as ANSI, or you can allow the router to autosense the LMI type.

Note: Each PVC exists as a point-to-point network on its own logical IP subnet. A partial configuration for SanJose1 is shown here:

```
SanJose1(config)#interface serial 0/0.17 point-to-point
SanJose1(config-subif)#ip address 192.168.193.1 255.255.255.0
SanJose1(config-subif)#frame-relay interface-dlci 17
SanJose1(config-fr-dlci)#exit
SanJose1(config-subif)#interface serial 0/0.18 point-to-point
SanJose1(config-subif)#ip address 192.168.192.1 255.255.255.0
SanJose1(config-subif)#frame-relay interface-dlci 18
```

Step 3

Test connectivity with extended pings between LANs at different regional sites. From SanJose1, use extended ping to test connectivity with London. Send several large packets (over 1000-byte datagram size) to measure throughput, and note the round-trip times in milliseconds:

```
SanJose1#ping
Protocol [ip]:
Target IP address: 192.168.200.1
Repeat count [5]: 55
Datagram size [100]: 1111
Timeout in seconds [2]:
Extended commands [n]: y
Source address or interface: 192.168.0.1
Type of service [0]:
Set DF bit in IP header? [no]:
Validate reply data? [no]:
Data pattern [0xABCD]:
Loose, Strict, Record, Timestamp, Verbose[none]:
Sweep range of sizes [n]:
Type escape sequence to abort.
Sending 55, 1111-byte ICMP Echos to 192.168.200.1, timeout is 2
       seconds:
!!!!!!!!!!!!!!!!!!!!!!!!!!!!!!!!!!!!!!!!!!!!!!!!!!!!!!!!!!!
Success rate is 100 percent (55/55), round-trip min/avg/max =
       176/179/192 ms
```

Issue extended pings, using the same parameters, to record round-trip times between regional LANs: From SanJose1 to Singapore and from Singapore to London.

Round-trip times will vary, primarily due to the WAN interface card in your router. The router probably contains either a WIC-2A/S supporting up to 128 Kbps or a WIC-2T supporting up to 2.048 Mbps. For the purposes of this lab, either WIC is fine. The round-trip times will become relevant when compared to the results of later tests.

Step 4

On Singapore and SanJose1, create a **map-class** in global configuration mode defining the CIR. A logical name must be assigned to uniquely identify each map-class. Use CIR as the name:

```
Singapore(config)#map-class frame-relay CIR
Singapore(config-map-class)#frame-relay traffic-rate 19200

SanJose1(config)#map-class frame-relay CIR
SanJose1(config-map-class)#frame-relay traffic-rate 19200
```

A Frame Relay map-class can be used by any Frame Relay interface. In this case, you will apply the map-class to Singapore's subinterface, as shown below. Because the map-class specifies rate enforcement, you must enable Frame Relay traffic-shaping on the major interface:

```
Singapore(config)#interface serial 0/0
Singapore(config-if)#frame-relay traffic-shaping
Singapore(config-if)#interface serial 0/0.16 point-to-point
Singapore(config-subif)#frame-relay class CIR
```

Configure the other end of this PVC, on SanJose1 by using the same commands:

```
SanJose1(config)#interface serial 0/0
SanJose1(config-if)#frame-relay traffic-shaping
SanJose1(config-if)#interface serial 0/0.17 point-to-point
SanJose1(config-subif)#frame-relay class CIR
```

Step 5

Test connectivity and throughput with extended pings as before, recording round-trip times. The average and round-trip times should have increased as traffic was buffered due to slow WAN links. Here are some sample results:

```
SanJose1#ping
<output ommited>
Sending 55, 1111-byte ICMP Echos to 192.168.232.1, timeout is 2
    seconds:
!!!!!!!!!!!!!!!!!!!!!!!!!!!!!!!!!!!!!!!!!!!!!!!!!!!!!!!!!!!
Success rate is 100 percent (55/55), round-trip min/avg/max =
    184/460/520 ms

London#ping
<output ommited>
Sending 55, 1111-byte ICMP Echos to 192.168.232.1, timeout is 2
    seconds:
!!!!!!!!!!!!!!!!!!!!!!!!!!!!!!!!!!!!!!!!!!!!!!!!!!!!!!!!!!!
Success rate is 100 percent (55/55), round-trip min/avg/max =
    356/464/540 ms
```

1. How are these ping results different from the first set of pings run in Step 3?

_____

_____

_____

Step 6

To observe detailed traffic shaping statistics, issue **show frame-relay pvc 18** on SanJose1. Although traffic-shaping is enabled, it is only active if traffic is buffered. For this reason, you might see "shaping inactive" in the output of this command:

```
SanJose1#show frame-relay pvc 18

PVC Statistics for interface Serial0/0 (Frame Relay DTE)

DLCI = 18, DLCI USAGE = LOCAL, PVC STATUS = ACTIVE, INTERFACE =
      Serial0/0.18

   input pkts 82              output pkts 80           in bytes 14127
   out bytes 13930           dropped pkts 1           in FECN pkts 0
   in BECN pkts 0            out FECN pkts 0          out BECN pkts
       0
   in DE pkts 0              out DE pkts 0
   out bcast pkts 66         out bcast bytes 12983
   pvc create time 00:39:54, last time pvc status changed 00:03:00
   cir 19200     bc 19200     be 0          limit 300    interval
       125
   mincir 9600     byte increment 300    BECN response no
   pkts 17         bytes 2828        pkts delayed 0         bytes
       delayed 0
   shaping inactive
   traffic shaping drops 0
   Serial0/0.18 dlci 18 is first come first serve default queueing

   Output queue 0/40, 0 drop, 0 dequeued
```

2. According to the output of this command, what is the CIR of this PVC?

_____

Lab 8-2: On-Demand Routing

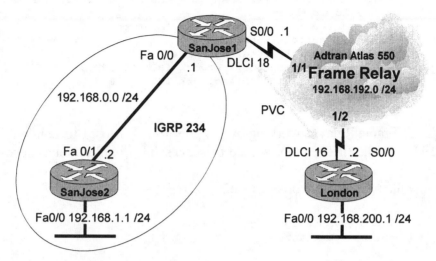

Objective

Configure and redistribute on-demand routing (ODR) over Frame Relay.

Scenario

As the network administrator for the International Travel Agency (ITA), you are responsible for establishing connectivity between company headquarters in San Jose and European regional headquarters (London). All LANs are directly connected to a single router in London with one Frame Relay WAN link. Because the London router is part of a stub network, it only needs a default route toward San Jose. Not using a routing protocol over the slow WAN link will save bandwidth. In order to send data back to London, a static route could be placed on SanJose1 and redistributed, but you know that the local administrators in London will be adding LANs in the coming weeks. Also, other regional sites are adding LANs. To reduce the burden on you and your staff, you decide to implement ODR as a way to dynamically add routes to the network without the overhead of routing protocols.

Step 1

Physically build the network as shown in the previous diagram. If you are using an Adtran Atlas 550 WAN emulator, ensure that the cables are connected to the correct ports.

Step 2

Configure IGRP on only the two San Jose routers. Also, use explicit commands configure Frame Relay between SanJose1 and London, as shown here:

```
SanJose1(config)#interface fastethernet 0/0
SanJose1(config-if)#ip address 192.168.0.1 255.255.255.0
```

```
SanJose1(config-if)#interface serial 0/0
SanJose1(config-if)#ip address 192.168.192.1 255.255.255.0
SanJose1(config-if)#encapsulation frame-relay
SanJose1(config-if)#frame-relay map ip 192.168.192.2 255.255.255.0
        18 broadcast
SanJose1(config-if)#frame-relay lmi-type ansi
SanJose1(config-if)#exit
SanJose1(config)#router igrp 234
SanJose1(config-router)#network 192.168.192.0
SanJose1(config-router)#network 192.168.0.0
```

Step 3

Verify Frame Relay is working by pinging from SanJose1 to London (192.168.192.2). The pings should be successful; troubleshoot as necessary.

View the routing table on SanJose2:

```
SanJose2#show ip route
<output omitted>

Gateway of last resort is not set

I    192.168.192.0/24 [100/80135] via 192.168.0.1, FastEthernet0/1
C    192.168.0.0/24 is directly connected, FastEthernet0/1
C    192.168.1.0/24 is directly connected, FastEthernet0/0
```

1. Does SanJose2's routing table include an entry for all networks in the diagram?

_____

SanJose2 has routes to all networks except the London LAN. Try pinging London's WAN interface (192.168.192.2) from SanJose2 this time.

2. Because SanJose2 has a route to the Frame Relay link, why are the pings failing?

_____

Verify that London has a route back to SanJose2, using the **show ip route** command:

```
London#show ip route
<output omitted>

Gateway of last resort is not set

C    192.168.192.0/24 is directly connected, Serial0/0
C    192.168.200.0/24 is directly connected, FastEthernet0/0
```

London has not learned any routes since it is not configured with a routing protocol. It doesn't make sense to run a dynamic routing protocol on a stub router, such as London. Simply configure a default route toward SanJose1.

```
London(config)#ip route 0.0.0.0 0.0.0.0 192.168.192.1
```

After you configure the default route, try to ping SanJose2's FastEthernet interface (192.168.1.1). This ping should now be successful; troubleshoot as necessary.

Now that London has all routing information needed to reach any network, check to see if SanJose1 has a complete routing table:

```
SanJose1#show ip route
<output omitted>

Gateway of last resort is not set

C    192.168.192.0/24 is directly connected, Serial0/0
C    192.168.0.0/24 is directly connected, FastEthernet0/0
I    192.168.1.0/24 [100/120] via 192.168.0.2, 00:00:54,
        FastEthernet0/0
```

Note: SanJose1 does not have a route to 192.168.200.0 (London's LAN).

Step 4

Users in London will never receive data until SanJose1 learns a route to their LAN. A static route to 192.168.200.0/24 could be entered in SanJose1. As more LANs are implemented in London or any other remote stub network, you need to add more static routes. To avoid this hassle, you can implement ODR.

Cisco routers send network IDs and subnet masks for adjacent networks in Cisco Discovery Protocol (CDP) frames. ODR tells the receiving router to build routes with the information. To configure ODR, simply enable it on the hub (receiving) router:

```
SanJose1(config)#router odr
```

After enabling ODR, check SanJose1's routing table again:

```
SanJose1#show ip route
Codes: C - connected, S - static, I - IGRP, R - RIP, M - mobile,
       B - BGP
       D - EIGRP, EX - EIGRP external, O - OSPF, IA - OSPF
       inter area
       N1 - OSPF NSSA external type 1, N2 - OSPF NSSA external
       type 2
       E1 - OSPF external type 1, E2 - OSPF external type 2,
       E - EGP
       i - IS-IS, L1 - IS-IS level-1, L2 - IS-IS level-2, ia -
       IS-IS inter area
       * - candidate default, U - per-user static route, o - ODR
       P - periodic downloaded static route

Gateway of last resort is not set

C    192.168.192.0/24 is directly connected, Serial0/0
C    192.168.0.0/24 is directly connected, FastEthernet0/0
I    192.168.1.0/24 [100/120] via 192.168.0.2, 00:00:34,
        FastEthernet0/0
```

3. Even after enabling ODR, there is still no route to the London LAN. Why?

Because ODR depends on CDP, verify that CDP is enabled. Issue the **show cdp** command on SanJose1:

```
SanJose1#show cdp
Global CDP information:
        Sending CDP packets every 60 seconds
        Sending a holdtime value of 180 seconds
        Sending CDPv2 advertisements is  enabled
```

CDP is enabled globally by default, with frames exchanged every 60 seconds. On SanJose1, view adjacent Cisco devices learned through CDP:

```
SanJose1#show cdp neighbors
Capability Codes: R - Router, T - Trans Bridge, B - Source Route
        Bridge
                    S - Switch, H - Host, I - IGMP, r - Repeater

Device ID       Local Intrfce     Holdtme     Capability  Platform
        Port ID
SanJose2        Fas 0/0           149           R         2621
        Fas 0/1
```

CDP does not appear to be running over the Frame Relay cloud between SanJose1 and London. CDP must also be enabled on the Frame Relay interfaces. Remember to configure *both* SanJose1 and London:

```
SanJose1(config)#interface serial 0/0
SanJose1(config-if)#cdp enable
```

After you enable CDP, view SanJose1's routing table again:

```
SanJose1#show ip route
Codes: C - connected, S - static, I - IGRP, R - RIP, M - mobile,
        B - BGP
        D - EIGRP, EX - EIGRP external, O - OSPF, IA - OSPF
        inter area
        N1 - OSPF NSSA external type 1, N2 - OSPF NSSA external
        type 2
        E1 - OSPF external type 1, E2 - OSPF external type 2,
        E - EGP
        i - IS-IS, L1 - IS-IS level-1, L2 - IS-IS level-2, ia -
        IS-IS inter area
        * - candidate default, U - per-user static route, o - ODR
        P - periodic downloaded static route

Gateway of last resort is not set

C    192.168.192.0/24 is directly connected, Serial0/0
o    192.168.200.0/24 [160/1] via 192.168.192.2, 00:00:32,
        Serial0/0
C    192.168.0.0/24 is directly connected, FastEthernet0/0
I    192.168.1.0/24 [100/120] via 192.168.0.2, 00:01:20,
        FastEthernet0/0
```

Note that SanJose1 finally has a route to the London LAN.

4. What is the administrative distance of the ODR route to the London LAN?

_____

Step 5

Finally, verify connectivity with an extended ping from SanJose2 to London:

```
SanJose2#ping
Protocol [ip]:
Target IP address: 192.168.200.1
Repeat count [5]:
Datagram size [100]:
Timeout in seconds [2]:
Extended commands [n]: y
Source address or interface: 192.168.1.1
Type of service [0]:
Set DF bit in IP header? [no]:
Validate reply data? [no]:
Data pattern [0xABCD]:
Loose, Strict, Record, Timestamp, Verbose[none]:
Sweep range of sizes [n]:
Type escape sequence to abort.
Sending 5, 100-byte ICMP Echos to 192.168.200.1, timeout is 2
    seconds:
.....
Success rate is 0 percent (0/5)
```

5. Why did the ping fail?

_____

_____

_____

View SanJose2's routing table:

```
SanJose2#show ip route
Codes: C - connected, S - static, I - IGRP, R - RIP, M - mobile,
    B - BGP
    D - EIGRP, EX - EIGRP external, O - OSPF, IA - OSPF
    inter area
    N1 - OSPF NSSA external type 1, N2 - OSPF NSSA external
    type 2
    E1 - OSPF external type 1, E2 - OSPF external type 2,
    E - EGP
    i - IS-IS, L1 - IS-IS level-1, L2 - IS-IS level-2,
    * - candidate default
    U - per-user static route, o - ODR, P - periodic
    downloaded static route
    T - traffic engineered route

Gateway of last resort is not set

I    192.168.192.0/24 [100/80135] via 192.168.0.1, FastEthernet0/1
C    192.168.0.0/24 is directly connected, FastEthernet0/1
C    192.168.1.0/24 is directly connected, FastEthernet0/0
```

Although SanJose1 and SanJose2 are sharing IGRP routes, SanJose1 is not forwarding the route learned through ODR. ODR only works between two routers for a total of one hop. ODR is intended as a low-maintenance way to implement hub-and-spoke topologies where routing protocols might utilize too much bandwidth. ODR is not a true routing protocol, though an ODR route can be redistributed into a routing protocol.

On SanJose1, provide default metrics for IGRP and redistribute ODR routes:

```
SanJose1(config)#router igrp 234
SanJose1(config-router)#default-metric 1000 100 250 100 1500
SanJose1(config-router)#redistribute odr
```

View the routing table on SanJose2 to confirm redistribution:

```
SanJose2#show ip route
Codes: C - connected, S - static, I - IGRP, R - RIP, M - mobile,
       B - BGP
       D - EIGRP, EX - EIGRP external, O - OSPF, IA - OSPF
       inter area
       N1 - OSPF NSSA external type 1, N2 - OSPF NSSA external
       type 2
       E1 - OSPF external type 1, E2 - OSPF external type 2,
       E - EGP
       i - IS-IS, L1 - IS-IS level-1, L2 - IS-IS level-2,
       * - candidate default
       U - per-user static route, o - ODR, P - periodic downloaded
       static route
       T - traffic engineered route

Gateway of last resort is not set

I    192.168.192.0/24 [100/80135] via 192.168.0.1, FastEthernet0/1
I    192.168.200.0/24 [100/10110] via 192.168.0.1, FastEthernet0/1
C    192.168.0.0/24 is directly connected, FastEthernet0/1
C    192.168.1.0/24 is directly connected, FastEthernet0/0
```

The London LAN appears as an IGRP route.

Step 6

The benefit of ODR is apparent as more LANs are created in London. Simulate another LAN in London by creating a loopback interface, as shown here:

```
London(config)#interface loopback 0
London(config-if)#ip address 192.168.208.1 255.255.255.0
```

Now view SanJose2's routing table:

```
SanJose2#show ip route
Codes: C - connected, S - static, I - IGRP, R - RIP, M - mobile,
       B - BGP
       D - EIGRP, EX - EIGRP external, O - OSPF, IA - OSPF
       inter area
       N1 - OSPF NSSA external type 1, N2 - OSPF NSSA external
       type 2
```

```
       E1 - OSPF external type 1, E2 - OSPF external type 2,
       E - EGP
       i - IS-IS, L1 - IS-IS level-1, L2 - IS-IS level-2,
       * - candidate default
       U - per-user static route, o - ODR, P - periodic downloaded
static route
       T - traffic engineered route

Gateway of last resort is not set

I    192.168.192.0/24 [100/80135] via 192.168.0.1, FastEthernet0/1
I    192.168.200.0/24 [100/10110] via 192.168.0.1, FastEthernet0/1
I    192.168.208.0/24 [100/10110] via 192.168.0.1, FastEthernet0/1
C    192.168.0.0/24 is directly connected, FastEthernet0/1
C    192.168.1.0/24 is directly connected, FastEthernet0/0
```

Note that the new network, 192.168.208.0/24 is dynamically added to both San Jose routers' tables.

Frame Relay Challenge Lab

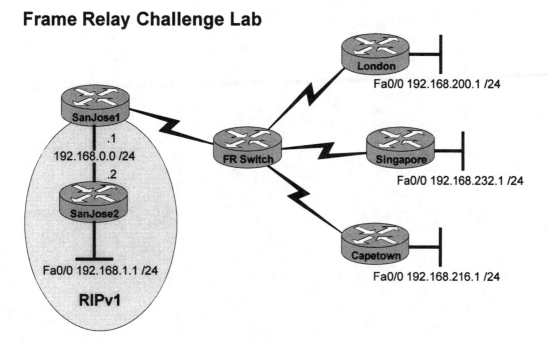

Objective

Provide connectivity using and ODR over Frame Relay point-to-point subinterfaces.

Scenario

As the network engineer for the International Travel Agency, you are responsible for connectivity between each regional site and headquarters in San Jose.

Design Considerations

To save money and have better control over your private Frame Relay network, you decide to lease multiple lines and configure a router as a Frame Relay switch. Most traffic will be between headquarters and each regional site. To save bandwidth, you have chosen on-demand routing (ODR) to stub networks to San Jose. The San Jose headquarters is running RIPv1.

Implementation Requirements

- All Frame Relay links are point-to-point subinterfaces. SanJose1 is the hub router in the hub-and-spoke topology.
- All routes from regional sites are sent via ODR. No other routing protocols on spoke routers.
- No default or static routes on San Jose routers.
- Implementation completion tests.
- View routes to all LANs in SanJose2's routing table.
- Successful extended ping among all LANs.

Lab 9-1: Configuring ISDN Dial Backup

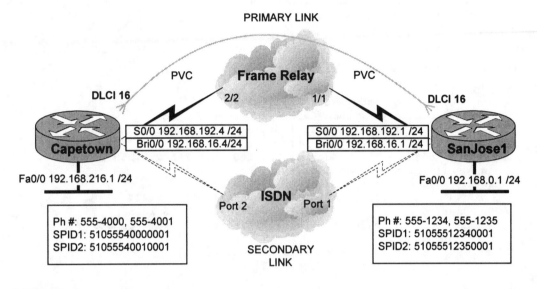

Objective

Configure ISDN dial backup for a fixed Frame Relay WAN link.

Scenario

As the network engineer for the International Travel Agency (ITA), you are responsible for full-time WAN connectivity between regional headquarters and San Jose company headquarters. You have provisioned Frame Relay permanent virtual circuits (PVCs) in a star topology, with SanJose1 as the hub router. To provide fault tolerance, each Frame Relay PVC is backed up with ISDN BRI.

Step 1

Build the network as shown in the previous diagram. If you are using the Atlas 550 as a WAN emulator, be sure to use the ports as indicated in the diagram. Before beginning this lab, it is recommended that you reload each router after erasing its startup configuration. This will prevent you from having problems caused by residual configurations.

Step 2

Configure and test ISDN BRI on Capetown, using CHAP authentication, as shown here:

```
Capetown(config)#isdn switch-type basic-ni
Capetown(config)#username SanJose1 password cisco
Capetown(config)#dialer-list 1 protocol ip permit
Capetown(config)#interface bri 0/0
Capetown(config-if)#ip address 192.168.16.4 255.255.255.0
Capetown(config-if)#encapsulation ppp
Capetown(config-if)#ppp authentication chap
Capetown(config-if)#isdn spid1 51055540000001 5554000
Capetown(config-if)#isdn spid2 51055540010001 5554001
```

```
Capetown(config-if)#dialer map ip 192.168.16.1 name SanJose1
      broadcast 5551234
Capetown(config-if)#dialer idle-timeout 60
Capetown(config-if)#dialer-group 1
```

Next, configure SanJose1. SanJose1 will only accept BRI calls, so do not configure a phone number with the **dialer map** statement:

```
SanJose1(config)#isdn switch-type basic-ni
SanJose1(config)#username Capetown password cisco
SanJose1(config)#dialer-list 1 protocol ip permit
SanJose1(config)#interface bri 0/0
SanJose1(config-if)#ip address 192.168.16.1 255.255.255.0
SanJose1(config-if)#encapsulation ppp
SanJose1(config-if)#ppp authentication chap
SanJose1(config-if)#isdn spid1 51055512340001 5551234
SanJose1(config-if)#isdn spid2 51055512350001 5551235
SanJose1(config-if)#dialer map ip 192.168.16.4 name Capetown
      broadcast
SanJose1(config-if)#dialer idle-timeout 60
SanJose1(config-if)#dialer-group 1
```

Ping across the ISDN link by sending a ping from Capetown to SanJose1 (192.168.16.1). This ping should be successful; troubleshoot as necessary.

Step 3

Configure and test Frame Relay connectivity on both routers. Capetown's configuration is shown here as an example:

```
Capetown(config)#interface s0/0
Capetown(config-if)#ip address 192.168.192.4 255.255.255.0
Capetown(config-if)#encapsulation frame-relay
Capetown(config-if)#frame-relay map ip 192.168.192.1 16 broadcast
```

Use ping to verify that the Frame link is operational. Ping one serial interface from the other.

Step 4

Configure and test static routing between the Capetown spoke router and the San-Jose1 hub router. Because Capetown supports a stub network, create a static route to all unknown networks pointing at SanJose1. SanJose1 will use a specific static route to return packets to the Capetown LAN, as shown here:

```
SanJose1(config)#ip route 192.168.216.0 255.255.255.0 192.168.192.4
```

```
Capetown(config)#ip route 0.0.0.0 0.0.0.0 192.168.192.1
```

Verify that the static routing configuration works by performing extended pings between LANs.

Step 5

Configure backup routing.

The Frame Relay link has adequate bandwidth for normal traffic. The ISDN BRI is deployed only for fault tolerance. Your service provider will be charging you per minute of ISDN call time if you exceed defined data transfer levels. Having a redundant path is worth the cost, but use of the line needs to be minimized to avoid associated charges.

Place floating static routes between SanJose1 and Capetown, utilizing the ISDN link:

```
Capetown(config)#ip route 0.0.0.0 0.0.0.0 192.168.16.1 222

SanJose1(config)#ip route 192.168.216.0 255.255.255.0 192.168.16.4
    222
```

View the routing tables, as shown here:

```
SanJose1#show ip route

Gateway of last resort is not set

C    192.168.192.0/24 is directly connected, Serial0/0
S    192.168.216.0/24 [1/0] via 192.168.192.4
C    192.168.16.0/24 is directly connected, BRI0/0
C    192.168.0.0/24 is directly connected, FastEthernet0/0


Capetown#show ip route

Gateway of last resort is 192.168.192.1 to network 0.0.0.0

C    192.168.192.0/24 is directly connected, Serial0/0
C    192.168.216.0/24 is directly connected, FastEthernet0/0
C    192.168.16.0/24 is directly connected, BRI0/0
S*   0.0.0.0/0 [1/0] via 192.168.192.1
```

1. Although you have configured two static routes on each router, only one of those routes is installed in each routing table. Why?

_____

_____

_____

The static routes using the Frame Relay link have a default administrative distance of 1, which is preferred over all routes except directly connected routes, which have an administrative distance of 0. If the Frame Relay link fails, associated routes will eventually be removed from the routing table, and ISDN routes with an administrative distance of 222 will be placed in the routing table. Connectivity will be restored, albeit at a much slower rate.

To make the ISDN link active only in the event of a Frame Relay link failure, make BRI 0/0 a backup interface to Serial0/0 on Capetown:

```
Capetown(config)#interface s0/0
Capetown(config-if)#backup interface bri0/0
Capetown(config-if)#backup delay 6 8
```

Only Capetown is configured with the **backup interface** and **backup delay** commands. The first backup delay value (6) represents the number of seconds between Serial 0/0 failure and the backup link (BRI 0/0) becoming active. The second value (8) is the number of seconds after Serial 0/0 is restored before bringing down the backup link. If you were to configure SanJose1's BRI as a backup interface, Capetown could not establish a dialup connection with SanJose1. SanJose1's BRI would either be in standby mode (shutdown) or trying to make a dialup call. In either case, Capetown would not be able to connect with it.

Take another look at Capetown's routing table:

```
Capetown#show ip route

Gateway of last resort is 192.168.192.1 to network 0.0.0.0

C    192.168.192.0/24 is directly connected, Serial0/0
C    192.168.216.0/24 is directly connected, FastEthernet0/0
S*   0.0.0.0/0 [1/0] via 192.168.192.1
```

The directly connected route for the ISDN link has disappeared. Check to see if the BRI is down by issuing the **show interface** command on Capetown:

```
Capetown#show int bri0/0
BRI0/0 is standby mode, line protocol is down
  Hardware is PQUICC BRI with U interface
  Internet address is 192.168.16.4/24
  MTU 1500 bytes, BW 64 Kbit, DLY 20000 usec,
     reliability 255/255, txload 1/255, rxload 1/255
  Encapsulation PPP, loopback not set
<output ommited>
```

The output of this command shows that the line is down, but standing by, in the event the serial interface goes down.

On Capetown, issue the **show backup** command:

```
Capetown#show backup
Primary Interface    Secondary Interface    Status
-----------------    -------------------    ------
Serial0/0            BRI0/0                 normal operation
```

Step 6

Test dial backup with an extended ping between Capetown and SanJose1. While the ping progresses, pull the serial cable from both routers:

```
Capetown#ping
Protocol [ip]:
Target IP address: 192.168.0.1
Repeat count [5]: 555
Datagram size [100]:
Timeout in seconds [2]: 1
Extended commands [n]: y
Source address or interface: 192.168.216.1
Type of service [0]:
Set DF bit in IP header? [no]:
Validate reply data? [no]:
Data pattern [0xABCD]:
Loose, Strict, Record, Timestamp, Verbose[none]:
Sweep range of sizes [n]:
Type escape sequence to abort.
Sending 555, 100-byte ICMP Echos to 192.168.0.1, timeout is 1
      seconds:
!!!!!!!!!!!!!!!!!!!!!!!!!!!!!!!!!!!!!!!!!!!!!!!!!!!!!!!!!!!!!!!!!!!!!
!!!!!!!!!!!!!!!!!!!!!!!!!!!!!!!!!!!!!!!!!!!!!!!!!!!!!!!!!!!!!!!!!!!!!
!!!!.........!!!!!!!!!!!!!!!!!!!!!!!!!!!!!!!!!!!!!!!!!!!!!!!!!!!!!!!!
!!!!!!!!!!!!!!!!!!!!!!!!!!!!!!!!!!!!!!!!!!!!!!!!!!!!!!!!!!!!!!!!!!!!!
!!!!!!!!!!!!!!!!!!!!!!!!!!!!!!!!!!!!!!!!!!!!!!!!!!!!!!!!!!!!!!!!!!!!!
!!!!!!!!!!!!!!!!!!!!!!!!!!!!!!!!!!!!!!!!!!!!!!!!!!!!!!!!!!!!!!!!!!!!!
!!!!!!!!!!!!!!!!!!!!!!!!!!!!!!!!!!!!!!!!!!!!!!!!!!!!!!!!!!!!!!!!!!!!!
!!!!!!!!!!!!!!!!!!!!!!!!!!!!!!!!!!!!!!!!!!!!!!!!!!!!!!!!!!!!!!!!!!!
Success rate is 98 percent (545/555), round-trip min/avg/max =
      32/39/60 ms
```

It took over five seconds for ISDN to become active after Frame Relay failed. While active, the backup interface is in backup mode. Issue the **show backup** command on Capetown, as shown here:

```
Capetown#show backup
Primary Interface     Secondary Interface     Status
-----------------     -------------------     ------
Serial0/0             BRI0/0                  backup mode
```

2. How did Capetown get to SanJose1 if the only route was through the failed Frame Relay link?

_____

_____

_____

To verify your answer to Question 2, issue **show ip route** on Capetown. The following route should now be in Capetown's routing table:

```
C    192.168.16.0/24 is directly connected, BRI0/0
```

When Serial 0/0 failed, its associated static route was removed from the routing table and replaced by the floating static route over the ISDN link.

Verify that SanJose1's ISDN interface is up by issuing the **show interface bri0/0** command:

```
SanJose1#show interface bri0/0
BRI0/0 is up, line protocol is up (spoofing)
  Hardware is PQUICC BRI with U interface
  Internet address is 192.168.16.1/24
  MTU 1500 bytes, BW 64 Kbit, DLY 20000 usec,
     reliability 255/255, txload 1/255, rxload 1/255
  Encapsulation PPP, loopback not set
<output ommited>
```

You have successfully implemented dial backup for WAN connectivity. Save your configurations from this lab; they will be used to complete the next lab exercise.

Lab 9-2: Using Secondary Links for On-Demand Bandwidth

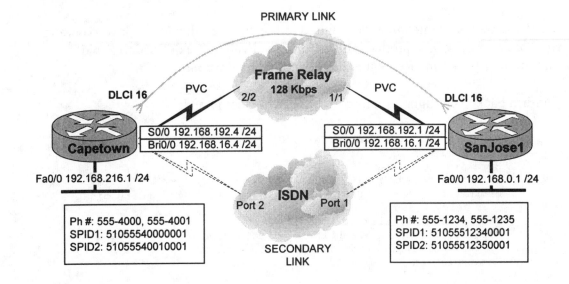

Objective

Configure ISDN dial-on-demand bandwidth supporting overload traffic from the primary Frame Relay link.

Scenario

The International Travel Agency has expanded, increasing traffic between Capetown and SanJose1. While waiting for your service provider to provision greater bandwidth on your Frame Relay link, you configure ISDN to carry traffic in case the Frame Relay link becomes saturated.

Step1

Build the network as shown in the previous diagram. If you are using the Atlas 550 as a WAN emulator, be sure to use the ports as indicated in the diagram.

Step 2

Load your saved configuration files from the completion of the previous lab. If you have not done the previous lab (Lab 9-1), do so now.

Step 3

As configured in the previous lab, ISDN will become active only if the Frame Relay link fails. Instead, you want ISDN to become active as the Frame Relay link reaches a predefined traffic threshold. Configure Capetown with the following syntax:

```
Capetown(config)#interface serial 0/0
Capetown(config-if)#no backup delay 6 8
Capetown(config-if)#backup load 2 1
```

The first number in the **backup load** command is the percentage of bandwidth utilization necessary on Serial 0/0 to trigger activation of backup interface BRI 0/0. The second number is the percentage of bandwidth utilization on Serial 0/0 deactivating

BRI 0/0. Due to the sporadic nature of data communications, percentages are evaluated, by default, during a sliding five-second window.

Note: The **backup load** values configured in this lab are ridiculously low to demonstrate functionality. In a production network, load values are defined to avoid saturation of the Frame Relay link. For example, **backup load 60 20**.

Confirm backup configuration using the following command:

```
Capetown#show interface serial 0/0
Serial0/0 is up, line protocol is up
  Hardware is PowerQUICC Serial
  Internet address is 192.168.192.4/24
  Backup interface BRI0/0, failure delay 0 sec, secondary disable
      delay 0 sec,
  kickin load 2%, kickout load 1%
  MTU 1500 bytes, BW 128 Kbit, DLY 20000 usec,
      reliability 255/255, txload 1/255, rxload 1/255
  Encapsulation FRAME-RELAY, loopback not set
```

Step 4

View the routing tables of both routers:

```
SanJose1#show ip route

Gateway of last resort is not set

C    192.168.192.0/24 is directly connected, Serial0/0
S    192.168.216.0/24 [1/0] via 192.168.192.4
C    192.168.16.0/24 is directly connected, BRI0/0
C    192.168.0.0/24 is directly connected, FastEthernet0/0


Capetown#show ip route

Gateway of last resort is 192.168.192.1 to network 0.0.0.0

C    192.168.192.0/24 is directly connected, Serial0/0
C    192.168.216.0/24 is directly connected, FastEthernet0/0
S*   0.0.0.0/0 [1/0] via 192.168.192.1
```

1. Which route will Capetown use to reach SanJose1 over the ISDN cloud?

_____

When the ISDN link only provided fault tolerance, floating static routes appeared in the routing table when a Frame Relay link failed and the route via Serial 0/0 was removed from the routing table. Only one route at a time was available; now both routes need to be available during times of excessive traffic. This can be accomplished with equal administrative distances. Modify the administrative distance for static routes associated with BRI 0/0 interfaces on both routers, as shown here:

```
Capetown(config)#no ip route 0.0.0.0 0.0.0.0 192.168.16.1 222
Capetown(config)#ip route 0.0.0.0 0.0.0.0 192.168.16.1
```

```
SanJose1(config)#no ip route 192.168.216.0 255.255.255.0 192.168.16.4
    222
SanJose1(config)#ip route 192.168.216.0 255.255.255.0 192.168.16.4
```

As the backup interface is activated, both routes can coexist in the routing table, which allows load balancing between the two equal cost paths.

Step 5

Test the dial-on-demand bandwidth by loading the Frame Relay link over 2 percent with an extended ping from Capetown to SanJose1. Watch the BRI router interface while you are pinging. You should see one channel light activate when ISDN is triggered. As soon as the ping is complete, issue the **show backup** and **show ip route** commands:

```
Capetown#ping
Protocol [ip]:
Target IP address: 192.168.0.1
Repeat count [5]: 55
Datagram size [100]: 1500
Timeout in seconds [2]: 1
Extended commands [n]: y
Source address or interface: 192.168.216.1
Type of service [0]:
Set DF bit in IP header? [no]:
Validate reply data? [no]:
Data pattern [0xABCD]:
Loose, Strict, Record, Timestamp, Verbose[none]:
Sweep range of sizes [n]:
Type escape sequence to abort.
Sending 55, 1500-byte ICMP Echos to 192.168.0.1, timeout is 1
    seconds:
!!!!!!!!!!!!!!!!!!!!!!!!!!!!!!..!!!!!!!!!!!!!!!!!!!!!!!!!!
Success rate is 96 percent (53/55), round-trip min/avg/max =
    380/418/444 ms

Capetown#show backup
Primary Interface     Secondary Interface     Status
-----------------     -------------------     ------
Serial0/0             BRI0/0                  overload mode


Capetown#show ip route

Gateway of last resort is 192.168.192.1 to network 0.0.0.0

C    192.168.192.0/24 is directly connected, Serial0/0
C    192.168.216.0/24 is directly connected, FastEthernet0/0
     192.168.16.0/24 is variably subnetted, 2 subnets, 2 masks
C       192.168.16.0/24 is directly connected, BRI0/0
C       192.168.16.1/32 is directly connected, BRI0/0
S*   0.0.0.0/0 [1/0] via 192.168.192.1
              [1/0] via 192.168.16.1
```

There are two parallel routes to SanJose1 while the BRI 0/0 interface is up. ISDN activated at about the same time the two packets were dropped due to congestion. Issue **show backup** after one minute, or after the BRI 0/0 channel light turns off:

```
Capetown#show backup
Primary Interface      Secondary Interface    Status
-----------------      -------------------    ------
Serial0/0              BRI0/0                 normal operation
```

The BRI 0/0 interface has deactivated and returned to standby. Another command you can use to to check interface status is **show ip interface brief**:

```
Capetown#show ip interface brief
Interface            IP-Address      OK? Method Status                 Protocol
FastEthernet0/0      192.168.216.1   YES NVRAM  up                     up
Serial0/0            192.168.192.4   YES NVRAM  up                     up
BRI0/0               192.168.16.4    YES NVRAM  standby mode           down
BRI0/0:1             unassigned      YES unset  administratively down  down
BRI0/0:2             unassigned      YES unset  administratively down  down
Serial0/1            unassigned      YES NVRAM  administratively down  down
```

You have successfully configured dial-on-demand bandwidth.

ISDN DDR and WAN Backup Challenge Lab

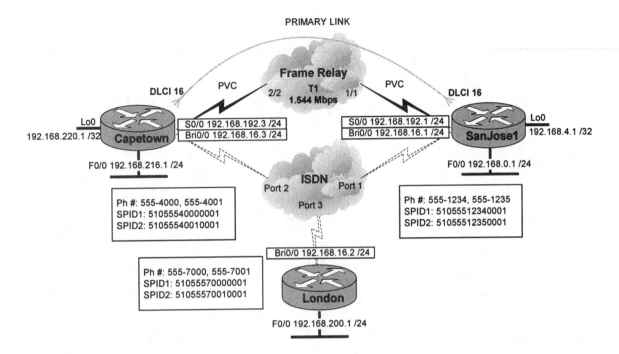

Objective

Configure backup interface and DDR to multiple destinations with a single ISDN interface using dialer profiles.

Scenario

The European regional headquarters, London, has connected to the International Travel Agency (ITA) WAN via ISDN. London and Capetown only need to connect with SanJose1, but Capetown must have fault tolerance. SanJose1 needs the ability to establish connectivity with either London or Capetown.

Implementation Requirements

- Dialer interfaces are used instead of legacy DDR.
- Full-time Frame Relay link between SanJose1 and Capetown.
- ISDN as backup to Frame Relay on Capetown (between SanJose1 and Capetown).
- DDR between SanJose1 and the other two sites, at up to128 Kbps if needed.
- PPP encapsulation with CHAP authentication over ISDN links.

Implementation Completion Tests

- Ability to ping among all LANs.
- When Frame Relay fails between Capetown and SanJose1, ISDN becomes active. Test: Remove both serial cables.
- An extended ping over ISDN can exceed 64 Kbps (with MLP configured correctly).

Lab 10-1: Configuring Weighted Fair Queuing

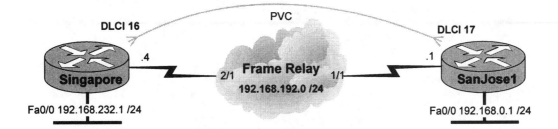

Objective

In this lab, you optimize weighted fair queuing (WFQ).

Scenario

As the network engineer for the International Travel Agency, you are responsible for WAN connectivity. As ITA has grown, traffic has increased on your Frame Relay network. Over the last few weeks, network technicians have reported unreliable Telnet access between San Jose and regional sites. After an investigation, you discover that average Frame Relay network utilization between Singapore and SanJose1 is near saturation. While investigating ways to increase bandwidth, you optimize WFQ as a temporary solution to meet the needs of all users.

Step 1

Build the network as shown in the previous diagram. If you are using the Atlas 550 as a WAN emulator, be sure to use the ports as indicated in the previous diagram. Before beginning this lab, it is recommended that you reload each router after erasing its startup configuration. This prevents you from having problems caused by residual configurations.

Step 2

Configure the network as shown in the diagram with Frame Relay, Ethernet and IGRP with autonomous system number 234.

Step 3

View the default queuing strategy on the Singapore Frame Relay link:

```
Singapore#show interfaces serial 0/0
Serial0/0 is up, line protocol is up
  Hardware is PowerQUICC Serial
  Internet address is 192.168.192.4/24
  MTU 1500 bytes, BW 128 Kbit, DLY 20000 usec,
     reliability 255/255, txload 1/255, rxload 1/255
  Encapsulation FRAME-RELAY, loopback not set
  Keepalive set (10 sec)
  LMI enq sent  385, LMI stat recvd 386, LMI upd recvd 0, DTE LMI up
  LMI enq recvd 0, LMI stat sent  0, LMI upd sent  0
  LMI DLCI 0  LMI type is ANSI Annex D  frame relay DTE
  Broadcast queue 0/64, broadcasts sent/dropped 745/0, interface
     broadcasts 418
```

```
Last input 00:00:02, output 00:00:02, output hang never
Last clearing of "show interface" counters 01:12:40
Input queue: 0/75/0/0 (size/max/drops/flushes); Total output drops:
    0
Queueing strategy: weighted fair
Output queue: 0/1000/64/0 (size/max total/threshold/drops)
    Conversations  0/1/32 (active/max active/max total)
    Reserved Conversations 0/0 (allocated/max allocated)
5 minute input rate 0 bits/sec, 0 packets/sec
5 minute output rate 0 bits/sec, 0 packets/sec
    852 packets input, 155960 bytes, 0 no buffer
    Received 0 broadcasts, 0 runts, 0 giants, 0 throttles
    0 input errors, 0 CRC, 0 frame, 0 overrun, 0 ignored, 0 abort
    1144 packets output, 252560 bytes, 0 underruns
    0 output errors, 0 collisions, 2 interface resets
    0 output buffer failures, 0 output buffers swapped out
    0 carrier transitions
DCD=up  DSR=up  DTR=up  RTS=up  CTS=up
```

1. According to the output of this command, what is the queuing strategy in use on this interface?

To view just the queuing configuration on the Frame Relay interface, issue **show queue interface Serial 0/0**:

```
SanJose1#show queue s0/0
  Input queue: 0/75/0 (size/max/drops); Total output drops: 0
  Queueing strategy: weighted fair
  Output queue: 0/1000/64/0 (size/max total/threshold/drops)
    Conversations  0/1/256 (active/max active/max total)
    Reserved Conversations 0/0 (allocated/max allocated)
```

2. According to the output of this command, what is the output queue threshold?

---

3. Does the output of the **show queue** command provide any information not displayed by the **show interface** command?

Since IOS 11.2, WFQ is the default queuing method on all interfaces with bandwidth of E1 (2.048 Mbps) or less. Earlier versions of IOS default to first-in, first-out (FIFO). FIFO queuing is preferred on high-bandwidth interfaces where saturation is uncommon.

If a router's serial interface is using FIFO, you can configure WFQ by issuing the **fair-queue** command:

```
Singapore(config)#interface serial 0/0
Singapore(config-if)#fair-queue
```

On a congested FIFO interface, low-volume, interactive sessions like Telnet are subject to intolerable delays, while high-bandwidth applications, such as FTP, monopolize available bandwidth. WFQ identifies and gives equal access to a variety of application protocols. WFQ can be thought of as statistically multiplexing all applications. Low-volume sessions are given the necessary bandwidth while high-volume sessions share the remainder. However, there is no guarantee of reserved bandwidth.

Interfaces overwhelmed with traffic can be forced to consistently drop packets. Queuing should not be seen as a solution to this problem. In such cases, more bandwidth is required. Queuing actually compounds performance problems because it demands additional router CPU cycles and forces the router to apply queuing logic to each packet. Thus, queuing is either a temporary fix, or a solution for those rare occasions when interactive sessions fail due to latency or dropped packets.

Each communication session between hosts creates a flow. The router understands a flow as a record of attributes, including source and destination addresses, port numbers, and the inbound interface. The router can then compare subsequent packets to existing flows. As packets are identified as belonging to a certain session, they are buffered accordingly.

To give each session equal router resources, a default maximum of 64 messages (packets) can be buffered by any one session. For ITA's network, you must increase the congestion threshold to 128 packets. This allows the router to buffer more packets per session, but decreases the number of sessions serviced in any period of time.

Note: Queuing is only active when congestion exists. Congestion exists when any interface has one or more packets buffered in its queue. If all interfaces are clear of buffered packets, queuing is idle.

Step 4

Increase the congestion threshold value to 128 packets on both routers' Frame Relay links:

```
Singapore(config)#interface serial 0/0
Singapore(config-if)#fair-queue 128

SanJose1(config)#interface serial 0/0
SanJose1(config-if)#fair-queue 128
```

Look again at the WFQ parameters on Serial 0/0:

```
SanJose1#show interfaces serial 0/0
Serial0/0 is up, line protocol is up
  Hardware is PowerQUICC Serial
  Internet address is 192.168.192.1/24
  MTU 1500 bytes, BW 1544 Kbit, DLY 20000 usec,
     reliability 254/255, txload 1/255, rxload 1/255
  Encapsulation FRAME-RELAY, loopback not set
```

```
         Keepalive set (10 sec)
         LMI enq sent  1155, LMI stat recvd 1156, LMI upd recvd 0, DTE LMI
            up
         LMI enq recvd 0, LMI stat sent  0, LMI upd sent  0
         LMI DLCI 0  LMI type is ANSI Annex D  frame relay DTE
         Broadcast queue 0/64, broadcasts sent/dropped 1141/0, interface
            broadcasts 592
         Last input 00:00:03, output 00:00:03, output hang never
         Last clearing of "show interface" counters 03:18:42
         Input queue: 0/75/0 (size/max/drops); Total output drops: 0
         Queueing strategy: weighted fair
         Output queue: 0/1000/128/0 (size/max total/threshold/drops)
            Conversations  0/1/256 (active/max active/max total)
            Reserved Conversations 0/0 (allocated/max allocated)
         5 minute input rate 0 bits/sec, 0 packets/sec
         5 minute output rate 0 bits/sec, 0 packets/sec
            1615 packets input, 143360 bytes, 0 no buffer
            Received 0 broadcasts, 0 runts, 0 giants, 0 throttles
            4 input errors, 0 CRC, 4 frame, 0 overrun, 0 ignored, 0 abort
            2308 packets output, 326118 bytes, 0 underruns
            0 output errors, 0 collisions, 7 interface resets
            0 output buffer failures, 0 output buffers swapped out
            0 carrier transitions
            DCD=up  DSR=up  DTR=up  RTS=up  CTS=up

      Singapore#show queue serial 0/0
         Input queue: 0/75/0/0 (size/max/drops/flushes); Total output drops:
            0
         Queueing strategy: weighted fair
         Output queue: 0/1000/128/0 (size/max total/threshold/drops)
            Conversations  0/1/32 (active/max active/max total)
            Reserved Conversations 0/0 (allocated/max allocated)
```

When the Frame Relay link is saturated, and queuing activates, each session will be able to buffer up to 128 packets before dropping any incoming packets. After the 128-packet discard threshold limit is reached for a particular flow, no packets will be buffered for that flow until the queue for that flow drops to 25% of the discard threshold. In this case, the queue must reach 32 packets (25% of 128). If packets are dropped, upper-layer protocols, such as TCP, can compensate and retransmit undelivered packets.

You have successfully changed the behavior of WFQ.

Lab 10-2: Configuring Priority Queuing

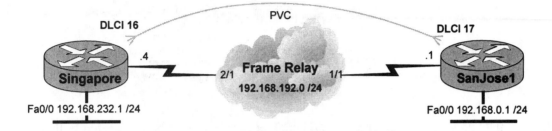

Objective

In this lab, you implement priority queuing.

Scenario

As the network engineer for the International Travel Agency, you are responsible for WAN connectivity. As ITA has grown, traffic has increased on your Frame Relay network. Additional bandwidth has not yet been provisioned for your Frame Relay permanent virtual circuits (PVCs). At peak traffic times during the workday, the network becomes sluggish and unreliable. Immediate action needs to be taken until more bandwidth can be acquired. You decide to implement priority queuing.

Step 1

Build the network as shown in the previous diagram. If you are using the Atlas 550 as a WAN emulator, be sure to use the ports as indicated in the diagram. Before you begin this lab, it is recommended that you reload each router after erasing its startup configuration. This prevents you from having problems caused by residual configurations.

Step 2

Priority queuing allows you to define types of traffic and associate each type of traffic with one of four queues: high, medium, normal, and low. Priority queuing will transmit all packets in the high queue first. When the high queue is empty, the medium queue is emptied, and the high queue is checked again for buffered packets. Only after all higher priority queues are emptied, lower queues are checked and emptied. It is possible that low queues will hold packets that never get transmitted, causing their associated sessions to time out.

There are three steps to configuring priority queuing: First, traffic is defined using access lists. Second, access lists are associated with queues using priority lists. Finally, priority lists are associated with interfaces.

You have defined three types of traffic you wish to assign priority to: TCP, UDP, and ICMP. All other traffic will be placed in the default queue, which is the normal queue.

Define three types of traffic with access lists on both routers, as shown here:

```
SanJose1(config)#access-list 111 permit tcp any any
SanJose1(config)#access-list 112 permit icmp any any
SanJose1(config)#access-list 113 permit udp any any

Singapore(config)#access-list 121 permit tcp any any
Singapore(config)#access-list 122 permit icmp any any
Singapore(config)#access-list 123 permit udp any any
```

Step 3

Priority lists now need to be created, and each access list must be associated with a queue. As with access lists, packets are compared to a priority list one line at a time, starting with the first line of the priority list. The first priority list line that matches the packet sends it to the associated queue. No following priority list statements are compared to the packet. For efficiency, structure your priority list so that a majority of packets are matched to the first few lines.

Give TCP traffic high priority, ICMP medium priority, and UDP low priority on both routers, as shown here:

```
Singapore(config)#priority-list 3 protocol ip high list 121
Singapore(config)#priority-list 3 protocol ip medium list 122
Singapore(config)#priority-list 3 protocol ip low list 123

SanJose1(config)#priority-list 5 protocol ip high list 111
SanJose1(config)#priority-list 5 protocol ip medium list 112
SanJose1(config)#priority-list 5 protocol ip high list 113
```

1. According to these commands, to what queue would FTP traffic be assigned?

_____

2. To what queue would TFTP traffic be assigned?

_____

Most of the configuration is complete, but queuing will never be applied until the priority list is associated with an interface. Apply the priority lists to the serial interfaces, as shown here:

```
SanJose1(config)#interface serial 0/0
SanJose1(config-if)#priority-group 5

Singapore(config)#interface serial 0/0
Singapore(config-if)#priority-group 3
```

Traffic output interface Serial 0/0 will be compared with **priority list** statements.

Confirm configuration with the **show queueing priority** command. *Note*: This command misspells the word *queuing*. When using the Cisco IOS, you must spell this word incorrectly (*queueing*) in order for the command to be recognized, as shown in this example:

```
SanJose1#show queueing priority
```

Current priority queue configuration:

```
List   Queue   Args
5      high    protocol ip          list 111
5      medium  protocol ip          list 112
5      high    protocol ip          list 113


Singapore#show queueing priority
Current priority queue configuration:

List   Queue   Args
3      high    protocol ip          list 121
3      medium  protocol ip          list 122
3      low     protocol ip          list 123
```

To view the quantity of packets in each queue per interface, issue **show queue** on each router:

```
Singapore#show queueing interface serial 0/0
Interface Serial0/0 queueing strategy: priority

Output queue utilization (queue/count)
        high/274 medium/560 normal/34 low/0
```

3. According to the previous output, what does the "high/272" mean?

```
SanJose1#show queueing interface serial 0/0
Interface Serial0/0 queueing strategy: priority

Output queue utilization (queue/count)
        high/306 medium/560 normal/88 low/0
```

As the link becomes saturated and some traffic has to wait, you have ensured that TCP traffic will always be transmitted first, medium traffic should get through, and normal and low traffic might get through. Because more packets will likely be buffered in the lower-priority queues, they are larger by default. The default queue sizes are high 20, medium 40, normal 60, and low 80.

Recall that the default queue for all undefined traffic is the normal queue. You decided to elevate the priority of undefined traffic by configuring the default queue as having medium priority on both routers:

```
SanJose1(config)#priority-list 5 default medium
```

Increase the number of records (packets) for the medium queue because that is now the default queue for all undefined traffic:

```
SanJose1(config)#priority-list 5 queue limit 20 90 60 80
```

Confirm queuing configuration, as shown here:

```
Singapore#show queueing priority
Current priority queue configuration:

List    Queue  Args
3       high   protocol ip          list 121
3       medium protocol ip          list 122
3       low    protocol ip          list 123
3       medium limit 90
```

Note: Only non-default queue sizes appear in the output.

You have successfully implemented and optimized priority queuing.

Lab 10-3: Configuring Custom Queuing

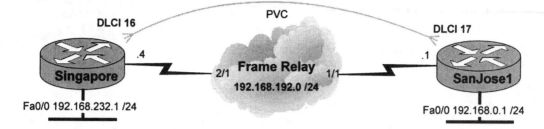

Objective

In this lab, you implement custom queuing.

Scenario

As the network engineer for the International Travel Agency, you are responsible for WAN connectivity. As ITA has grown, traffic has increased on your Frame Relay network. ITA partners, including airlines and hotel chains, have begun to complain about the speed of your Web site. Also, file uploads, downloads, Web sessions, and database synchronizations time out on a regular basis. Though additional bandwidth has been ordered from the service provider, you have been directed to ensure partners and customers are not affected by bandwidth problems in the interim. If necessary, internal users will suffer during peak traffic times. After monitoring the network, you decide to allocate bandwidth, giving Voice over IP (VoIP) 40 percent, FTP 20 percent, and HTTP 20 percent, with all other traffic sharing the remaining 20 percent.

Step 1

Build the network as shown in the previous diagram. If you are using the Atlas 550 as a WAN emulator, be sure to use the ports as indicated in the diagram. Before you begin this lab, it is recommended that you reload each router after erasing its startup configuration. This prevents you from having problems caused by residual configurations.

Step 2

Configure the network as shown in the previous diagram with Frame Relay, Ethernet and IGRP with autonomous system number 234.

Step 3

Custom queuing attempts to remedy some of the potentially devastating effects other queuing methods can have on low-priority traffic. Recall that some applications might never get serviced when priority queuing is used.

Custom queuing will "multiplex" bandwidth to assure that all queues get the pre-defined proportion of bandwidth. Seventeen different queues exist, of which 1-16 can be associated with traffic types. Queue 0 is the system queue, used by essential traffic, such as interface keepalives. Queue 0 is always serviced first. The remaining queues are serviced in a round-robin fashion, with each queue completely emptied in turn. Proportions of bandwidth are expressed as the maximum number of bytes a queue can hold. Queues that can buffer a relatively large number of bytes will have the opportunity to transmit more data per unit of time than queues buffering a relatively small number of bytes. Because custom queuing allocates bandwidth based on the maximum number of bytes rather than on time, bandwidth is not wasted. As soon as a queue is empty, the router moves to the next queue.

Define traffic for each queue with queue lists, as shown here:

```
Singapore(config)#queue-list 1 protocol ip 1 tcp ftp
Singapore(config)#queue-list 1 protocol ip 2 tcp www
Singapore(config)#queue-list 1 default 3
```

1. According to the previous configuration, to what queue would FTP traffic be assigned?

_____

2. To what queue would TFTP traffic be assigned?

_____

Because VoIP uses TCP and UDP, you need to reference an extended access list that will define VoIP traffic. Create the access list first.

```
Singapore(config)#access-list 111 permit tcp any any eq 1720
Singapore(config)#access-list 111 permit udp any any range 16380
    16480
```

Now reference the access list from the queue list:

```
Singapore(config)#queue-list 1 protocol ip 4 list 111
```

The queue number within the queue list is only a unique identifier; it's not an indication of any hierarchy or preference. What matters is the relative number of bytes a queue can hold.

Step 4

When the Frame Relay link is saturated, assuming all queues are full, bandwidth will be divided relative to queue size. Again, you want to allocate bandwidth to applications based on the following percentages: VoIP 40 percent, FTP 20 percent, HTTP 20 percent, and all other traffic sharing the remaining 20 percent.

The default queue size is 1500 bytes. If 1500 bytes are assumed to equal 20 percent of bandwidth, then doubling the VoIP queue will yield 40 percent. To figure out what percentage of bandwidth a queue is receiving in times of congestion, divide the queue size by the sum of all queues. For example, 3000 bytes/7500 bytes = 0.4 (or 40 percent).

Define queue limits on both routers, as shown here:

```
Singapore(config)#queue-list 1 queue 1 byte-count 1500
Singapore(config)#queue-list 1 queue 2 byte-count 1500
Singapore(config)#queue-list 1 queue 3 byte-count 1500
Singapore(config)#queue-list 1 queue 4 byte-count 3000
```

Step 5

Now that the traffic is defined and associated with a queue, and the maximum bytes are defined for each queue, configure both Frame Relay interfaces to use custom queuing.

```
Singapore(config)#interface serial 0/0
Singapore(config-if)#custom-queue-list 1
```

Step 6

Verify your configuration with the **show queueing custom** and **show interface** command.

Note: Remember to use the incorrect spelling: *queueing*.

```
SanJose1#show queueing custom
Current custom queue configuration:

List   Queue   Args
1      3       default
1      1       protocol ip          tcp port ftp
1      2       protocol ip          tcp port www
1      4       protocol ip          list 111
1      4       byte-count 3000


Singapore#show interfaces serial 0/0
Serial0/0 is up, line protocol is up
  Hardware is PowerQUICC Serial
  Internet address is 192.168.192.4/24
  MTU 1500 bytes, BW 1544 Kbit, DLY 20000 usec,
     reliability 255/255, txload 5/255, rxload 5/255
  Encapsulation FRAME-RELAY, loopback not set
  Keepalive set (10 sec)
  LMI enq sent  1917, LMI stat recvd 1919, LMI upd recvd 0, DTE LMI
     up
  LMI enq recvd 0, LMI stat sent  0, LMI upd sent  0
  LMI DLCI 0  LMI type is ANSI Annex D  frame relay DTE
  Broadcast queue 0/64, broadcasts sent/dropped 794/0, interface
     broadcasts 240
  Last input 00:00:00, output 00:00:00, output hang never
  Last clearing of "show interface" counters 05:19:42
  Input queue: 1/75/0 (size/max/drops); Total output drops: 0
  Queueing strategy: custom-list 1
  Output queues: (queue #: size/max/drops)
      0: 0/20/0 1: 0/20/0 2: 0/20/0 3: 0/20/0 4: 0/20/0
      5: 0/20/0 6: 0/20/0 7: 0/20/0 8: 0/20/0 9: 0/20/0
      10: 0/20/0 11: 0/20/0 12: 0/20/0 13: 0/20/0 14: 0/20/0
      15: 0/20/0 16: 0/20/0
  5 minute input rate 31000 bits/sec, 4 packets/sec
  5 minute output rate 31000 bits/sec, 4 packets/sec
      6383 packets input, 1956197 bytes, 0 no buffer
```

```
Received 0 broadcasts, 0 runts, 0 giants, 0 throttles
0 input errors, 0 CRC, 0 frame, 0 overrun, 0 ignored, 0 abort
6534 packets output, 1960423 bytes, 0 underruns
0 output errors, 0 collisions, 7 interface resets
0 output buffer failures, 0 output buffers swapped out
0 carrier transitions
DCD=up  DSR=up  DTR=up  RTS=up  CTS=up
```

The command output shows statistics for each queue. Queuing will become active when Frame Relay becomes saturated and thresholds have to be enforced.

You have successfully implemented custom queuing.

Lab 11-1: Configuring Static NAT

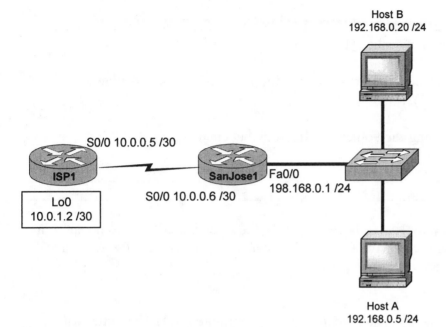

Host B
192.168.0.20 /24

S0/0 10.0.0.5 /30

ISP1

Lo0
10.0.1.2 /30

SanJose1 Fa0/0
198.168.0.1 /24

S0/0 10.0.0.6 /30

Host A
192.168.0.5 /24

Objective

Configure Network Address Translation (NAT) static translation to provide reliable outside access to three shared company servers.

Scenario

When the International Travel Agency (ITA) expanded and updated their network, they chose to use the 192.168.0.0 /24 private addresses and NAT to handle connectivity with the outside world. In order to secure the outside IP addresses from their ISP, ITA must pay a monthly fee per IP address. ITA has asked you to set up a series of prototypes that would demonstrate NAT's capabilities to meet ITA's requirements. The company hopes to be able to get by with 14 real IP addresses (42.0.0.48 /28). For a variety of reasons including security concerns, the company wishes to hide the internal network from the outside.

Step 1

Build and configure the network according to the previous diagram. This configuration requires the use of subnet zero, so you might need to enter the **ip subnet-zero** command, depending on the version of IOS you are using.

Configure SanJose1 to use a default route to ISP1, as shown here:

```
SanJose1(config)#ip route 0.0.0.0 0.0.0.0 10.0.0.5
```

Host A represents one of the proposed shared servers that will be part of an Ethernet LAN attached to SanJose1. Host B represents a user in the ITA network.

Step 2

Verify your configurations with the **show run** command.

Verify that SanJose1 can ping ISP1's serial interface (10.0.0.5) and that ISP1 can ping SanJose1's serial interface (10.0.0.6).

At this time, ISP1 cannot ping either workstation or SanJose1's FastEthernet interface (192.168.0.1).

1. Both workstations can ping each other and 10.0.0.6, but cannot ping 10.0.0.5. Why does the latter ping fail?

_____

_____

In fact, the ping request should be getting to 10.0.0.5. Because ISP1 has no entry in its routing table for the 192.168.0.0 /24, ISP1 cannot reply. You configure a static route to solve this problem in Step 7.

Step 3

SanJose1 is the boundary router where you will configure NAT. The router will be translating the inside local addresses to inside global addresses, essentially converting the internal private addresses into legal public addresses for use on the Internet.

On SanJose1, create static translations between the inside local addresses (the servers to be shared) and the inside global addresses using the following commands:

```
SanJose1(config)#ip nat inside source static 192.168.0.3 42.0.0.49
SanJose1(config)#ip nat inside source static 192.168.0.4 42.0.0.50
SanJose1(config)#ip nat inside source static 192.168.0.5 42.0.0.51
```

2. If you needed a static translation for a fourth server, 192.168.0.6, what would be the appropriate command?

_____

Step 4

Next, specify an interface on SanJose1 to be used by inside network hosts requiring address translation:

```
SanJose1(config)#interface fastethernet0/0
SanJose1(config-if)#ip nat inside
```

You must also specify an interface to be used as the outside NAT interface:

```
SanJose1(config)#interface serial0/0
SanJose1(config-if)#ip nat outside
```

Step 5

To see the translations, use the **show ip nat translations** command. The results should look something like this:

```
SanJose1#show ip nat translations
Pro Inside global      Inside local      Outside local     Outside global
---  42.0.0.49          192.168.0.3       ---               ---
---  42.0.0.50          192.168.0.4       ---               ---
---  42.0.0.51          192.168.0.5       ---               ---
```

To see what NAT activity has occurred, use the **show ip nat statistics** command. The results should look something like this:

```
SanJose1#show ip nat statistics
Total active translations: 3 (3 static, 0 dynamic; 0 extended)
Outside interfaces:
  Serial0/0
Inside interfaces:
  FastEthernet0/0
Hits: 0  Misses: 0
Expired translations: 0
Dynamic mappings:
SanJose1#
```

Note that the Hits value is currently 0.

Step 6

From Host A, ping 10.0.0.5 (ISP1's serial interface). The pings should still fail because ISP1 has no route for 192.168.0.0 /24 in its routing table.

Return to the console connection to SanJose1 and type **show ip nat statistics**, as shown here:

```
SanJose1#show ip nat statistics
Total active translations: 3 (3 static, 0 dynamic; 0 extended)
Outside interfaces:
  Serial0/0
Inside interfaces:
  FastEthernet0/0
Hits: 4  Misses: 0
Expired translations: 0
Dynamic mappings:
```

You should now see the hits equal 4. This tells you that the translation was made even though you didn't get a response. Remember that the ping replies are not sent because ISP1 does not have route back to SanJose1. It's time to remedy this.

Step 7

On ISP1, configure the following static route to the global addresses used by SanJose1 for NAT:

```
ISP1(config)#ip route 42.0.0.48 255.255.255.240 10.0.0.6
```

The subnet mask defines the pool of IP addresses as 42.0.0.48 /28.

You should now be able to successfully ping 42.0.0.51. This is the translated address or 192.168.0.5, the shared server.

The **show ip route** command confirms that the static route is present, as shown here:

```
ISP1#show ip route
Codes: C - connected, S - static, I - IGRP, R - RIP, M - mobile,
       B - BGP
       D - EIGRP, EX - EIGRP external, O - OSPF, IA - OSPF inter area
       N1 - OSPF NSSA external type 1, N2 - OSPF NSSA external type 2
       E1 - OSPF external type 1, E2 - OSPF external type 2, E - EGP
       i - IS-IS, L1 - IS-IS level-1, L2 - IS-IS level-2, ia - IS-IS
       inter area
       * - candidate default, U - per-user static route, o - ODR
       P - periodic downloaded static route

Gateway of last resort is not set

     42.0.0.0/28 is subnetted, 1 subnets
S       42.0.0.48 [1/0] via 10.0.0.6
     10.0.0.0/30 is subnetted, 2 subnets
C       10.0.1.0 is directly connected, Loopback0/0
C       10.0.0.4 is directly connected, Serial0/0
```

Step 8

From Host A, ping the ISP1 router at 10.0.0.5. This ping should now be successful.

You should also be able to ping ISP1's loopback address, 10.0.1.2.

From the console connection to SanJose1, issue the **show ip nat statistics** command and look over the statistics. The number of hits should be much larger than before.

Try the **show ip nat translations verbose** command. The results should look something like this:

```
SanJose1#show ip nat translations verbose
Pro Inside global     Inside local      Outside local      Outside global
--- 42.0.0.49         192.168.0.3       ---                ---
    create 00:40:25, use 00:40:25,
    flags:
static, use_count: 0
--- 42.0.0.50         192.168.0.4       ---                ---
    create 00:40:25, use 00:40:25,
    flags:
static, use_count: 0
--- 42.0.0.51         192.168.0.5       ---                ---
    create 00:40:25, use 00:06:46,
    flags:
static, use_count: 0
```

Note: The verbose option includes information about how recently each translation was used.

Step 9

From SanJose1, use the **show ip nat statistics** command and make a note of the number of hits.

From Host B, ping both 10.0.0.5 and 10.0.1.2.

3. Both should fail. Why?

_____

_____

_____

From SanJose1, issue the **show ip nat statistics** command again and note that the number of hits hasn't changed. The problem is that NAT did not translate Host B's IP address (192.168.0.20) to one of the global addresses. The **show ip nat translations** command should confirm this.

You haven't set up a static translation for Host B, which represents a LAN user. While you could quickly configure a static translation for this single end user, configuring a static translation for every user on the LAN could be a huge task, resulting in hundreds of configuration commands. Dynamic NAT allows you to configure the router to assign global addresses dynamically, on an as-needed basis. While static translation might be appropriate for servers, dynamic translation is almost always used with end-user stations. You explore dynamic NAT in the next lab exercise.

Lab 11-2: Configuring Dynamic NAT

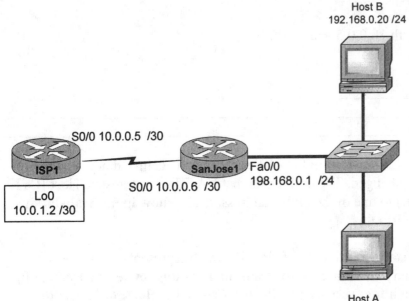

Objective

Configure dynamic NAT to provide privately addressed users with access to outside resources.

Scenario

When the International Travel Agency (ITA) expanded and updated their network, they chose to use the 192.168.0.0 /24 private addresses and NAT to handle connectivity with the outside world. In securing the outside IP addresses from their ISP, ITA has to pay a monthly fee per IP address. ITA has asked you to set up a series of prototypes that would demonstrate NAT's capabilities to meet ITA's requirements. The company hopes to be able to get by with 14 real IP addresses (42.0.0.48 /28). For a variety of reasons including security concerns, the company wishes to hide the internal network from the outside.

ITA is hoping to limit user access to the Internet and other outside resources by limiting the number of connections. You have been asked to prototype the basic dynamic translation to see if it will meet ITA's objectives.

Step 1

Build and configure the network according to the previous diagram. This configuration requires the use of subnet zero, so you may need to enter the **ip subnet-zero** command, depending on the IOS version you are using. Both Host A and Host B represent users on the ITA network.

Configure SanJose1 to use a default route to ISP1:

```
SanJose1(config)#ip route 0.0.0.0 0.0.0.0 10.0.0.5
```

On ISP1, configure a static route to the global addresses used by SanJose1 for NAT:

```
ISP1(config)#ip route 42.0.0.48 255.255.255.240 10.0.0.6
```

Step 2

Define a pool of global addresses to be allocated by the dynamic NAT process. Issue the following command on SanJose1:

```
SanJose1(config)#ip nat pool MYNATPOOL 42.0.0.55 42.0.0.55 netmask
     255.255.255.240
```

The name MYNATPOOL is the name of the address pool. If you prefer, you can use a different word of your choosing. The first 42.0.0.55 in the command is the first IP address in the pool. The second 42.0.0.55 is the last IP address in the pool. The previous command creates a pool that contains only a single address. Typically, you will configure a larger range of addresses in a pool. For now, only one address will be used.

Next, you must configure a standard access list to define which internal source addresses can be translated. Because you are translating any users on the ITA network, use the following command:

```
SanJose1(config)#access-list 2 permit 192.168.0.0 0.0.0.255
```

To establish the dynamic source translation, you must link the access list to the name of the NAT pool, as shown here:

```
SanJose1(config)#ip nat inside source list 2 pool MYNATPOOL
```

Finally, specify an interface on SanJose1 to be used by inside network hosts requiring address translation:

```
SanJose1(config)#interface fastethernet0/0
SanJose1(config-if)#ip nat inside
```

You must also specify an interface to be used as the outside NAT interface:

```
SanJose1(config)#interface serial0/0
SanJose1(config-if)#ip nat outside
```

Step 3

On SanJose1, enter the **show ip nat translations** command, which should result in no output. Unlike static translations, which are permanent and always remain in the translations table, dynamic translations are only assigned as needed, and only appear when active.

From Host A, ping ISP1's serial and loopback IP addresses. Both pings should work; troubleshoot as necessary.

Issue the **show ip nat translations** command on SanJose1 again. You should now get a single translation for that workstation. The result might look like this:

```
SanJose1#show ip nat trans
Pro Inside global      Inside local      Outside local      Outside global
--- 42.0.0.55          192.168.0.21      ---                ---
```

From Host B, ping ISP1's serial and loopback IP addresses. They should both fail. The one available IP address in the pool is being used by the other workstation. If you had assigned a larger pool of addresses, Host B could be assigned an address from the pool.

Step 4

Issue the **show ip nat translations verbose** command and examine the output:

```
SanJose1#show ip nat translations verbose
Pro Inside global      Inside local      Outside local      Outside global
--- 42.0.0.55          192.168.0.21      ---                ---
    create 00:13:18, use 00:13:06, left 23:46:53,
    flags: none, use_count: 0
```

1. According to the output of this command, how much time is left before the dynamic translation times out?

_____

The default timeout value for dynamic NAT translations is 24 hours. This means the second workstation will have to wait until the next day before it can be assigned the address.

Next, issue the **show ip nat statistics** command. Notice that it summarizes the translation information, shows the pool of global addresses, and indicates that only one address has been allocated (translated), as shown here:

```
SanJose1#show ip nat statistics
Total active translations: 1 (0 static, 1 dynamic; 0 extended)
Outside interfaces:
  Serial0/0
Inside interfaces:
  FastEthernet0/0
Hits: 45  Misses: 0
Expired translations: 0
Dynamic mappings:
-- Inside Source
access-list 2 pool MYNATPOOL refcount 1
 pool MYNATPOOL: netmask 255.255.255.240
         start 42.0.0.55 end 42.0.0.55
         type generic, total addresses 1, allocated 1 (100%), misses 4
```

To change the default NAT timeout value from 24 hours (86,400 seconds) to 120 seconds, issue the following command:

```
SanJose1(config)#ip nat translation timeout 120
```

You must clear the existing address allocation before the new timer can take effect. Type **clear ip nat translation *** to immediately clear the translation table.

Now, from Host B, try pinging either interface of ISP1 again. The ping should be successful.

Use the **show ip nat translations** and **show ip nat translations verbose** commands to confirm the translation and to see that the new translations expire in two minutes.

Next, perform a ping from Host B and issue the **show ip nat translations verbose** command again. You should see that the "time left" timer has been reset. This means that additional hosts won't be allocated an address until a translation has been inactive for the timeout period.

Step 5

In this step, configure the NAT pool to include the complete range of global addresses available to ITA. Issue the following command on SanJose1:

```
SanJose1(config)#ip nat pool MYNATPOOL 42.0.0.55 42.0.0.62 netmask
    255.255.255.240
```

The preceding command redefines MYNATPOOL to include a range of eight addresses. You should now be able to ping ISP1 from both workstations.

The **show ip nat translations** command confirms that two translations have occurred, as shown here:

```
SanJose1#show ip nat translations
Pro Inside global     Inside local      Outside local     Outside global
--- 42.0.0.55         192.168.0.20      ---               ---
--- 42.0.0.56         192.168.0.21      ---               ---
```

Increasing the address range in the pool allows more hosts to be translated. However, if every address in the pool is allocated, the timeout period must expire before any other hosts can be allocated an address. As you saw in the last step, an allocated address cannot be released until its host is inactive for the duration of the timeout period.

In the next lab, you learn to use many-to-one NAT, or NAT overload. An overload configuration can allow hundreds of hosts to use a handful of global addresses, without hosts waiting for timeouts.

Lab 11-3: Configuring NAT Overload

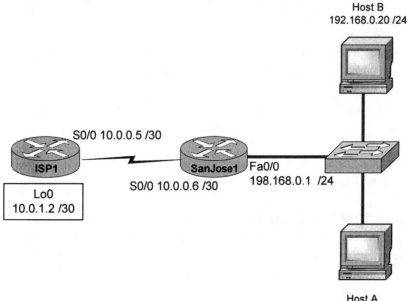

Host B
192.168.0.20 /24

S0/0 10.0.0.5 /30

ISP1

Lo0
10.0.1.2 /30

SanJose1 Fa0/0

S0/0 10.0.0.6 /30

198.168.0.1 /24

Host A
192.168.0.21 /24

Objective

Configure dynamic NAT with overload.

Scenario

When the International Travel Agency (ITA) expanded and updated their network, they chose to use the 192.168.0.0 /24 private addresses and NAT to handle connectivity with the outside world. In securing the outside IP addresses from their ISP, ITA is having to pay a monthly fee per IP address. ITA has asked you to set up a series of prototypes that would demonstrate NAT's capabilities to meet ITA's requirements. The company hopes to be able to get by with 14 real IP addresses (42.0.0.48 /28). For a variety of reasons including security concerns, the company wishes to hide the internal network from the outside.

It appears that the basic dynamic NAT translations will be too limiting and cumbersome to meet ITA's needs, so you are asked to modify the prototype to use the overload feature.

Step 1

Build and configure the network according to the previous diagram. This configuration requires the use of subnet zero, so you might need to enter the **ip subnet-zero** command, depending on the IOS version that you are using. Both Host A and Host B represent users on the ITA network.

Configure SanJose1 to use a default route to ISP1:

```
SanJose1(config)#ip route 0.0.0.0 0.0.0.0 10.0.0.5
```

On ISP1, configure a static route to the global addresses used by SanJose1 for NAT:

```
ISP1(config)#ip route 42.0.0.48 255.255.255.240 10.0.0.6
```

Define a pool of global addresses to be allocated by the dynamic NAT process. Issue the following command on SanJose1:

```
SanJose1(config)#ip nat pool MYNATPOOL 42.0.0.55 42.0.0.62 netmask
    255.255.255.240
```

Configure a standard access list to define which internal source addresses can be translated. Because you are translating all users on the ITA network, use the following command:

```
SanJose1(config)#access-list 2 permit 192.168.0.0 0.0.0.255
```

Specify an interface on SanJose1 to be used by inside network hosts requiring address translation:

```
SanJose1(config)#interface fastethernet0/0
SanJose1(config-if)#ip nat inside
```

You must also specify an interface to be used as the outside NAT interface:

```
SanJose1(config)#interface serial0/0
SanJose1(config-if)#ip nat outside
```

Step 2

In the last exercise, you saw that a pool of "real" global IP addresses can be used to provide internally addressed hosts with access to the Internet and other outside resources. However, in your previous implementation, each global address could be allocated to only one host at a time.

The most powerful feature of NAT is address overloading, or port address translation (PAT). Overloading allows multiple inside addresses to map to a single global address. With PAT, literally hundreds of privately addressed nodes can access the Internet using only one global address. The NAT router keeps track of the different conversations by mapping TCP and UDP port numbers.

Configure address overloading on SanJose1 with the following commands:

```
SanJose1(config)#ip nat inside source list 2 pool MYNATPOOL overload
```

After you configure the overload feature, ping both interfaces of ISP1 (10.0.1.2 and 10.0.0.5) from Host A. The pings should be successful. Next, issue the **show ip nat translation** command:

```
SanJose1#show ip nat translation
Pro Inside global      Inside local       Outside local      Outside global
icmp 42.0.0.55:1536    192.168.0.21:1536  10.0.0.5:1536      10.0.0.5:1536
icmp 42.0.0.55:1536    192.168.0.21:1536  10.0.1.2:1536      10.0.1.2:1536
```

1. What port number is the source of the ping?

_____

2. What port number is the destination of the ping?

_____

In addition to tracking the IP addresses translated, the translations table also records the port numbers being used. Also notice that the first column (Pro) shows the protocol used.

Now look at the output of the **show ip nat translation verbose** command:

```
SanJose1#show ip nat translation verbose
Pro Inside global      Inside local      Outside local     Outside global
icmp 42.0.0.55:1536    192.168.0.21:1536  10.0.0.5:1536     10.0.0.5:1536
    create 00:00:09, use 00:00:06, left 00:00:53,
    flags:
extended, use_count: 0
icmp 42.0.0.55:1536    192.168.0.21:1536  10.0.1.2:1536     10.0.1.2:1536
    create 00:00:04, use 00:00:01, left 00:00:58,
    flags:
extended, use_count: 0
```

Note: The timeout for these overloaded dynamic translations of ICMP is 60 seconds. Note also that each session has its own timeout timer. New activity only resets one specific session's timer. You may need to ping again to see the result on your router.

From the MS-DOS prompt of Host A, quickly issue the following commands and then return to the SanJose1 console to issue the **show ip nat translation** command. You must work fast because you are racing against the 60-second timeout:

```
HostA:\>ping 10.0.0.5
HostA:\>telnet 10.0.0.5     (Do not login. Return to command window)
HostA:\>ftp: 10.0.0.5           (It will fail. Don't worry about it)
```

Note: To quit the Windows FTP program, type bye and press Enter.

After you initiate these three sessions, the output of the **show ip nat translation** command should look something like the following:

```
SanJose1#show ip nat translation
Pro Inside global      Inside local      Outside local     Outside global
icmp 42.0.0.55:1536    192.168.0.21:1536  10.0.0.5:1536     10.0.0.5:1536
tcp 42.0.0.55:1095     192.168.0.21:1095  10.0.0.5:21       10.0.0.5:21
tcp 42.0.0.55:1094     192.168.0.21:1094  10.0.0.5:23       10.0.0.5:23
```

Although the NAT router has a pool of eight IP addresses to work with, it chooses to continue to use the 42.0.0.55 for both workstations. The Cisco IOS continues to overload the first address in the pool until it is maxed out, and then moves to the second address, and so on.

Step 3

In this step, you examine the timeout values in more detail. From Host A, initiate FTP and HTTP sessions with ISP1 at 10.0.0.5. Because ISP1 is not configured as an FTP server or Web server, both sessions will fail:

```
HostA:\>ftp: 10.0.0.5
```

To open an HTTP session, type ISP1's IP address in the URL field of a Web browser window.

After you attempt both FTP and HTTP sessions, use the **show ip nat translation verbose** command and examine the time left entries, as shown here:

```
SanJose1# show ip nat translation verbose
Pro Inside global      Inside local      Outside local      Outside global
icmp 42.0.0.55:1536    192.168.0.21:1536  10.0.0.5:1536      10.0.0.5:1536
    create 00:00:29, use 00:00:26, left 00:00:33,
    flags:
extended, use_count: 0
tcp 42.0.0.55:1114     192.168.0.21:1114  10.0.0.5:21        10.0.0.5:21
    create 00:00:16, use 00:00:15, left 00:00:44,
    flags:
extended, timing-out, use_count: 0
tcp 42.0.0.55:1113     192.168.0.21:1113  10.0.0.5:23        10.0.0.5:23
    create 00:00:22, use 00:00:22, left 23:59:37,
    flags:
extended, use_count: 0
tcp 42.0.0.55:1115     192.168.0.21:1115  10.0.0.5:80        10.0.0.5:80
    create 00:00:12, use 00:00:11, left 23:59:48,
    flags:
extended, use_count: 0
```

Some of the TCP transactions are using a 24-hour timeout timer. To see the other timers that can be set, use the **ip nat translation ?** command while in global configuration mode, as shown here:

```
SanJose1(config)#ip nat translation ?
  dns-timeout     Specify timeout for NAT DNS flows
  finrst-timeout  Specify timeout for NAT TCP flows after a FIN or
      RST
  icmp-timeout    Specify timeout for NAT ICMP flows
  max-entries     Specify maximum number of NAT entries
  port-timeout    Specify timeout for NAT TCP/UDP port specific flows
  syn-timeout     Specify timeout for NAT TCP flows after a SYN and
      no further
                  data
  tcp-timeout     Specify timeout for NAT TCP flows
  timeout         Specify timeout for dynamic NAT translations
  udp-timeout     Specify timeout for NAT UDP flows
```

The actual timeout options vary with versions of the IOS. The defaults for some of the more common times are

- **dns-timeout**   DNS session (60 seconds)
- **finrst-timeout**   TCP session after a FIN or RST / end of session (60 seconds)
- **icmp-timeout**   ICMP session (60 seconds)
- **tcp-timeout**   TCP port session (86,400 seconds – 24 hours)
- **timeout**   Dynamic NAT translations (86,400 seconds – 24 hours)
- **udp-timeout**   UDP port session (300 seconds – 5 minutes)

The **finrst-timeout** timer makes sure that TCP sessions close the related port 60 seconds after the TCP termination sequence.

Dynamic NAT sessions can only be initiated by an internal host. It is not possible to initiate a NAT translation from outside the network. To some extent, this adds a level of security to the internal network. It might also help to explain why the dynamic timeout timer for overload sessions is so short. The window of opportunity stays open just long enough to make sure that legitimate replies like Web pages, FTP and TFTP sessions, and ICMP messages can get in.

You saw in Lab 11-1 that outside hosts can ping our static NAT translations at any time, provided the inside host is up. This is so you can share Web, FTP, TFTP, DNS, and other types of servers with the outside world.

With dynamic NAT configured for overload, the translation stays up for 24 hours and could allow an outside host to try to access the translation and therefore the host. But with overload option, the outside host has to be able to recreate the NAT IP address plus the port number, thereby reducing the likelihood of an unwanted host gaining access to your system.

Step 4

To see the actual translation process and troubleshoot NAT problems, you can use the **debug ip nat** command and its related options.

Remember, as with all **debug** commands, this can seriously impair the performance of your production router and should be used judiciously. The **undebug all** command turns off all debugging.

On SanJose1, use the **debug ip nat** command to turn on the debug feature.

On Host A, ping ISP1's serial interface (10.0.0.5), as shown here:

```
SanJose1#debug ip nat
IP NAT debugging is on
06:37:40: NAT:  s=192.168.0.21->42.0.0.55, d=10.0.0.5 [63]
06:37:40: NAT*: s=10.0.0.5, d=42.0.0.55->192.168.0.21 [63]
06:37:41: NAT*: s=192.168.0.21->42.0.0.55, d=10.0.0.5 [64]
06:37:41: NAT*: s=10.0.0.5, d=42.0.0.55->192.168.0.21 [64]
```

```
06:37:42: NAT*: s=192.168.0.21->42.0.0.55, d=10.0.0.5 [65]
06:37:42: NAT*: s=10.0.0.5, d=42.0.0.55->192.168.0.21 [65]
06:37:43: NAT*: s=192.168.0.21->42.0.0.55, d=10.0.0.5 [66]
06:37:43: NAT*: s=10.0.0.5, d=42.0.0.55->192.168.0.21 [66]
06:38:43: NAT: expiring 42.0.0.55 (192.168.0.21) icmp 1536 (1536)
```

Turn off debugging:

```
SanJose1#undebug all
All possible debugging has been turned off
```

Notice that you can see both translations as the pings pass both ways through the NAT router. Note that the number at the end of the row is the same for both translations of each ping. The s= indicates the source, d= indicates the destination, and -> shows the translation.

The **06:38:43** entry shows the expiration of the NAT translation.

The **detailed** option can be used with **debug ip nat** to provide the port numbers as well as the IP address translations, as shown here:

```
SanJose1#debug ip nat detailed
IP NAT detailed debugging is on
07:03:50: NAT:  i: icmp (192.168.0.21, 1536) -> (10.0.0.5, 1536)
      [101]
07:03:50: NAT:  address not stolen for 192.168.0.21, proto 1 port
      1536
07:03:50: NAT:  ipnat_allocate_port: wanted 1536 got 1536
07:03:50: NAT*: o: icmp (10.0.0.5, 1536) -> (42.0.0.55, 1536) [101]
07:03:51: NAT*: i: icmp (192.168.0.21, 1536) -> (10.0.0.5, 1536)
      [102]
07:03:51: NAT*: o: icmp (10.0.0.5, 1536) -> (42.0.0.55, 1536) [102]
07:03:52: NAT*: i: icmp (192.168.0.21, 1536) -> (10.0.0.5, 1536)
      [103]
07:03:52: NAT*: o: icmp (10.0.0.5, 1536) -> (42.0.0.55, 1536) [103]
07:03:53: NAT*: i: icmp (192.168.0.21, 1536) -> (10.0.0.5, 1536)
      [104]
07:03:53: NAT*: o: icmp (10.0.0.5, 1536) -> (42.0.0.55, 1536) [104]
```

Lab 11-4: Configuring TCP Load Distribution

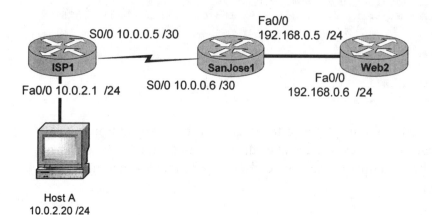

Objective

In this lab, you configure NAT with the TCP Load Distribution option. You also learn to use the **prefix-length** option as an alternative to the **netmask** option of the **ip nat pool** command.

Scenario

When the International Travel Agency (ITA) expanded and updated their network, they chose to use the 192.168.0.0 /24 private addresses and NAT to handle connectivity with the outside world. In securing the outside IP addresses from their ISP, ITA is having to pay a monthly fee per IP address. ITA asked you to set up a series of prototypes that demonstrate NAT's capabilities to meet ITA's requirements. The company hopes to be able to get by with 14 real IP addresses (42.0.0.48 /28). For a variety of reasons including security concerns, the company wishes to hide the internal network from the outside.

ITA's Web server (192.168.0.5) is overwhelmed by outside traffic. You are asked to create a pool of two mirrored servers to handle the load. These servers will be addressed as 192.168.0.5 and 192.168.0.6.

Outside users and DNS use the global IP address, 42.0.0.51, to access the Web server. ITA would like to continue using the single address and have the NAT router distribute the requests among the two mirrored servers. You are asked to create a prototype that demonstrates TCP load distribution using NAT.

Step 1

Build and configure the network according to the previous diagram. Host A represents a user outside of ITA's network; be sure to configure Host A with the correct default gateway. Note that SanJose1's FastEthernet interface should be configured with the IP address 192.168.0.5 /24. This is for testing purposes, so that SanJose1 can respond to HTTP requests directed to 192.168.0.5.

Configure SanJose1 to use a default route to ISP1:

```
SanJose1(config)#ip route 0.0.0.0 0.0.0.0 10.0.0.5
```

On ISP1, configure a static route to the global addresses used by SanJose1 for NAT:

```
ISP1(config)#ip route 42.0.0.48 255.255.255.240 10.0.0.6
```

Specify an interface on SanJose1 to be used by inside network hosts requiring address translation:

```
SanJose1(config)#interface fastethernet0/0
SanJose1(config-if)#ip nat inside
```

You must also specify an interface to be used as the outside NAT interface:

```
SanJose1(config)#interface serial0/0
SanJose1(config-if)#ip nat outside
```

Verify that both workstations can ping 10.0.0.5 and 10.0.0.6. Troubleshoot as necessary.

Step 2

For testing purposes, configure SanJose1 as a Web server at 192.168.0.5, as shown here:

```
SanJose1(config)#ip http server
```

For the purposes of this lab, another router will act as the second Web server. Configure this router, as shown here:

```
Router(config)#hostname Web2
Web2(config)#enable password cisco
Web2(config)#ip default-gateway 192.168.0.5
Web2(config)#no ip routing
Web2(config)#interface fastethernet0/0
Web2(config-if)#ip address 192.168.0.6 255.255.255.0
Web2(config-if)#exit
Web2(config)#ip http server
```

Step 3

Create a NAT pool to represent the planned Web servers, as shown here:

```
SanJose1(config)#ip nat pool WebServers 192.168.0.5 192.168.0.6
        prefix-length 24 type rotary
```

Note: In the preceding command, the keyword **prefix-length** is used instead of the keyword **netmask**. Both keywords specify the subnet mask; the prefix-length option allows you to specify the mask as a bitcount (24 instead of 255.255.255.0). The **type rotary** sets up a round-robin rotation through the designated pool. The name **Web-Servers** is a user-defined variable, so it can be any useful word.

Next, create an access list to define the global address that will be used to access the server pool. Remember, you are to use 42.0.0.51, which was the original Web server IP address that is known to the outside users:

```
SanJose1(config)#access-list 50 permit 42.0.0.51
```

The command that links the pool and the global address is

```
SanJose1(config)#ip nat inside destination list 50 pool
        WebServers
```

The **inside destination** indicates that the NAT translations will be established from the outside network to the inside network.

Step 4

Ping 42.0.0.51 from Host A. The ping should fail because ping uses ICMP and not TCP, which is the only protocol supported by the NAT load distribution feather. To test your configuration, have Host A open a Web browser window.

Type 42.0.0.51 into the address line of the Web browser on Host A. When the following screen appears, use any username and cisco as the password (it's case-sensitive). If the router is not configured with cisco as the enable secret/password, enter the password that it is configured with instead.

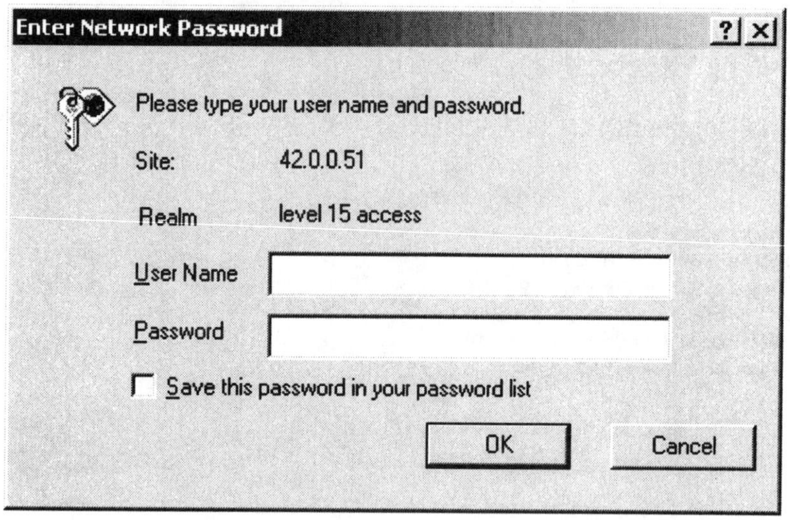

After you authenticate to the router, you should see a page similar to the following:

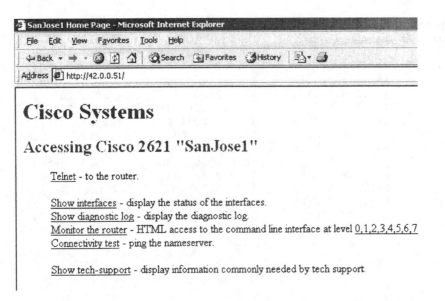

1. What is the inside address of the router whose Web server you are viewing?

_____

Click the Refresh button of the Web browser. A new page should appear, as shown in the following figure.

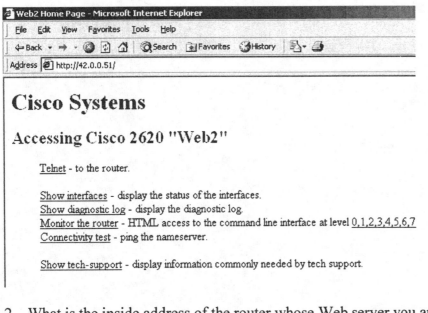

2. What is the inside address of the router whose Web server you are viewing?

_____

3. If you click Refresh again, what will happen?

_____

_____

To verify that SanJose1 is distributing the TCP load among itself and Web2, issue the **show ip nat translation** command, as shown here:

```
SanJose1#show ip nat translation
Pro Inside global      Inside local       Outside local      Outside global
tcp 42.0.0.51:80       192.168.0.5:80     10.0.2.20:1322     10.0.2.20:1322
tcp 42.0.0.51:80       192.168.0.6:80     10.0.2.20:1323     10.0.2.20:1323
tcp 42.0.0.51:80       192.168.0.5:80     10.0.2.20:1324     10.0.2.20:1324
tcp 42.0.0.51:80       192.168.0.6:80     10.0.2.20:1325     10.0.2.20:1325
tcp 42.0.0.51:80       192.168.0.5:80     10.0.2.20:1326     10.0.2.20:1326
tcp 42.0.0.51:80       192.168.0.6:80     10.0.2.20:1327     10.0.2.20:1327
tcp 42.0.0.51:80       192.168.0.5:80     10.0.2.20:1328     10.0.2.20:1328
tcp 42.0.0.51:80       192.168.0.6:80     10.0.2.20:1329     10.0.2.20:1329
tcp 42.0.0.51:80       192.168.0.5:80     10.0.2.20:1330     10.0.2.20:1330
tcp 42.0.0.51:80       192.168.0.6:80     10.0.2.20:1331     10.0.2.20:1331
tcp 42.0.0.51:80       192.168.0.5:80     10.0.2.20:1332     10.0.2.20:1332
tcp 42.0.0.51:80       192.168.0.6:80     10.0.2.20:1333     10.0.2.20:1333
```

NAT Challenge Lab

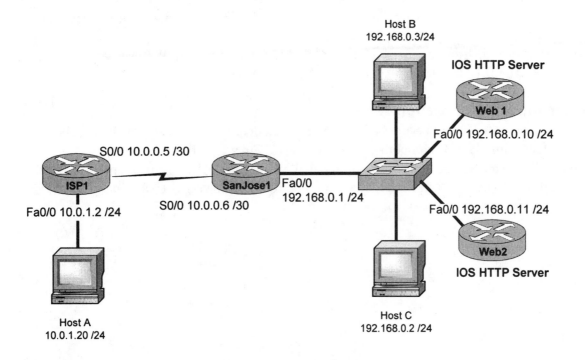

Objective

Configure SanJose1 to use static NAT, dynamic NAT, and TCP load distribution.

Scenario

As the network engineer for the International Travel Agency (ITA), you are responsible for configuring the NAT boundary router. Your ISP has allocated only 14 global addresses for your company's use (42.0.0.48 /28). You must configure NAT to allow over 200 internally addressed hosts to communicate with the outside world using this pool of global addresses.

Design Considerations

You must configure SanJose1 so that all LAN clients in the 192.168.0.0 /24 network can reach the ISP1 router using dynamic NAT. In addition, you must configure static mapping for SanJose1's FastEthernet address (192.168.0.1), so you can manage the router remotely via Telnet. Finally, you need to configure TCP load distribution to distribute HTTP traffic among a pair of mirrored Web servers, represented by the routers Web1 and Web2. Because they are acting only as Web servers, Web1 and Web2 should both be configured with the following commands: **ip default-gateway 192.168.0.1**, **no ip routing**, and **ip http server**.

Implementation Requirements

- Static NAT maps SanJose1's FastEthernet interface to a global IP.
- Dynamic NAT allows any host on the 192.168.0.0 /24 network to communicate with outside hosts.
- TCP load distribution maps a single global IP address to both Web servers (192.168.0.10 and 192.168.0.11).

Implementation Completion Tests

- Host A can Telnet to SanJose1 by using the statically mapped global IP address.
- Host B and Host C can both ping Host A and Telnet to ISP1.
- Host A can browse both Web servers at Web1 and Web2 by using a single global IP address. The Web page alternates from one router to the other each time the browser window is refreshed.

Lab 12-1: Router Security and AAA Authentication

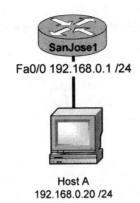

SanJose1

Fa0/0 192.168.0.1 /24

Host A
192.168.0.20 /24

Objectives

In this lab, use the **login local** command to configure authentication and access levels.

Also, you are introduced to the Cisco IOS AAA security authentication features, including custom prompts and debug features.

Scenario

The International Travel Agency (ITA) is concerned about the security of their routers and switches. You are asked to create a prototype of Cisco's login security features including AAA.

Step 1

Before beginning this lab, it is recommended that you reload the routers after erasing their startup configuration. This prevents you from having problems caused by residual configurations.

Build and configure the network according to the previous diagram. Use the following commands to configure SanJose1:

```
SanJose1(config)#enable password cisco
SanJose1(config)#line vty 0 4
SanJose1(config-line)#login
SanJose1(config-line)#password cisco
SanJose1(config-line)#line aux 0
SanJose1(config-line)#login
SanJose1(config-line)#password cisco
SanJose1(config-line)#exit
```

Verify that the router can ping the workstation.

Step 2

Security for the user EXEC mode can be configured for each of the three access methods: VTY (Telnet), AUX, and console. VTYs and AUX port access require a login password by default. If no password is set, the router does not establish a session. Instead, it returns an error message explaining that a password is required but not set.

By default, the console port is not configured to request a login password. Typically, it is a smart idea to configure the console port with the **login** command, so that a password is required. Without password security, anyone with a laptop and a console cable can gain access to the device easily.

The following table shows each of the three access methods, their associated command syntax, and an example using the same password for each method. It is possible (and recommended) to set different passwords for each access method.

Password Type	Access Method	Syntax	Example
Console session	Console port	line con 0 password *password* login	line con 0 password cisco login
Telnet session	VTY interfaces (example syntax sets all five virtual interfaces at once)	line vty 0 4 password *password* login	line vty 0 4 password cisco login
AUX session	AUX port (if present, can be accessed via a modem)	line AUX 0 password *password* login	line AUX 0 password cisco login

The **login** command requires that the user authenticate when connecting to the line. When the **login** command is used without optional keywords, the password must be defined by the **password** command, as shown in the Example column of the table.

Telnet to SanJose1 from Host A. Verify that you must supply the password, cisco, to gain user-level access to the router.

Step 3

It is possible to require a username and a password for logins to the router. Moreover, you can configure different username/password combinations for different users. These username/password combinations can be stored locally, in the router's database, or remotely, on a specialized security server.

Configure a local username/password database for SanJose1, as shown here:

```
SanJose1(config)#username remote password access
SanJose1(config)#username scott password wolfe
```

Add an entry with your first name as the username and your last name as the password.

To finish the configuration, issue the **login local** command for line con 0, as shown here:

```
SanJose1(config)#line con 0
SanJose1(config-line)#login local
```

The keyword **local** instructs the router to check username/password combinations against the local database. Now only the defined combinations of usernames and passwords can be used to access the user mode from the router's console. Like all passwords in the Cisco IOS, these passwords are case sensitive and can include text and/or numbers. The usernames are not case-sensitive.

Exit out of the session and then log in to SanJose1 from the console port. The new access prompts will look like this:

```
User Access Verification

Username: remote
Password:
SanJose1>exit

User Access Verification

Username: ScOtT
Password:
% Login invalid          (Used the wrong case on the password)

Username: ScOtT
Password:
SanJose1>                (Used the correct case on the password)
```

From Host A, Telnet to SanJose1 and confirm that you are prompted only for a password. The password cisco should still work.

You can also configure the AUX and VTYs to check username/password combinations against the local database. Enter the following commands, on SanJose1:

```
SanJose1(config)#line aux 0
SanJose1(config-line)#login local
SanJose1(config)#line vty 0 4
SanJose1(config-line)#login local
```

From Host A, Telnet to SanJose1 and confirm that you need to enter one of the username/password combinations.

Step 4

The Cisco IOS AAA feature offers several security measures. In this step, you examine the authentication feature. The AAA authentication feature is used to validate users.

Warning: It is important to have a plan when configuring AAA because configuration commands take effect immediately. It is possible to lock yourself out of the router.

Enter the following lines in SanJose1:

```
SanJose1(config)#aaa new-model
SanJose1(config)#username admin password aaacisco
SanJose1(config)#aaa authentication login default local enable
```

The **aaa new-model** command enables AAA. After this command is entered, the console, VTY, AUX, and TTY ports require a username and password for access.

The **aaa authentication login default** command defines how the username/password will be checked. Multiple options can be used with this command. The first option, which, in this case, is "local," will be tried first. In the event the attempt to check a username/password using this method returns an error, the second method will be tried, and so on. It is important to note that an authentication failure is not an error. An error results only if the specified source, such as a remote server, cannot be read. The available options for the **aaa authentication login default** command are

```
SanJose1(config)#aaa authentication login default ?
  enable       Use enable password for authentication.
  group        Use Server-group   (used to access TACACS or RADIUS
     servers)
  line         Use line password for authentication.
  local        Use local username authentication.
  local-case   Use case-sensitive local username authentication.
```

If you had a TACACS+ server configured with username/password combinations, you could configure the router with the command, **aaa authentication login default group tacacs+ local enable.** The **group** keyword indicates a server group while the **tacacs+** parameter specifies the type of security server. As the second specified option in this example command, the local database would only be used if the TACACS+ server could not be reached.

From Host A, Telnet to SanJose1 and confirm that you are prompted for a username and password. Confirm that **admin** and **aaacisco** grant you access to the router.

Disconnect from SanJose1 and then attempt to log in again. This time, verify that the username is not case-sensitive but the password is.

In some cases, you might want usernames to be case-sensitive. You can configure AAA to make usernames case-sensitive by issuing the following command on SanJose1:

```
SanJose1(config)#aaa authentication login default local-case enable
```

After entering this command, log out and then log back in to the router. Verify that both the username and password are now case sensitive.

Step 5

The default login prompt looks like this:

```
User Access Verification

Username:
```

When using AAA, you have the option of presenting a more specific and/or user-friendly prompt. Issue the following command on SanJose1:

```
SanJose1(config)#aaa authentication username-prompt "Enter your NT
    username:"
```

To verify the new prompt, exit out of the console session and log back in.

Step 6

In this step, you look at the **debug aaa authentication** command feature. On SanJose1 activate the debug feature with the following command:

```
SanJose1#debug aaa authentication
AAA Authentication debugging is on
```

From Host A, Telnet to SanJose1 and press Enter the first time you are prompted for a username. The second time, use a bogus username/password combination. On the third and final attempt, log in correctly.

A partial display of the **debug** output will look like the following lines. The first four lines set up the login session. Note that the number (1421093628) tracks the session until the failed password and a new tracking number are generated.

```
02:48:32: AAA: parse name=tty2 idb type=-1 tty=-1
02:48:32: AAA: name=tty2 flags=0x11 type=5 shelf=0 slot=0 adapter=0
        port=2 chann
el=0
02:48:32: AAA/MEMORY: create_user (0x1FEC44) user='' ruser=''
        port='tty2' rem_ad
dr='192.168.0.10' authen_type=ASCII service=LOGIN priv=1
02:48:32: AAA/AUTHEN/START (1421093628): port='tty2' list=''
        action=LOGIN servic
e=LOGIN
02:48:32: AAA/AUTHEN/START (1421093628): using "default" list
02:48:32: AAA/AUTHEN/START (1421093628): Method=LOCALCASE
02:48:32: AAA/AUTHEN (1421093628): status = GETUSER
```

```
02:48:33: AAA/AUTHEN/CONT (1421093628): continue_login
        (user='(undef)')
02:48:33: AAA/AUTHEN (1421093628): status = GETUSER
02:48:33: AAA/AUTHEN/CONT (1421093628): Method=LOCALCASE
02:48:33: AAA/AUTHEN/LOCAL (1421093628): no username: GETUSER
02:48:33: AAA/AUTHEN (1421093628): status = GETUSER
SanJose1#
02:48:45: AAA/AUTHEN/CONT (1421093628): continue_login (user='')
02:48:45: AAA/AUTHEN (1421093628): status = GETUSER
02:48:45: AAA/AUTHEN/CONT (1421093628): Method=LOCALCASE
02:48:45: AAA/AUTHEN (1421093628): User not found, emulating local-
        override
02:48:45: AAA/AUTHEN (1421093628): status = ERROR
02:48:45: AAA/AUTHEN/START (297482216): port='tty2' list=''
        action=LOGIN service
=LOGIN
```

The (297482216) attempt ends up as a failed attempt – bad password, as shown here:

```
        (lines omitted)
02:48:49: AAA/AUTHEN (297482216): password incorrect
02:48:49: AAA/AUTHEN (297482216): status = FAIL
```

The following lines are a partial display of the successful attempt:

```
        (lines omitted)
02:48:57: AAA/AUTHEN/CONT (782251026): continue_login (user='bob')
02:48:57: AAA/AUTHEN (782251026): status = GETPASS
02:48:57: AAA/AUTHEN/CONT (782251026): Method=LOCALCASE
02:48:57: AAA/AUTHEN (782251026): status = PASS
```

Use **undebug all** to turn off all debugging.

Lab 12-2: Configuring AAA Authorization and Accounting

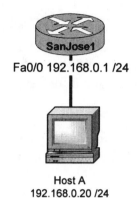

Fa0/0 192.168.0.1 /24

Host A
192.168.0.20 /24

Objectives

In this lab, you use the **exec-timeout** command to control the amount of time before an idle Telnet or console session is terminated.

You are also introduced to the Cisco IOS AAA security authorization and accounting features, which can be implemented to limit the EXEC commands that a user is permitted to use.

Scenario

The International Travel Agency (ITA) is concerned about the security of its routers and switches. You are asked to create a prototype of Cisco's login security features including AAA and CiscoSecure.

Step 1

Before beginning this lab, it is recommended that you reload the routers after erasing their startup configuration. This prevents you from having problems caused by residual configurations.

Build and configure the network according to the above diagram. Use the following commands to configure SanJose1:

```
SanJose1(config)#line con 0
SanJose1(config-line)#exec-timeout 0 0
SanJose1(config-line)#password cisco
SanJose1(config-line)#logging synchronous
SanJose1(config-line)#transport input none
SanJose1(config-line)#enable password cisco
SanJose1(config-line)#line vty 0 4
SanJose1(config-line)#login
SanJose1(config-line)#password cisco
SanJose1(config-line)#exec-timeout 0 0
SanJose1(config-line)#line aux 0
SanJose1(config-line)#exec-timeout 0 0
SanJose1(config-line)#login
SanJose1(config-line)#password cisco
```

The **exec-timeout 0 0** commands configure the amount of time a router will wait before terminating an idle EXEC session. The first number specifies the number of minutes, and the second number specifies the number of seconds. Thus, the command **exec-timeout 0 45** would configure the idle timer to 45 seconds. Using two zeros, as previously shown, configures the router so that EXEC sessions never time out. Such a configuration is a security risk, because unattended sessions will remain open, and could potentially be exploited by a malicious user. While configuring **exec-timeout 0 0** is uncommon on production routers, it is a useful configuration when performing lab exercises.

It is possible to set different timeout values for each of the CON, VTY, and AUX sessions. The default timeout for all three of these lines is 10 minutes.

Step 2

The AAA feature can be used to limit a user's options based on the username/password entered during login.

By default, there are three privilege levels on the router:

Privilege Level	Result
1	User level only (prompt is router>), the default level for login
15	Privileged level (prompt is router#), the level after going into enable mode
0	Seldom used, but includes five commands: disable, enable, exit, help, and logout

You can define levels 2-14 by "moving" commands from one of the default privilege levels to the new level. Configuring custom privilege levels can involve significant administration on the router.

To determine your current privilege level, type the **show privilege** command:

```
SanJose1#show privilege
Current privilege level is 15
```

1. While in user EXEC mode, what is your privilege level?

_____

2. While in privileged EXEC mode, what is your privilege level?

_____

To configure a custom privilege level (in this case, level 7), add the following entries to the authentication database on SanJose1:

```
SanJose1(config)#username cisco0 privilege 0 password cisco0
SanJose1(config)#username cisco15 privilege 15 password cisco15
SanJose1(config)#username cisco7 privilege 7 password cisco7
SanJose1(config)#aaa new-model
SanJose1(config)#aaa authentication login default local
```

Now exit out completely from EXEC mode and log back into the router using the username cisco15 and password cisco15. By logging in with privilege level 15, you will prevent the router from locking you out when you begin to configure AAA authorization.

Note: You must log in as a user with privilege level 15 in order to begin modifying the default privilege level of IOS commands. Failure to do so will result in console session lockout when you enter the **aaa authorization exec default local** command.

After you authenticate as cisco15, you can configure AAA authorization and create a custom privilege level. First, enter the following configuration command:

```
SanJose1(config)#aaa authorization exec default local
```

Next, specify which commands will be authorized. On SanJose1, issue the following commands from the console:

```
SanJose1(config)#aaa authorization commands 0 default local
SanJose1(config)#aaa authorization commands 15 default local
SanJose1(config)#aaa authorization commands 7 default local
```

After issuing these commands, a user must be "authorized" to use commands in privilege levels 0, 7, and 15.

The command to configure the router to query a TACACS+ server first would be **aaa authorization commands 0 default group tacacs+ local enable**. The **group** key-word indicates a server group while the **tacacs+** keyword indicates the type of security server. If configured with this command, the local database on SanJose1 would only be used if the TACACS+ server were unavailable.

The final step is to specify which commands will exist in privilege level 7. On SanJose1, issue the following commands from the console:

```
SanJose1(config)#privilege configure level 7 snmp-server host
SanJose1(config)#privilege configure level 7 snmp-server enable
SanJose1(config)#privilege configure level 7 snmp-server
SanJose1(config)#privilege exec level 7 ping
SanJose1(config)#privilege exec level 7 configure terminal
SanJose1(config)#privilege exec level 7 configure
```

Now enter the **debug aaa authorization** command so you can observe the authoriza-tion process.

Step 3

From Host A, Telnet to SanJose1 and log in as cisco15. Note that, because you have logged on with privilege level 15, you are immediately given privileged EXEC access.

Type the **show privilege** command and verify your privilege level. Enter global configuration mode, and note the debug results on SanJose1's console session.

Exit out of the Telnet session.

Now log back into the router as cisco0.

3. After you authenticate as cisco0, can you enter privileged EXEC mode?

_____

As cisco0, enter the **?** command at the router prompt.

4. How many commands are available to privilege level 0?

_____

Exit out of the Telnet session, and log in as cisco7. Note that this user, like cisco15, begins an EXEC session in privileged mode.

Enter global configuration and use the **?** command to see which commands are available in privilege level 7, as shown here:

```
SanJose1#config terminal
```

Enter configuration commands, one per line. End with Ctrl+Z.

```
SanJose1(config)#?
Configure commands:
  default      Set a command to its defaults
  end          Exit from configure mode
  exit         Exit from configure mode
  help         Description of the interactive help system
  no           Negate a command or set its defaults
  snmp-server  Modify SNMP parameters
```

Note the debug output on SanJose1. Use the **undebug all** command to turn off all debugging.

Step 4

In this step, you configure AAA accounting on SanJose1. If you do not have a TACACS+ server, the results will not be stored but the recording will occur.

```
SanJose1(config)# aaa accounting exec default start-stop group
     tacacs+
SanJose1(config)# aaa accounting commands 15 default start-stop group
     tacacs+
SanJose1(config)# aaa accounting network default start-stop group
     tacacs+
SanJose1(config)# aaa accounting connection default start-stop group
     tacacs+
SanJose1(config)# aaa accounting system default start-stop group
     tacacs+
```

The following is a brief description of each of the previous command options:

Option	Result
AAA	Identifies an AAA command.
accounting	Accounting – or tracking feature of AAA.
exec	Tracks EXEC commands on the device
commands 15	Tracks commands by privilege level 15 users (can be 0-15)
network	Tracks network services like PPP
connection	Tracks outbound Telnet sessions
system	Tracks system events like reload
start-stop	Include both Start and Stop recordings (compared to *stop-only*)
default	Use the default list as compared to a custom list
group	Use a group of servers
TACACS+	Use TACACS+ instead of a RADIUS server

On SanJose1, enable **debug aaa accounting** with the following command:

```
SanJose1#debug aaa accounting
AAA Accounting debugging is on
```

From Host A, Telnet to SanJose1 and authenticate as cisco15. In the Telnet session, perform a couple of simple commands, such as **show run**. Return to the console session on SanJose1 and examine the debug output. The following debug output resulted from cisco15 entering the **show running-config** and **copy running-config startup-config** commands:

```
01:04:59: AAA/ACCT/CMD: User cisco15, Port tty2, Priv 15:
        "show running-config <cr>"
01:04:59: AAA/ACCT/CMD: Found list "default"
01:04:59: AAA/ACCT: user cisco15, acct type 3 (3901449983):
      Method=tacacs+ (tacacs+)
01:05:20: AAA/ACCT/CMD: User cisco15, Port tty2, Priv 15:
        "copy running-config startup-config <cr>"
01:05:20: AAA/ACCT/CMD: Found list "default"
01:05:20: AAA/ACCT: user cisco15, acct type 3 (2545785330):
      Method=tacacs+ (tacacs+)
```

Lab 12-3: Using a TACACS+ Server

Fa0/0 192.168.0.1 /24

TACACS+ Server
(CiscoSecure)

Objective

In this lab, you configure AAA to use a TACACS+ server.

Scenario

The International Travel Agency (ITA) has set up and configured a CiscoSecure
TACACS+ server and needs to place the routers under the control of the TACACS+
server. You might need to modify the hostname and IP address of your router.

Step 1

The host shown in the previous diagram can be running CiscoSecure software to
provide TACACS+ services. Configure SanJose1 using the following commands as
an example:

```
SanJose1(config)#line con 0
SanJose1(config-line)#exec-timeout 0 0
SanJose1(config-line)#password cisco
SanJose1(config-line)#logging synchronous
SanJose1(config-line)#transport input none
SanJose1(config-line)#enable password cisco
SanJose1(config-line)#line vty 0 4
SanJose1(config-line)#login
SanJose1(config-line)#password cisco
SanJose1(config-line)#exec-timeout 0 0
SanJose1(config-line)#line aux 0
SanJose1(config-line)#exec-timeout 0 0
SanJose1(config-line)#login
SanJose1(config-line)#password cisco
```

Confirm that SanJose1 can ping the TACACS+ server.

Your instructor will provide the IP address of the TACACS+ server and an encryp-
tion key, which is required to establish a connection between the router and the
server. Your instructor will also provide you with a username/password combination
(already entered in the CiscoSecure database).

Step 2

On SanJose1, add the following configuration lines:

```
SanJose1(config)#aaa new-model
SanJose1(config)#username admin password aaacisco
SanJose1(config)#aaa authentication login default group tacacs+ local
    enable
SanJose1(config)#tacacs-server host xxx.xxx.xxx.xxx    (ip address of
    tecacs+ server)
SanJose1(config)#tacacs-server key xxxxx                (get key from
    the instructor)
```

Exit from SanJose1 and then try to log in with the username of nobody and the password nothing. This should fail if you have a working connection to the TACACS+ server. If the login does not fail, reload the routers and try again.

After the login using **nobody** fails, log in as the user assigned to you by your instructor. This login should work, indicating that SanJose1 has successfully queried the TACACS+ server, and authenticated your username and password.

1. If you did not know any of the valid username/password combinations stored on the TACACS+ server, how could you gain access to the router?

_____

_____

Simulate a network outage by disconnecting the cable from SanJose1's FastEthernet interface. Attempt to log in to the router a second time via the console port.

2. Because the router's attempt to query the TACACS+ server will fail, which authentication method will be used? Why?

_____

_____

When you attempt to log in, SanJose1 will try to query the TACACS+ server first. Because the network connection to the server is unavailable, this query returns an error. The second method of authentication defined by the **aaa authentication** command specifies that the local database should be consulted next. Thus, you should be able to authenticate as **admin** using the password **aaacisco**.

Once you have authenticated, enter the following command on SanJose1:

```
SanJose1(config)#no username admin password aaacisco
```

3. If no TCP/IP connection to the TACACS+ server is available, and no local username/password database exists on the router, which authentication method will be used? Why?

_____

_____

Exit the console session on SanJose1 and log back in again. Eventually, you will be prompted for a username. Enter the username **admin**, and—when prompted—enter the password of **aaacisco**. This authentication attempt will return an error, because there is no local username/password database. Remember, an error is not the same as an authentication failure. A failure occurs when the authentication method is operational, but the username/password combination is found to be invalid.

The third method of authentication defined by the **aaa authentication** command specifies that the enable password (or secret, if it exists) should be used in the event the first two authentication methods return an error.

You should be able to access the router using the enable password, cisco.

Appendix A

Command Reference

Labs 2

Configuration Commands

Command	Definition
Router(config-if)#**physical-layer** {**sync** | **async**}	Specifies the mode of a slow-speed serial interface on a router as either synchronous or asynchronous.
Router(config)#**line** [**aux** | **console** | **tty** | **vty**] *line number* [*ending-line-number*]	Identifies a specific line for configuration and starts the line configuration mode.
Router(config-line)#**login** [**local** | **tacacs**]	Enables password checking at login.
Router(config-line)#**speed** *bps*	Sets the terminal baud rate.
Router(config-line)#**flowcontrol** {**none** | **software** [**lock**] [**in** | **out**] | **hardware** [**in** | **out**]}	Sets the method of data flow control between the terminal or other serial device and the router.
Router(config-line)#**modem inout**	Configures a line for both incoming and outgoing calls.
Router(config-line)#**transport input** {**all** | **lat** | **mop** | **nasi** | **none** | **pad** | **rlogin** | **telnet** | **v120**}	Defines which protocols to use to connect to a specific line of the router.
Router(config-line)# **stopbits** {**1** | **1.5** | **2**}	Sets the number of stop bits transmitted per byte.
Router#**telnet** *host* [*port*] [*keyword*]	Logs on to a host that supports Telnet.
Router# **disconnect** [*connection*]	Disconnects a line.
Router(config)#**modem autoconfigure discovery**	Configures a line to discover what kind of modem is connected to the router and configure that modem automatically.
Router(config)#**async mode dedicated**	Places a line into dedicated asynchronous mode using SLIP or PPP encapsulation.
Router(config-if)#**dialer in-band** [**no-parity** | **odd-parity**]	Specifies that dial-on-demand routing (DDR) is to be supported.
Router(config-if)#**dialer idle-timeout** *seconds*	Specifies the idle time before the line is disconnected.
Router(config-if)#**dialer wait-for-carrier-time** *seconds*	Specifies the length of time the interface waits for a carrier.
Router(config-if)#**dialer hold-queue** *packets*	Allows interesting outgoing packets to be queued until a modem connection is established.
Router(config-if)#**dialer-group** *group-number*	Controls access by configuring an interface to belong to a specific dialing group.

Command	Definition
Router(config-if)#**dialer map** *protocol next-hop-address* [name *hostname*] [**spc**] [speed 56 | 64] [broadcast] [modem-script *modem-regexp*] [system-script *system-regexp*] [*dial-string*[:*isdn-subaddress*]]	Configures a serial interface or ISDN interface to call one or more sites or to receive calls from multiple sites.
Router(config)#**chat-script** *script-name expect-send*	Creates a script that will place a call over a modem.
Router(config)#**dialer-list** *dialer-group* **protocol** *protocol-name* {**permit** | **deny** | list *access-list-number* | *access-group*}	Defines a DDR dialer list to control dialing by protocol or by a combination of protocol and access list.

show Commands

Command	Definition
Router#**show line** [*line-number*]	Displays a terminal line's parameters.
Router# **show dialer** [**interface** *type number*]	Displays general diagnostic information for interfaces configured for DDR.

debug Commands

Command	Definition
Router#**debug confmodem**	Displays information associated with the discovery and configuration of the modem attached to the router.

Labs 3

Configuration Commands

Command	Definition
Router(config-if)# **peer default ip address** {*ip-address* | **dhcp** | **pool** [*pool-name*]}	Specifies an IP address from a specific IP address pool, or an address from the DHCP mechanism to be returned to a remote peer connecting to this interface.
Router(config-line)#**autoselect** {**arap** | **ppp** | **slip** | **during-login**}	Configures a line to start an ARA, PPP, or SLIP session, use [[using?]] the **autoselect** line configuration command.
Router#**ppp** {/**default** | {*remote-ip-address* | *remote-name*} [@*tacacs-server*]} [/**routing**]	Starts an asynchronous connection using PPP.
Router(config-if)# **ppp authentication** {**chap** | **chap pap** | **pap chap** | **pap**} [**if-needed**] [*list-name* | **default**] [**callin**]	Specifies the order in which the CHAP or PAP protocols are requested on the interface.
Router(config-if)#**ppp compress** [**predictor** | **stac**]	Configures software compression for PPP encapsulation.
Router(config-if)# **ip tcp header-compression** [**on** | **off** | **passive**]	Configures TCP header compression on the asynchronous link.

Command	Definition
Router(config-if)#**ppp callback** {**accept** | **request**}	Enables a dialer interface that is not a data terminal ready (DTR) interface to function either as a callback client that requests callback or as a callback server that accepts callback requests.
Router(config-if)#**dialer callback-secure**	Enables callback security.
Router(config-if)#**dialer callback-server** [**username** **dialstring**]	Enables an interface to make return calls when callback is successfully negotiated.
Router(config)# **map-class dialer** *classname*	Defines a class of shared configuration parameters for PPP callback.
Router(config-if)# **ppp pap sent-username** *username* **password** *password*	Enables remote PAP support for an interface and uses the **sent-username** and **password** elements in the PAP authentication request packet to the peer.

show Command

Command	Definition
Router#**show compress**	Displays compression statistics.

debug Commands

Command	Definition
Router# **debug ppp** {**packet** | **negotiation** | **error** | **authentication** | **compression** | **cbcp**}	Displays information on traffic and exchanges in an internetwork implementing the PPP.
Router#**debug dialer**	Displays debugging information about the packets received on a dialer interface.

Labs 5

Configuration Commands

Command	Definition
Router(config)#**isdn switch-type** *switch-type*	Specifies the central office switch type on the ISDN interface.
Router(config-if)#**isdn spid1** *spid-number* [*ldn*]	Defines the service profile identifier (SPID) number that has been assigned by the ISDN service provider for the B1 channel.
Router(config-if)#**isdn spid2** *spid-number* [*ldn*]	Defines the service profile identifier (SPID) number that has been assigned by the ISDN service provider for the B1 channel.
Router#**show isdn** {**active** | **history** | **memory** | **status** [*dsl* | *interface-type number*] | **timers**}	Displays the information about calls, history, memory, status, and Layer 2 and Layer 3 timers.
Router#**clear interface** *type number* .	Resets the hardware logic on an interface.
Router(config-if)# **snapshot server** *active-time* [**dialer**]	Configures a server router for snapshot routing.

Command	Definition
Router(config-if)#**dialer map snapshot** *sequence-number dial-string*	Defines a dialer map for Cisco's snapshot routing protocol on a client router connected to a DDR interface.
Router(config-if)#**snapshot client** *active-time quiet-time* [**suppress-statechange-updates**] [**dialer**]	Configures a client router for snapshot routing.
Router(config-if)#**ppp multilink**	Enables multilink PPP on an interface.
Router(config-if)# **dialer load-threshold** *load* [**outbound** | **inbound** | **either**]	Configures bandwidth on demand by setting the maximum load before the dialer places another call to a destination.

show Commands

Command	Definition
Router#**show snapshot** [*type number*]	Displays snapshot routing parameters associated with an interface.
Router #**show ppp multilink**	Display bundle information for multilink PPP bundles.

debug Commands

Command	Definition
Router#**debug isdn event**	Displays ISDN events occurring on the user side (on the router) of the ISDN interface.

Labs 6

Configuration Commands

Command	Definition
Router(config-if)# **dialer pool-member** *number* [**priority** *priority*] [**min-link** *minimum*] [**max-link** *maximum*]	Configures a physical interface to be a member of a dialer profile dialing pool.
Router(config-if)# **dialer pool** *number*	Specifies, for a dialer interface, which dialing pool to use to connect to a specific destination subnetwork.
Router(config-if)# **dialer remote-name** *username*	Specifies for a dialer interface the authentication name of the remote router on the destination subnetwork.
Router(config-if)#**dialer string** *dial-string* [**class** *class-name*]	Specifies the string (telephone number) to be used when placing a call from an interface.
Router#**isdn disconnect interface** *interface* {**b1** | **b2** | **all**}	Disconnects an ISDN data call without bringing down the interface.
Router#**interface dialer** *number*	Specifies the string (telephone number) to be used when placing a call from an interface.

Labs 7

Configuration Commands

Command	Definition
Router(config)#**x25 routing [tcp-use-if-defs]**	Enables X.25 switching or tunneling.
Router(config-if)#**encapsulation x25 [dte | dce]** **[ddn | bfe] | [ietf]**	Specifies a serial interface's operation as an X.25 device.
Router(config)#**x25 route** [#*position*] [*selection*] [*modification*] *disposition* [*xot-keepalive*]	Creates an entry in the X.25 routing table.
Router(config-if)#**x25 address** *x121-address*	Sets the X.121 address of a particular network interface.
Router(config-if)#**x25 map** *protocol address* [*protocol2 address2*[...[*protocol9 address9*]]] *x121-address* [*option*]	Configures the LAN protocols-to-remote host mapping.
Router(config-if)#**x25 ltc** *circuit-number*	Sets the lowest two-way virtual circuit number.
Router(config-if)#**x25 htc** *circuit-number*	Sets the highest two-way virtual circuit number.
Router(config-if)#**x25 pvc** *circuit protocol address* [*protocol2 address2*[...[*protocol9 address9*]]] *x121-address* [*option*]	Establishes an X.25 permanent virtual circuit (PVC).

show Commands

Command	Definition
show x25 route	Displays the X.25 routing table.
show x25 vc [*lcn*]	Displays information about active switched virtual circuits (SVCs) and PVCs.

Labs 8

Configuration Commands

Command	Definition
Router(config-if)#**encapsulation frame-relay** **[cisco | ietf]**	Enables Frame Relay encapsulation.
Router(config-if)#**frame-relay lmi-type** **{ansi | cisco | q933a}**	Configures the Local Management Interface (LMI) type.
Router#**clear frame-relay-inarp**	Clears dynamically created Frame Relay maps, which are created by the use of Inverse Address Resolution Protocol (Inverse ARP).
Router(config-if)#**frame-relay interface-dlci** *dlci* **[ietf | cisco]** [voice-encap size]	Assigns a data link connection identifier (DLCI) to a specified Frame Relay subinterface on the router or access server.
Router(config-if)#**frame-relay map** *protocol* *protocol-address dlci* **[broadcast] [ietf | cisco]**	Defines the mapping between a destination protocol address and the DLCI used to connect to the destination address.
Router(config-if)#**frame-relay inverse-arp** [*protocol*] [*dlci*]	Enables Inverse ARP on a specified interface or subinterface.

Command	Definition
Router(config-if)#**ip split-horizon**	Enables the split horizon mechanism.
Router(config)#**map-class frame-relay** *map-class-name*	Specifies a map class to define quality of service (QOS) values for an SVC.
Router(config-map-class)#**frame-relay adaptive-shaping** {**becn** | foresight}	Configures a router to respond to either BECN or ForeSight backward congestion notification messages.
Router(config-if)#**frame-relay traffic-shaping**	Enables both traffic shaping and per-virtual circuit queuing for all PVCs and SVCs on a Frame Relay interface
Router(config-if)#**frame-relay class** *name*	Associates a map class with an interface or subinterface.

show Commands

Command	Definition
Router# **show frame-relay lmi** [*type number*]	Displays the statistics about the Local Management Interface.
Router# **show frame-relay map**	Displays the current map entries and information about the connections.
Router# **show frame-relay pvc** [*type number* [*dlci*]]	Displays statistics about PVCs for Frame Relay interfaces.

Labs 9

Configuration Commands

Command	Definition
Router(config-if)#**backup interface** *type number*	Configures an interface as a secondary or dial backup.
Router(config-if)# **backup delay** {*enable-delay* | **never**} {*disable-delay* | **never**}	Defines how much time should elapse before a secondary line status changes after a primary line status has changed.
Router(config-if)# **backup load** {*enable-threshold* | **never**} {disable-threshold | **never**}	Sets a traffic load threshold for dial backup service.

show Command

Command	Definition
Router#**show backup**	Displays the backup interface and the status.

Labs 10

Configuration Commands

Command	Definition
Router(config-if)# **fair-queue** [congestive-discard-threshold [dynamic-queues [reservable-queues]]]	Enables weighted fair queuing for an interface.

Command	Definition
Router(config)# **priority-list** list-number **protocol** protocol-name {**high** | **medium** | **normal** | **low**} queue-keyword keyword-value	Establishes queuing priorities based upon the protocol type.
Router(config)# **priority-list** list-number **interface** interface-type interface-number {**high** | **medium** | **normal** |**low**}	Establishes queuing priorities on packets entering from a given interface.
Router(config)# **priority-list** list-number **default** {**high** | **medium** | **normal** | **low**} -	Assigns a priority queue for those packets that do not match any other rule in the queue list.
Router(config)# **priority-list** list-number **queue-limit** [high-limit [medium-limit [normal-limit [low-limit]]]	Designates the queue length limit for a queue.
Router(config-if)# **priority-group** list-number	Assigns the specified priority list to an interface.
Router(config-if)#**custom-queue-list** list	Assigns a custom queue list to an interface.
Router(config)#**queue-list** *list-number* **default** *queue-number*	Assigns a priority queue for those packets that do not match any other rule in the queue list.
Router(config)#**queue-list** list-number **queue** queue-number **limit** limit-number	Designates the queue length limit for a queue.
Router(config)#**queue-list** list-number **queue** queue-number **byte-count** byte-count-number	Specifies how many bytes the system allows to be delivered from a given queue during a particular cycle.
Router(config)#**queue-list** list-number **protocol** protocol-name queue-number queue-keyword keyword-value	Establishes queuing priority based upon the protocol type.
Router(config)#**queue-list** list-number **interface** interface-type interface-number queue-number	Establishes queuing priorities on packets entering on an interface.

show Commands

Command	Definition
Router# **show queueing** [**custom** | **fair** | **priority** | **red**]	Lists all or selected configured queuing strategies.
Router# **show interfaces** [interface] **fair-queue**	Displays information and all statistics about weighted fair queuing for a VIP-based interface.

Labs 11

Configuration Commands

Command	Definition
Router(config)#**ip nat inside source** {**list** {*access-list-number* | *name*} {**pool** *name* | **interface** *dialer-name*} [**overload**] | **static** *local-ip global-ip*}	Enables NAT of the inside source address.
Router(config-if)#**ip nat** {**inside** | **outside**}	Designates that traffic originating from or destined for the interface is subject to NAT.

Command	Definition
Router(config)#**ip nat pool** *name start-ip end-ip* {**netmask** *netmask* | **prefix-length** *prefix-length*}[**type rotary**]	Defines a pool of IP addresses for NAT.
Router(config-if)#**ip nat inside source** {**list** {*access-list-number* | *name*} **pool** *name* [**overload**] | **static** *local-ip global-ip*}	Enables NAT of the inside source address.
Router(config)#**ip http server**	Enables the Cisco IOS Web server.

show Commands

Command	Definition
show ip nat translations [**verbose**]	Displays active NAT translations.
show ip nat statistics	Displays NAT statistics.

Labs 12

Configuration Commands

Command	Definition
Router(config)#**aaa new-model**	Enables the AAA access control model.
Router(config)# **tacacs-server host hostname** [**single-connection**] [**port integer**] [**timeout integer**] [**key string**]	Specifies a TACACS host.
Router(config)#**tacacs-server key** *key*	Sets the authentication encryption key used for all TACACS+ communications between the access server and the TACACS+ daemon.
Router(config)# **radius-server host** {*hostname* | *ip-address*} [**auth-port** *port-number*] [**acct-port** *port-number*]	Specifies a RADIUS server host.
Router(config)#**radius-server key** {*string*}	Sets the authentication and encryption key for all RADIUS communications between the router and the RADIUS daemon.
Router(config)# **aaa authentication login** {**default** | *list-name*} *method1* [*method2...*]	Sets AAA authentication at login, using the AAA authentication login global configuration command.
Router(config)# **aaa authentication arap** {**default** | *list-name*} *method1* [*method2...*]	Enables an AAA authentication method for AppleTalk Remote Access (ARA) using RADIUS or TACACS+.
Router(config)# **aaa authentication enable default** *method1* [*method2...*]	Enables AAA authentication to determine if a user can access the privileged command level.
Router(config)#**aaa authentication local-override**	Configures the Cisco IOS software to check the local user database for authentication before attempting another form of authentication.
Router(config)# **aaa authentication login** {**default** | *list-name*} *method1* [*method2...*]	Sets AAA authentication at login.

Command	Definition
Router(config)# **aaa authentication nasi** {**default** | *list-name*} *method1* [*method2...*]	Specifies AAA authentication for NetWare Asynchronous Services Interface (NASI) clients connecting through the access server.
Router(config)# **aaa authentication password-prompt** *text-string*	Changes the text displayed when users are prompted for a password.
Router(config)# **aaa authentication ppp** {**default** | *list-name*} *method1* [*method2...*]	Specifies one or more AAA authentication methods for use on serial interfaces running Point-to-Point Protocol (PPP).
Router(config)# **aaa authentication username-prompt** *text-string*	Changes the text displayed when users are prompted to enter a username.
Router(config)# **aaa authorization** {**network** | **exec** | **commands** *level* | **reverse-access**} {**default** | *list-name*} [*method1* [*method2...*]]	Sets the parameters that restrict a user's network access.
Router(config)# **aaa accounting** {**system** | **network** | **exec** | **connection** | **commands** *level*} {**default** | *list-name*} {**start-stop** | **wait-start** | **stop-only** | **none**} [*method1* [*method2...*]]	Enables AAA accounting of requested services for billing or security purposes when you use RADIUS or TACACS+.

show Command

Command	Definition
Router#**show privilege**	Displays your current level of privilege.

debug Commands

Command	Definition
Router#**debug aaa authentication**	Displays what methods of authentication are being used and what the results of these methods are.
Router#**debug aaa authorization**	Displays what methods of authorization are being used and what the results of these methods are.
Router#**debug aaa accounting**	Displays information on accountable events as they occur.

Appendix B

Adtran Atlas 550 Reference

CCNP Cisco Networking Academy Atlas 550 Configuration

The labs in this companion assume that you have access to a WAN emulator; specifically, the Adtran Atlas 550. A general-purpose configuration file for the Atlas 550 is available to authorized Cisco Networking Academy instructors at cisco.netacad.net. The following sections provide important Layer-2 addressing information that is essential for successful completion of the lab exercises in this book.

Atlas 550 Frame Relay Configuration

Using this configuration file, you can create three different Frame Relay topologies. You can create a partial-mesh topology by using four routers, each connected to one of the four V.35 ports on the Atlas 550. In order to create a full-mesh or hub-and-spoke topology, you must connect three routers to specific ports. The following diagrams can be used as a guide when building Frame Relay labs with the Atlas.

Frame Relay DLCIs – Partial Mesh   **Frame Relay DLCIs– Full Mesh**

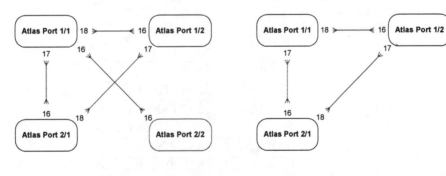

Frame Relay DLCIs – Hub-and-Spoke

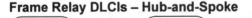

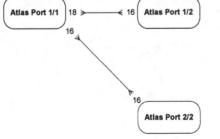

Atlas 550 POTS Configuration

The base configuration file allows you to connect up to eight modems or telephones in the Octal FXS module. Use the following table as a guide when building POTS labs with the Atlas.

Octal FXS Module	
Port #	Phone #
Port 1	5556001
Port 2	5556002
Port 3	5556003
Port 4	5556004
Port 5	5556005
Port 6	5556006
Port 7	5556007
Port 8	5556008

Atlas 550 ISDN Configuration

The base configuration file allows you to connect up to four ISDN BRIs to the ISDN module. Additionally, you can use the T1 Network module on the Atlas to connect a PRI. When working with ISDN in the lab, use the following table of phone numbers and SPIDs as a reference.

ISDN BRI Module		
Port #	Phone #	SPIDs
BRI 1	5551234	55512340001
	5551235	55512350001
BRI 2	5554000	55540000001
	5554001	55540010001
BRI 3	5557000	55570000001
	5557001	55570010001
BRI 4	5558000	55580000001
	5558001	55580010001

ISDN BRI Module	
Port #	Phone #
PRI	5555000

Notes for Doing ISDN Labs with the Atlas 550 and Cisco IOS

This section provides important information regarding the interaction between the Adtran Atlas 550 and the Cisco IOS when using ISDN.

Random Timer

Cisco routers use a random-length time delay in the range of 1 to 300 seconds to prevent mass power failures from overwhelming network ISDN switches when power returns and all the devices start up at the same time. To force a Cisco router connected to a National ISDN BRI switch to wait a random time interval before activating the Layer 2 interface when the switch starts up, use the **isdn twait-disable interface configuration** command. This is enabled by default and the delay is between 1 and 300 seconds.

SPID Negotiation and Status

Assume that the Cisco routers are configured with National ISDN as the switch type (basic-ni). It is also assumed all the basic settings have been configured for ISDN on the BRI interface (no dialer profiles).

Once configured and after turning off the routers (not the Atlas) for a few seconds and powering them up, the routers sync up to the Atlas (this can take up to five minutes depending on the *random time* that routers choose when bringing up the interface and polling the Atlas). Note that the default setting on the router (isdn tei powerup in the global configuration mode) is for ISDN TEI negotiation to occur when the router is first powered on. After the D-channel goes down, the routers and the Atlas are not able to spontaneously renegotiate the TEIs required prior to the SPIDs being negotiated. The Cisco routers do not let go of their previously negotiated Layer 2 configuration, so this has to be forced, as described next.

After the routers are set up, check that the SPIDs have been properly negotiated with the show isdn status command. If one or more of the SPIDs does not appear "valid" or "established" in the output, reloading the routers will ensure a base negotiation with the Atlas. A much easier alternative and a thoroughly tested procedure is to use the **clear interface bri** command; however, it might be necessary to execute this command up to three times in a row. The output of **show isdn status** should look something like this when all is well with Layers 1 and 2 (prior to any calls taking place):

```
router#show isdn status
Global ISDN Switchtype = basic-ni
ISDN BRI0/0 interface
        dsl 0, interface ISDN Switchtype = basic-ni
    Layer 1 Status:
        DEACTIVATED
    Layer 2 Status:
        TEI = 64, Ces = 1, SAPI = 0, State = TEI_ASSIGNED
        TEI = 65, Ces = 2, SAPI = 0, State = TEI_ASSIGNED
    Spid Status:
        TEI 64, ces = 1, state = 8(established)
            spid1 configured, spid1 sent, spid1 valid
            Endpoint ID Info: epsf = 0, usid = 70, tid = 1
```

```
        TEI 65, ces = 2, state = 8(established)
            spid2 configured, spid2 sent, spid2 valid
            Endpoint ID Info: epsf = 0, usid = 70, tid = 2
    Layer 3 Status:
        0 Active Layer 3 Call(s)
    Activated dsl 0 CCBs = 0
    The Free Channel Mask:   0x80000003
    Total Allocated ISDN CCBs = 0
```

After shutting down the BRI interface and bringing it back up, or after a period of inactivity, the SPID states might change to "terminal down" or "init." In these cases, it might again be necessary to use the **clear interface bri** command up to three times. Multiple shut/no shut attempts might also work, but the (multiple) **clear interface bri** command alternative has proven more reliable. Unplugging and replugging the cable from the router and/or Atlas will *not* force a base negotiation of Layer 2 parameters. Again, use the **show isdn status** command to verify the state of Layer 1 and Layer 2 connections between the router and the Atlas.

Note: If only one SPID is valid, you might still be able to complete Layer 3 connectivity for that channel.

Authentication

Depending on your configuration and IOS version, you might notice that pings will be unsuccessful across the Atlas even though all router configurations are correct. You might even notice that routing updates are working despite the problem with pings. If you do a **debug ip packet** and see "encapsulation failed" appear in the output (assuming all router configurations are correct), it is due to a missing authentication configuration–which is a bug in the IOS. To solve this problem, you need to configure authentication on each router. Under typical circumstances, you should not have to configure authentication, but on some versions of the IOS, you will have no choice. If problems still exist after configuring authentication, they are probably due to a mistake in the authentication configuration. The **debug ppp authentication** command helps to verify errors.

Dialer Maps

Dialer maps are put on both the remote and central sides of the circuit, but a destination phone number is put in the dialer map on the remote side only (TAC recommendation). Think of it as a remote site calling into a central site where only the remote site initiates the call. If destination phone numbers are put on both sides of the circuit, there might be *mixed results* with one side calling, then the other side seeing the interesting packet that brought up the connection and making a call back on the other channel. Configuring destination phone numbers on both sides with dialer maps might be problematic.

Debug IP Packet

To see if pings are traversing the Atlas, issue the **debug ip packet** command on the destination router and ping across from the source router. If you see ICMP packets with the source IP displayed and you see echo reply packets sourced from the destination router and destined for the source router, all is well. However, keep in mind that if authentication is not configured, you might still have failed pings appearing on the source router.

Channel Status

In the Atlas, the status of D channels and B channels can be viewed under "Channel Status"–keeping in mind that D means active D channel and A means active B channel. An Atlas 550 debug output can be viewed and redirected to a syslog server, just as on the router. By using this feature, detailed and prescriptive debug information can be viewed. This subject, however, is beyond the scope of this document.

SPID Validity

A cosmetic bug is in some versions of the Cisco IOS–12.0(7)T in particular. The router will display the SPIDs as being invalid with the show isdn status command even when they are valid. One way to check that the SPIDs are valid (other than Layer 3 connectivity tests like ping) is to look at debug output in the Atlas OS or to view the Channel Status on the Atlas.

Caveat for Cisco IOS 12.0

The following is a caveat listed on CCO for ISDN with PPP encapsulation running IP that might be of interest.

Dial-in ISDN clients spontaneously lose IP connectivity. The Cisco router located at the central site stops detecting incoming IP packets, while PPP level still reports encapsulated IP packets ("debug ppp packet," type 0x21) and new clients can pass PPP negotiation and authentication. ISDN remains in "multiple frame established" mode, and the central router can still send out IP packets. Workaround: Restart the router.

Alarm Lights

The red alarm lights that appear on the Adtran Atlas 550 have no effect on the functionality of the labs. The lights come on whenever there is an ISDN BRI or PRI port on the Atlas 550 that is configured (via the downloaded configuration file), but not in use. There are two ways to turn off the red lights: (1) Connect up all ISDN BRI and PRI ports with the appropriate cables to technology-compatible router interfaces or (2) in the Atlas configuration file, delete the configuration associated with the unused ISDN port.

Internet Explorer Versus Netscape Navigator

Some people have reported problems with TFTPing the Atlas configuration file after downloading it from the Web using Netscape. If you have problems with TFTP failures after downloading the Atlas 550 config using Netscape, try downloading the file by using Internet Explorer.

Lab C-1: Configuring CHAP Authentication on a 700 Series Router

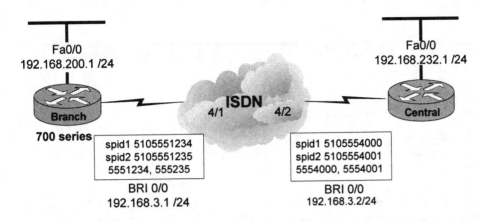

Objective

Configure a Cisco 700 series router to dial an IOS router using PPP encapsulation and authenticate with CHAP.

Scenario

The International Travel Agency (ITA) hired employees who will be working from their homes. ITA asked you to give these telecommuters access to the corporate network. Because the telecommuters do not need constant-access network resources, you decide to implement dial-on-demand routing on Cisco 770 routers. In this lab, the remote 700 series router will use the CHAP authentication method.

Step 1

Before you begin, it is recommended that you erase and reload both routers after erasing their startup configuration. Use the **set default** command to erase the configuration on the 700 series router. Wire the network according to the previous diagram and configure Central's FastEthernet 0/0 interface with the appropriate IP address. Be sure to connect each router's BRI interface to its appropriate port on the Atlas 550.

Step 2

Configure the 700 series router.

To set the hostname of the router, enter the following command:

```
>set system Branch
```

Set the ISDN switch type and the SPID numbers by using the following commands:

```
Branch>set switch ni-1
Branch>set 1 spid 51055512340001
Branch>set 2 spid 51055512350001
Branch>set 1 directory 5551234
Branch>set 2 directory 5551235
```

The **set directory** command sets the router's local directory number assigned by the ISDN service provider for each ISDN B channel.

Step 3

Configure an IP address for the Ethernet port by using the following commands:

```
Branch>cd lan
Branch:LAN>set ip address 192.168.1.1
Branch:LAN>set ip netmask 255.255.255.0

Branch:LAN>set ip routing on
Branch:LAN>set bridging off
Branch:LAN>cd
```

The **set ip routing on** command turns the IP routing engine on for a profile. The **set bridging off** command disables the bridging engine for a profile. The **cd** command, also known as the **change directory** command, creates a profile, enters an existing profile, and/or returns to system mode.

To create a user-defined profile named **Central** and to set specific parameters to the profile, use the following commands:

```
Branch>set user Central
Branch:Central>set ip address 192.168.3.1
Branch:Central>set ip netmask 255.255.255.0
Branch:Central>set number 5554000
Branch:Central>set ip routing on
Branch:Central>set ip route destination 0.0.0.0/0 gateway 192.168.3.2
Branch:Central>set bridging off
Branch:Central>cd
```

Set PPP authentication to CHAP and set the secret client password to cisco using the following commands:

```
Branch>set ppp authentication out chap
Branch>set ppp authentication in chap
Branch>set ppp secret client
```

The **set ppp authentication in** and the **set ppp authentication out** commands configure PPP authentication for outgoing and incoming ISDN calls. The **set ppp secret client** command configures the passwords used for PPP CHAP authentication. To configure the password for PPP PAP authentication you can use the **set ppp password client** command.

Next, configure the expected host password to cisco:

```
Branch>cd Central
Branch:Central>set ppp secret host
```

The **set ppp secret host** will expect the remote router to supply cisco as the password to successfully pass CHAP authentication.

Finally, set the Central profile as the active profile:

```
Branch>set active Central
```

Step 4

Configure Central to accept incoming PPP calls and force CHAP authentication:

```
Central(config)#username Branch password cisco
Central(config)#dialer-list 1 protocol ip permit
Central(config)#isdn switch-type basic-ni
Central(config)#interface BRI0/0
Central(config-if)#ip address 192.168.3.2 255.255.255.0
Central(config-if)#encapsulation ppp
Central(config-if)#ppp authentication chap
Central(config-if)#dialer map ip 192.168.3.1 name Branch 5551234
Central(config-if)#dialer-group 1
Central(config-if)#isdn spid1 51055540000001 5554000
Central(config-if)#isdn spid2 51055540010001 5554001
Central(config-if)#no shutdown
```

Configure a static route to the Ethernet network connected to the 700 series branch router:

```
Central(config)#ip route 192.168.1.0 255.255.255.0 192.168.3.1
```

From the branch router's console, ping Central's FastEthernet interface.

The pings should be successful. If the pings fail, troubleshoot as necessary.

Lab C-2: Configuring Multilink PPP on a Cisco 700 Series Router

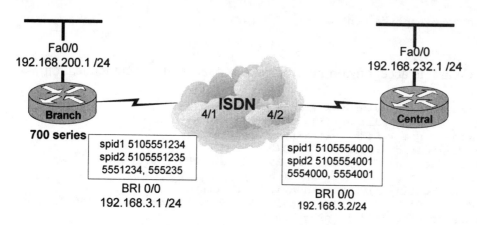

Objective

Configure PPP multilink on a Cisco 700 series router.

Scenario

The International Travel Agency (ITA) hired employees who will be working from their homes. ITA asked you to give these telecommuters access to the corporate network. Because the telecommuters do not need full-time access to network resources, you decide to implement dial-on-demand routing on Cisco 700 series routers to connect to ITA's network. You must configure the remote router to authenticate with CHAP and then enable multilink PPP.

Step 1

Before you begin, it is recommended that you erase and reload both routers after erasing their startup configuration. Use the **set default** command to erase the configuration on the 700 series router. Wire the network according to the previous diagram and configure Central's FastEthernet 0/0 interface with the appropriate IP address. Be sure to connect each router's BRI interface to its appropriate port on the Atlas 550.

Step 2

Use the following command to set the hostname of the router:

```
>set system Branch
```

Set the ISDN switch type and the SPID numbers by using the following commands:

```
Branch>set switch ni-1
Branch>set 1 spid 51055512340001
Branch>set 2 spid 51055512350001
Branch>set 1 directory 5551234
Branch>set 2 directory 5551235
```

The **set directory** command sets the router's local directory number assigned by the ISDN service provider for each ISDN B channel.

Step 3

Configure an IP address for the Ethernet port using the following commands:

```
Branch>cd lan
Branch:LAN>set ip address 192.168.1.1
Branch:LAN>set ip netmask 255.255.255.0

Branch:LAN>set ip routing on
Branch:LAN>set bridging off
Branch:LAN>cd
```

The **set ip routing on** command turns the IP routing engine on for a profile. The **set bridging off** command disables the bridging engine for a profile. The **cd** command, also known as the **change directory** command, creates a profile, enters an existing profile, and/or returns to system mode.

To create a user-defined profile named **Central** and to set specific parameters to the profile, use the following commands:

```
Branch>set user Central
Branch:Central>set ip address 192.168.3.1
Branch:Central>set ip netmask 255.255.255.0
Branch:Central>set number 5554000
Branch:Central>set ip routing on
Branch:Central>set ip route destination 0.0.0.0/0 gateway 192.168.3.2
Branch:Central>set bridging off
Branch:Central>cd
```

Set PPP authentication to CHAP and set the client password to cisco using the following commands:

```
Branch>set ppp authentication out chap
Branch>set ppp authentication in chap
Branch>set ppp secret client
```

The **set ppp authentication in** and the **set ppp authentication out** commands configure PPP authentication for outgoing and incoming ISDN calls. The **set ppp secret client** command configures the passwords used for PPP CHAP authentication. To configure the password for PPP PAP authentication, you can use the **set ppp password client** command.

Next, configure the expected host password to cisco:

```
Branch>cd Central
Branch:Central>set ppp secret host
```

The **set ppp secret host** command will expect the remote router to supply cisco as the password to successfully pass CHAP authentication.

Next, set the Central profile as the active profile:

```
Branch>set active Central
```

Finally, configure the 700 series router for PPP multilink using the following command:

```
Branch>set ppp multilink on
Branch>demand 2 threshold 1 duration 1 source both
```

The **demand 2** command specifies the threshold at which the second B channel will be brought up. In this case, the second channel will become active if 1 kbps is sent during a one-second interval (duration).

To verify your **demand** configuration, issue the **show demand** command:

```
Branch>show demand
Demand Calling Parameters          Link D        Link 1        Link 2
  Connection Type                  Auto OFF      Auto ON         Auto ON
  Permanent                            OFF           OFF
      OFF
  Threshold                          0 kbs         0 kbs             1
      kbs
  Duration                           1 sec         1 sec             1
      sec
  Source                               LAN           LAN
      BOTH
Timeout (call tear down) Parameters
  Threshold                          0 kbs         0 kbs            48
      kbs
  Duration                             OFF           OFF
      OFF
  Source                               LAN           LAN
      BOTH
```

Step 4

Configure Central to accept incoming PPP calls and force CHAP authentication:

```
Central(config)#username Branch password cisco
Central(config)#dialer-list 1 protocol ip permit
Central(config)#isdn switch-type basic-ni
Central(config)#interface BRI0/0
Central(config-if)#ip address 192.168.3.2 255.255.255.0
Central(config-if)#encapsulation ppp
Central(config-if)#ppp authentication chap
Central(config-if)#ppp multilink
Central(config-if)#dialer map ip 192.168.3.1 name Branch 5551234
Central(config-if)#dialer-group 1
Central(config-if)#dialer load-threshold 1 either
Central(config-if)#isdn spid1 51055540000001 5554000
Central(config-if)#isdn spid2 51055540010001 5554001
Central(config-if)#no shutdown
```

Configure a static route to the Ethernet network connected to the 700 series branch router:

```
Central(config)#ip route 192.168.1.0 255.255.255.0 192.168.3.1
```

Ping Central's Ethernet interface from the Branch router. The pings should be successful.

If the pings fail, troubleshoot as necessary. To verify PPP multilink configurations, use the **show status** command on the Branch and the **show ppp multilink** command on the Central router.

Lab C-3: Configuring DHCP Server on a Cisco 700 Series Router

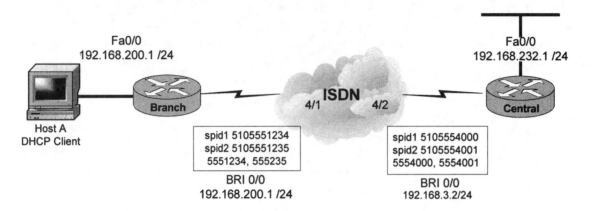

Objective

Configure the DHCP server on a Cisco 700 series router.

Scenario

The International Travel Agency (ITA) hired employees who will be working from their homes. ITA asked you to give these telecommuters access to the corporate network. Because the telecommuters do not need full-time access to network resources, you decide to implement dial-on-demand routing on Cisco 700 routers to connect to ITA's network. You must configure the remote router to authenticate with CHAP. Finally, you need to configure the router to act as a DHCP server with a pool of 50 addresses.

Step 1

Before you begin, it is recommended that you erase and reload both routers after erasing their startup configuration. Use the **set default** command to erase the configuration on the 700 series router. Wire the network according to the previous diagram and configure Central's FastEthernet 0/0 interface with the appropriate IP address. Be sure to connect each router's BRI interface to its appropriate port on the Atlas 550.

Step 2

Use the following command to set the hostname of the router:

```
>set system Branch
```

Set the ISDN switch type and the SPID numbers by using the following commands:

```
Branch>set switch ni-1
Branch>set 1 spid 51055512340001
Branch>set 2 spid 51055512350001
Branch>set 1 directory 5551234
Branch>set 2 directory 5551235
```

The **set directory** command sets the router's local directory number assigned by the ISDN service provider for each ISDN B channel.

Step 3

Configure an IP address for the Ethernet port by using the following commands:

```
Branch>cd lan
Branch:LAN>set ip address 192.168.1.1
Branch:LAN>set ip netmask 255.255.255.0

Branch:LAN>set ip routing on
Branch:LAN>set bridging off
Branch:LAN>cd
```

The **set ip routing on** command turns the IP routing engine on for a profile. The **set bridging off** command disables the bridging engine for a profile. The **cd** command, also known as the **change directory** command, creates a profile, enters an existing profile, and/or returns to system mode.

To create a user-defined profile named **Central** and to set specific parameters to the profile, use the following commands:

```
Branch>set user Central
Branch:Central>set ip address 192.168.3.1
Branch:Central>set ip netmask 255.255.255.0
Branch:Central>set number 5554000
Branch:Central>set ip routing on
Branch:Central>set ip route destination 0.0.0.0/0 gateway 192.168.3.2
Branch:Central>set bridging off
Branch:Central>cd
```

Set PPP authentication to CHAP and set the client password to cisco by using the following commands:

```
Branch>set ppp authentication out chap
Branch>set ppp authentication in chap
Branch>set ppp secret client
```

The **set ppp authentication in** and the **set ppp authentication out** commands configure PPP authentication for outgoing and incoming ISDN calls. The **set ppp secret client** command configures the passwords used for PPP CHAP authentication. To configure the password for PPP PAP authentication, you can use the **set ppp password client** command.

Next, configure the expected host password to cisco:

```
Branch>cd Central
Branch:Central>set ppp secret host
```

The **set ppp secret host** will expect the remote router to supply cisco as the password to successfully pass CHAP authentication.

Next, set the Central profile as the active profile:

```
Branch>set active Central
```

Configure the 700 series router as a DHCP server by using the following commands:

```
BranchRouter>set dhcp server
BranchRouter>set dhcp address 192.168.1.2 50
BranchRouter>set dhcp netmask 255.255.255.0
BranchRouter>set dhcp gateway rimary 192.168.1.1
```

Step 4

Configure Central to accept incoming PPP calls and force CHAP authentication:

```
Central(config)#username Branch password cisco
Central(config)#dialer-list 1 protocol ip permit
Central(config)#isdn switch-type basic-ni
Central(config)#interface BRI0/0
Central(config-if)#ip address 192.168.3.2 255.255.255.0
Central(config-if)#encapsulation ppp
Central(config-if)#ppp authentication chap
Central(config-if)#dialer map ip 192.168.3.1 name Branch 5551234
Central(config-if)#dialer-group 1
Central(config-if)#isdn spid1 51055540000001 5554000
Central(config-if)#isdn spid2 51055540010001 5554001
Central(config-if)#no shutdown
```

Configure a static route to the Ethernet network connected to the 700 series branch router.

```
Central(config)#ip route 192.168.1.0 255.255.255.0 192.168.3.1
```

Ping Central's FastEthernet interface from the Branch router.

The pings should be successful. If the pings fail, troubleshoot as necessary.

Step 5

Release and renew Host A's IP configuration using **ipconfig /release_all** and **ipconfig /renew_all** command in MS-DOS prompt.

Verify that Host A received the correct IP configuration from the 700 series router; troubleshoot as necessary.

Notes

Notes

Notes

Notes